# Tolley's Practical Risk Assessment Handbook

by
Mike Bateman
BSc, MIOSH, RSP
Health and Safety Consultant

Butterworths Tolley

Published by Butterworths Tolley
2 Addiscombe Road
Croydon CR9 5AF England
0208 686 9141

Typeset in Great Britain
by
YHT Ltd

Printed in Great Britain
by
The Bath Press



ISBN 0 75450 749-1

# Foreword

This handbook is intended to help not only those involved in carrying out risk assessments but also those who simply need to know what risk assessment is all about - health and safety specialists, safety representatives, managers at all levels and directors, together with owners of small and medium sized businesses.

Whilst inevitably references must be made to legal requirements, the handbook adopts a practical approach to risk assessment and contains a variety of checklists, risk assessment forms and examples of what completed risk assessments might look like. It aims to remove much of the mystique about risk assessment and demonstrate that it is a process in which everyone with an awareness of the risks and precautions associated with their work activities can play a part.

The book assumes that the reader is likely to already have a general awareness, although not necessarily a detailed knowledge, of health and safety legislation. Risk assessment requirements introduced by specific regulations (eg COSHH, noise, manual handling) form a large part of the handbook, although those with detailed specialist needs in these areas may also need to consult the additional references provided in those sections.

# Contents

# 1 Introduction

**In this chapter:**

**The background to risk assessment**

Key requirements of HASAWA 1974
What is 'reasonably practicable'?
Practicable and absolute requirements
The Management of Health and Safety at Work Regulations ('the Management Regulations')

**Regulations requiring risk assessment**

Control of Substances Hazardous to Health Regulations 1999 ('COSHH 1999')
Noise at Work Regulations 1989
Manual Handling Operations Regulations 1992
Health and Safety (Display Screen Equipment) Regulations 1992
Personal Protective Equipment at Work Regulations 1992
Fire Precautions (Workplace) Regulations 1997
Control of Lead at Work Regulations 1998
Control of Asbestos at Work Regulations 1987
Genetic Manipulation Regulations 1989
Genetically Modified Organisms (Contained Use) Regulations 1992
Supply of Machinery (Safety) Regulations 1992
Control of Major Accident Hazard Regulations 1999 ('COMAH 1999')
Ionising Radiations Regulations 1999

**Related health and safety management concepts**

Safe systems of work
'Dynamic risk assessment'
Permits to work
CDM health and safety plans
Method statements

**References**

## The background to risk assessment

**1.1** The term 'risk assessment' probably first came into common use as a result of the *Control of Substances Hazardous to Health Regulations 1988* (commonly known as the *'COSHH Regulations'* and revised several times since) which required employers to make a 'suitable and sufficient assessment of the risks created' by work liable to expose any employees to any substance hazardous to health. Similar requirements had actually previously been contained in both the *Control of Lead at Work Regulations 1980* and the *Control of Asbestos at Work Regulations 1987*.

In practice a type of risk assessment had already been necessary for some years particularly as a result of the use of the qualifying clause 'so far as is reasonably practicable' in a number of the *sections* of the *Health and Safety at Work etc Act 1974* (*'HASAWA 1974'*).

## Key requirements of HASAWA 1974

Previously most Acts and Regulations dealing with health and safety had been extremely prescriptive in their requirements and narrow in their scope. The report of the Robens Committee (published in 1972) recommended major changes including:

- the replacement of specific legal requirements by general obligations;
- legislation to cover everyone at work, including the self-employed (rather than just those in factories, offices etc as was previously the case);
- introduction of requirements for employers (and the self-employed) to take account not just of employees but also of others, including the public.

These recommendations were implemented through the passing of *HASAWA 1974* in 1974. The Act applies to everyone 'at work' – employers, self-employed and employees (with the exception of domestic servants in private households).

*Section 2* sets out general duties of employers to their employees, with the most general contained in *Section 2(1)*:

> 'It shall be the duty of every employer to ensure, so far as is reasonably practicable, the health, safety and welfare at work of all his employees'.

This 'catch-all' requirement is all-embracing in its scope, although it is qualified by the term 'reasonably practicable'. *Section 2(2)* goes on to detail more specific requirements relating to:

- provision and maintenance of plant and systems of work;
- use, handling, storage and transport of articles and substances;
- provision of information, instruction, training and supervision;
- places of work and means of access and egress;
- the working environment, facilities and welfare arrangements.

These are also qualified by the term 'reasonably practicable'.

*Section 2(3)* requires employers with 5 or more employees to prepare a written health and safety policy statement, together with the organisation and arrangements for carrying it out, and to bring this to the notice of employees.

*Section 3* places general duties on both employers and the self-employed in respect of persons other than their employees. *Section 3(1)* states:

> 'It shall be the duty of every employer to conduct his undertaking in such a way as to ensure, so far as is reasonably practicable, that persons not in his employment who may be affected thereby are not exposed to risks to their health or safety'.

Employers thus have duties to contractors (and their employees), visitors, customers, members of the emergency services, neighbours, passers-by and the public at large. This may (up to a point) extend to include trespassers. Once again these duties are subject to the 'reasonably practicable' qualification.

Self-employed persons are put under a similar duty by *Section 3(2)* and must also take care of themselves. (If they have employees then *Section 2* will also apply to them).

*Section 4* of the Act places duties on each person who has to any extent control of non-domestic premises used for work purposes in respect of those who are not their employees. Such persons may include landlords or managing agents. Each such person is required by *Section 4(2)*,

> 'to take such measures as it is reasonable for a person in his position to take to ensure, so far as is reasonably practicable, that the premises, all means of access thereto or egress therefrom available for use by persons using the premises, and any plant or substance in the premises or, as the case may be, provided for

use there, is or are safe and without risks to health'.

This requirement also is subject to the qualification of 'so far as is reasonably practicable'.

*Section 6* places a number of duties on those who design, manufacture, import or supply articles for use at work, or articles of fairground equipment and those who manufacture, import or supply substances. Many of these obligations also contain the 'reasonably practicable' qualification. (It is not the intention of this handbook to develop further upon the duties contained in *Section 6*).

## What is 'reasonably practicable'?

**1.3** The phrase 'reasonably practicable' is not just included in the key *sections* of *HASAWA 1974* but is contained in many requirements of a wide variety of Regulations. Lord Justice Asquith provided a definition in his judgement on the case of *Edwards v National Coal Board* (1949) in which he stated:

> ' "Reasonably practicable" is a narrower term than "physically possible" and seems to me to imply that a computation must be made by the owner in which the quantum of risk placed on one scale and the sacrifice involved in the measures necessary for averting risk (whether in money, time or trouble) is placed in the other, and that, if it be shown that there is a gross disproportion between them – the risk being insignificant in relation to the sacrifice – the defendants discharge the onus on them. Moreover, this computation falls to be made by the owner at a point in time anterior to the accident.'

*Section 40* of *HASAWA 1974* places the burden of proof in respect of what was or was not 'reasonably practicable' (or 'practicable' – see below) on the person charged with failure to comply with a duty or requirement. To a certain extent this reverses the usual onus of proof although defendants need only establish that they satisfied the duty or requirement on the balance of probabilities (not beyond all reasonable doubt, as is normally the case in criminal courts).

Quite clearly it would be both impractical and undesirable to decide what precautions are appropriate for every work situation by making submissions to a court of law. Employers (and the self-employed) must make their own decisions – this is what the Robens report proposed – a large degree of self-regulation by employers rather than increasingly complex and specific legal requirements. The level of risk must be established and the various options as to precautions considered by the duty holder in order to determine what is 'reasonably practicable' – in effect the employer must carry out a form of risk assessment.

Two aspects of 'reasonably practicable' merit further emphasis. For a precaution not to be reasonably practicable, the risk must be insignificant in relation to the sacrifice involved in taking the precaution. The abilities of the duty holder to meet the sacrifice involved in averting the risk should not be a consideration. In other words the precaution must represent reasonable value in health and safety terms – whether the duty holder can afford the cost (or time or trouble) should not be an issue. Taking account of employers' differing abilities to bear the costs of precautions would obviously lead to extremely inconsistent application of the law.

## Practicable and absolute requirements

**1.4** Not all health and safety law is qualified by the phrase 'reasonably practicable'. Some requirements must be carried out 'so far as is practicable'. 'Practicable' is a tougher standard to meet than 'reasonably practicable'. However, its meaning is different from 'physically possible'. The precautions must be possible in the light of current knowledge and invention (*Adsett v K and L Steelfounders & Engineers Ltd.* (1953)). Once a precaution is practicable it must be taken even if it is inconvenient or expensive. However, it is not practical to take precautions against a danger which is not yet known to exist (*Edwards v National Coal Board* (1949)), although it may be practicable once the danger is recognised. As stated in 1.3 above, *Section 40* of *HASAWA 1974* places the burden of proving what may or may not be practicable on the duty holder.

Many health and safety duties are subject to neither 'practicable' nor 'reasonably practicable' qualifications. These absolute requirements usually state that something 'shall' or 'shall not' be done. However, even these duties often contain other words which are subject to a certain amount of interpretation – 'suitable', 'sufficient', 'adequate', 'efficient', 'appropriate' etc.

Once again a duty holder cannot hope to determine whether requirements have been met 'so far as is practicable' or whether the precise wording of an absolute requirement has been complied with unless a proper evaluation of the risks and the effectiveness of the precautions has been made ie a form of risk assessment has been carried out.

## The Management of Health and Safety at Work Regulations ('the Management Regulations')

**1.5** The *Management Regulations* were introduced in 1992 and revised in 1999. They were intended to implement the European Framework Directive (89/391) on the introduction of measures to encourage improvements in the safety and health of workers at work. *Regulation 3* of the *Management Regulations* 1992 required employers and the self-employed to make a suitable and sufficient assessment of the risks to both employees and persons not in their employment (in the latter case arising out of or in connection with the employer's or self-employed person's undertaking). The purpose of the assessment being the identification of the measures needed 'to comply with the requirements and prohibitions imposed ... by or under the relevant statutory provisions.' ie identifying what is needed to comply with the law.

Given the extremely broad obligations contained in *Sections 2, 3, 4* and *6* of *HASAWA 1974*, all risks arising from work activities should be considered as part of the risk assessment process (although some risks may be dismissed as being insignificant). Compliance with more specific requirements of Regulations must also be assessed – whether these are absolute obligations or subject to 'practicable' or 'reasonably practicable' qualifications.

The requirement for risk assessment introduced in the *1992 Management Regulations* simply formalised what employers should have been doing all along – identifying what precautions they needed to take to comply with the law. (A separate obligation in the *Management Regulations* required effective arrangements to be made to ensure these precautions were actually implemented). However, in addition *Regulation 3* also required all employers with five or more employees to record the significant findings of their assessments ie they had to be able to demonstrate that they had actually gone through a systematic risk assessment process.

The 1999 version of the *Management Regulations* contained similar requirements and also consolidated various amendments which had been made to the original Regulations. The most significant of these were that special attention must be given during the risk assessment process to risks to:

- New and expectant mothers;
- Children and young persons.

More detailed guidance on these aspects and on the whole process of risk assessment is contained later in the handbook but the process can be summarised as establishing:

1. What risks arise from the work activities;
2. What precautions are in place;
3. Whether those precautions are enough to comply with the law;
4. If not, what additional precautions need to be introduced.

Any such additional precautions must then be implemented (*Regulation 5* of the *Management Regulations* 1999 contains requirements relating to the effective implementation of precautions).

## Regulations requiring risk assessment

**1.6** An increasing number of codes of Regulations contain requirements for risk assessments. Several of these Regulations are of significance to a wide range of work activities and are dealt with in some detail elsewhere in the handbook. These are:

### Control of Substances Hazardous to Health Regulations 1999 ('COSHH 1999')

**1.7** *Regulation 6* requires employers to make a suitable and sufficient assessment of the risks created by work liable to expose any employees to any substance hazardous to health and of the steps that need to be taken to meet the requirements of the Regulations.

### Noise at Work Regulations 1989

**1.8** *Regulation 4* requires employers to make a noise assessment which is adequate for the purposes of:

- identifying which employees are exposed to noise above defined action levels;
- providing information to comply with other duties under the Regulations (reduction of noise exposure, provision of ear protection, establishment of ear protection zones and informing employees).

### Manual Handling Operations Regulations 1992

**1.9** Employers are required by *Regulation 4* to make a suitable and sufficient assessment of all manual handling operations at work which involve a risk of employees being injured and to take appropriate steps to reduce the risk to the lowest level reasonably practicable. (They must avoid such manual handling operations if it is reasonably practicable to do so).

## Health and Safety (Display Screen Equipment) Regulations 1992

**1.10** *Regulation 2* requires employers to perform a suitable and sufficient analysis of display screen equipment ('DSE') workstations for the purpose of assessing risks to 'users' or 'operators' as defined in the Regulations. Risks identified in the assessment must be reduced to the lowest extent reasonably practicable.

## Personal Protective Equipment at Work Regulations 1992

**1.11** Under *Regulation 6* employers must ensure that an assessment is made to determine risks which have not been avoided by other means and identify personal protective equipment ('PPE') which will be effective against these risks. The Regulations also contain other requirements relating to the provision of PPE; its maintenance and replacement; information, instruction and training; and the steps which must be taken to ensure its proper use.

## Fire Precautions (Workplace) Regulations 1997

**1.12** These Regulations, taken together with the *Management Regulations 1999*, make it quite explicit that employers must carry out an assessment of fire risks and fire precautions. Part II of the Regulations contains specific requirements relating to fire safety which must be included in the assessment.

Amendments to the Regulations in 1999 removed the exemption from risk assessment requirements originally given to holders of Fire Certificates (under the *Fire Precautions Act 1971* and other legislation). They too are required to carry out fire risk assessments.

Some codes of Regulations requiring risk assessments are of rather more specialist application and have not been included in the handbook. However, references to key HSE publications of relevance are included at the end of this chapter. These Regulations include:

## Control of Lead at Work Regulations 1998

**1.13** The 1980 version of these Regulations provided a basis for the original *COSHH Regulations*. *Regulation 5* of the 1998 Regulations requires an assessment to be made to determine the nature and degree of exposure of employees to lead. (*Regulation 3* also requires the exposure of others to be taken into account). An assessment of the adequacy of control measures is required by the *Management Regulations*. (See REF. 1.)

## Control of Asbestos at Work Regulations 1987

**1.14** *Regulation 5* requires that,

> 'an employer shall not carry out any work which exposes or is liable to expose any of his employees to asbestos unless he has made an adequate assessment of that exposure.'

The *Regulation* stipulates that the assessment must:

- identify the type of asbestos involved;
- determine the nature and degree of exposure;
- set out the steps to be taken to prevent or reduce the exposure to the lowest level reasonably practicable.

Whilst the principles adopted within the remainder of the Regulations are similar to the *COSHH Regulations*, there are other detailed requirements relating to plans of work, notification of work with asbestos, designated areas, labelling etc. (See REFS. 2, 3 and 4).

## Genetic Manipulation Regulations 1989

**1.15** These Regulations require various activities involving genetic manipulation to be notified to the Health and Safety Executive (HSE). An assessment must be made by HSE approved methods to determine whether the activity falls within designated containment levels or warrants 'only the use of good large-scale practice.'

## Genetically Modified Organisms (Contained Use) Regulations 1992

**1.16** *Regulation 7* requires a risk assessment to be carried out before:

- premises are used for activities involving genetic modification for the first time
- any activity involving genetic modification is undertaken.

Schedule 3 to the Regulations sets out parameters which may be taken into account in risk assessments and the Regulations and other schedules contain many other detailed requirements (See reference 5).

## Supply of Machinery (Safety) Regulations 1992

**1.17** The Regulations include a variety of procedures which must be followed in assessing conformity of machinery with essential health and safety requirements set out in the Machinery Directive. This assessment must be co-ordinated by the 'responsible person' – normally the manufacturer or his representative. However, where employers import machinery directly from outside the EC or where they assemble machinery or parts to form 'relevant machinery', they too are likely to have duties under the Regulations. (See references 6 and 7).

## Control of Major Accident Hazard Regulations 1999 ('COMAH 1999')

**1.18** The Regulations only apply to sites containing specified quantities of dangerous substances. They require the preparation of both on-site and off-site emergency plans with the objectives of:

- containing and controlling incidents so as to minimise their effects, and to limit damage to persons, the environment and property;
- implementing the measures necessary to protect persons and the environment from the effects of major accidents;
- communicating the necessary information to the public and to the emergency services and authorities concerned in the area;
- providing for the restoration and clean-up of the environment following a major accident.

Such plans can only be prepared utilising risk assessment techniques and the HSE have provided considerable guidance on the methodology to be followed and the parameters to be taken into account. (See references 8, 9 and 10).

## Ionising Radiations Regulations 1999

**1.19** *Regulation* 7 requires employers to carry out a risk assessment before commencing any new activity involving work with ionising radiation. The assessment must be:

> 'sufficient to demonstrate that:
>
> all hazards with the potential to cause a radiation accident have been identified; and

the nature and magnitude of the risks to employers and other persons arising from those hazards have been evaluated.'

Where such radiation risks are identified, all reasonably practicable steps must be taken to:

- prevent any such accident;
- limit its consequences should such an accident occur;
- provide employees with necessary information, instruction, training and equipment necessary to restrict their exposure.

An HSE booklet contains an Approved Code of Practice and Guidance on the Regulations (see REF. 11). This includes an explanation of the inter-relationship between the above requirements and the risk assessments required by the *Management Regulations 1999.*

## Related health and safety management concepts

**1.20** Risk assessment techniques are an essential part of many health and safety management concepts and several of these are explored in some detail within the handbook.

### Safe systems of work

**1.21** Employers are required under *section 2(2)(a)* of *HASAWA 1974* to provide and maintain 'systems of work that are, so far as is reasonably practicable, safe and without risks to health'.

*Regulation 4(2)* of the *Confined Spaces Regulations 1997* contains a similar requirement for safe systems of work. *Regulation 8(1)* of the *Lifting Operations and Lifting Equipment Regulations 1998* ('LOLER') requires lifting operations to be carried out in a safe manner, the accompanying Approved Code of Practice (ACOP) referring to the need for a safe system of work in certain circumstances. A safe system of work can only be established through the process of risk assessment.

### 'Dynamic risk assessment'

**1.22** Even applying the formalised risk assessment approaches described in the handbook it will be impossible for employers to take account of every possible variable and eventuality in work activities in advance. A degree of reliance must be placed on employees to make their own judgements in respect of health and safety. For example:

- How does a maintenance fitter gain access to carry out work on a fan motor –
  - does he use a ladder, a tower scaffold or a mobile elevating work platform (eg a 'cherrypicker')?
- Is it safe to plough a sloping field given the prevailing ground and weather conditions?
- What precautions need to be taken before going to survey a semi-derelict building in a deprived part of a city?

The term 'dynamic risk assessment' is often used to describe the process employees are expected to follow in such situations. However, it is essential that employers ensure that employees have the necessary knowledge and experience to make such judgements. The employer's 'generic risk assessments' must have identified the types of risks which might be present in these variable situations, established a framework of precautions (procedures, equipment etc) which are likely to be necessary and provided guidance on which precautions are appropriate for which situations.

## Permits to work

**1.23** A permit to work system is a formalised method for identifying a safe system of work (usually for a high risk activity) and ensuring that this system is followed.

The Permit Issuer is expected to carry out a dynamic risk assessment of the work activity. The Permit Issuer should be more competent in identifying the risks and the relevant precautions than those carrying out the work and in many situations the types of precautions required will have been identified in advance.

## CDM health and safety plans

**1.24** A key component of the *Construction (Design and Management) Regulations 1994* ('CDM 1994') is the requirement for a health and safety plan. The framework of the plan is prepared initially by the 'Planning Supervisor' (who is appointed by the client) and the plan is then developed in much more detail by the 'Principal Contractor' for the project, who is also responsible for its implementation. Essentially this process requires a risk assessment in relation to the CDM project:

- What risks are likely to be involved in the project?
- What precautions are likely to be required to control these risks?
- How will these precautions be implemented?
- Are the precautions proving effective?
- If not, what improvements need to be made?

## Method statements

**1.25** The term method statement is being used increasingly, particularly in relation to construction work. Method statements usually involve a description of how a particular task or operation is to be carried out. In the context of a CDM health and safety plan the method statement should identify all the components of a safe system of work – arrived at through a process of risk assessment. However, the method statement may go much further – identifying specification standards for the work being carried out, or equipment being installed and providing details on materials being used.

# *References*

## (All HSE publications)

**1.26**


| | | |
|---|---|---|
| 1 | COP 2 | Control of lead at work. (1998) |
| 2 | L 27 | The control of asbestos at work. *Control of Asbestos at Work Regulations* 1987 & ACOP Third Edition (1999). |
| 3 | L 28 | Work with asbestos insulation, asbestos coating and asbestos insulating board. *Control of Asbestos at Work Regulations* 1987 ACOP Third Edition (1999). |
| 4 | L 11 | A guide to the *Asbestos (Licensing) Regulations* 1983. Guidance on Regulations (1999). |
| 5 | L 29 | A guide to the *Genetically Modified Organisms (Contained Use) Regulations* 1992. (2000) |
| 6 | INDG 270 | Supplying new machinery. Advice to suppliers (1998) – free leaflet |

| | | |
|---|---|---|
| 7 | INDG 271 | Buying new machinery. A short guide to the law (1998) – free leaflet |
| 8 | L 111 | A guide to the *Control of Major Accident Hazard Regulations* 1999 (1999) |
| 9 | HSG 190 | Preparing safety reports. *Control of Major Accident Hazard Regulations* 1999 (1999) |
| 10 | HSG 191 | Emergency planning for major accidents. *Control of Major Accident Hazard Regulations* (1999) |
| 11 | L 121 | Work With Ionising Radiation. *Ionising Radiations Regulations* 1999 ACOP & Guidance (2000) |

# 2 What the Management Regulations require

## Introduction

**2.1** A general requirement for risk assessment is contained in the *Management of Health and Safety at Work Regulations 1999* (the *Management Regulations 1999*), *Regulation 3*. Changes to the original Regulations passed in 1992 mean that the risk assessment must now include fire risks and precautions (see CHAPTER 14: FIRE RISK ASSESSMENTS) and also risks to both young persons (under 18s) and new and expectant mothers (see CHAPTER 3: SPECIAL CASES). Other Regulations require more specific types of risk assessment, eg of hazardous substances (COSHH), noise, manual handling operations, display screen equipment and personal protective equipment (these are dealt with in Chapters 9 to 13 of the handbook).

*Regulation 3(1)* of the *Management Regulations 1999* states:

> 'every employer shall make a suitable and sufficient assessment of:
>
> (a) the risks to the health and safety of his employees to which they are exposed whilst they are at work; and
>
> (b) the risks to the health and safety of persons not in his employment arising out of or in connection with the conduct by him of his undertaking,
>
> for the purpose of identifying the measures he needs to take to comply with the requirements or prohibitions imposed upon him by or under the relevant statutory provisions and by Part II of the Fire Precautions (Workplace) Regulations 1997.'

*Regulation 3(2)* imposes similar requirements on self-employed persons.

*Regulation 3(3)* requires a risk assessment to be reviewed if:

- there is reason to suspect that it is no longer valid; or
- there has been a significant change in the matters to which it relates.

*Regulation 3(4)* requires a risk assessment to be made or reviewed before an employer employs a young person and *regulation 3(5)* identifies particular issues which must be taken into account in respect of young persons (especially their inexperience, lack of awareness of risks and immaturity). Further requirements in respect of young persons are contained in *Regulation 19.*

*Regulation 16* contains specific requirements on the factors which must be taken into account in risk assessments in relation to new and expectant mothers. These relate to processes, working conditions and physical, biological or chemical agents. The 'special cases' of young persons and new or expectant mothers are dealt with in CHAPTER 3: SPECIAL CASES.

*Regulation 3(6)* requires employers with five or more employees to record:

- the significant findings of their risk assessments; and
- any group of employees identified as being especially at risk.

Many different methods of recording assessments are described in CHAPTER 5: ASSESSMENT RECORDS.

The HSE have published a booklet (*L21 Management of health and safety at work. Management of Health and Safety at Work Regulations 1999. Approved code of practice (2000)*) which contains the *Management Regulations* in full, the associated approved code of practice ('ACOP') and guidance on the Regulations.

## *Hazards and risks*

**2.2** The ACOP to the Regulations provides definitions of both hazard and risk.

A *hazard* is something with the potential to cause harm.

A *risk* is the likelihood of potential harm from that hazard being realised.

The *extent of the risk* will depend on:

- the likelihood of that harm occurring;
- the potential severity of that harm (resultant injury or adverse health effect);
- the population which might be affected by the hazard, ie the number of people who might be exposed;

**Example 1: Pedestrians crossing a roadway**

*Hazard:* A pedestrian being injured through being hit by traffic.

*Extent of the risk* is determined by factors such as:

- the volume of traffic;
- the number of pedestrians having to cross the road;
- the layout of the roadway (designated crossing points, warning signs, lighting, lines of visibility);
- the speed of the traffic;
- the nature of the traffic (pedal cycles will cause less injury than heavy goods vehicles);
- the capabilities and awareness of those crossing the road (children probably being at greater risk than adults).

**Example 2: Falling objects during maintenance work**

*Hazard:* A person at ground level being struck by a falling object during maintenance work.

*Extent of the risk* is determined by factors such as:

- the frequency of maintenance at elevated levels;
- the presence of persons in areas below;
- the numbers of such persons;
- the security of tools used in the maintenance work;
- measures taken to secure other items, eg equipment and components;
- the degree of care exercised by maintenance workers;
- the size and weight of objects which may fall;
- the potential distance objects might fall;
- the presence of openings in the working platform;
- the availability of edge protection;
- whether persons at ground level are wearing head protection.

## Evaluation of precautions

**2.3** The ACOP clearly states that the risk assessment involves 'identifying the hazards present ... and evaluating the extent of the risks involved, taking into account existing precautions and their effectiveness.'

The evaluation of the effectiveness of precautions is an integral part of the risk assessment process. This is overlooked by some organisations who concentrate on the identification (and often the quantification) of risks without checking whether the intended precautions are actually being taken in the workplace and whether these precautions are proving effective.

Taking the previous examples to illustrate this principle:

In *Example 1: Pedestrians crossing a roadway*, the risk assessment must include consideration of whether:

- pedestrians are using available crossing points;
- warning signs are of adequate size and suitably positioned;
- lighting levels are adequate;
- speed limits are being observed.

Similarly in *Example 2: Falling objects during maintenance work*, the risk assessment must take account of whether:

- barriers and/or warning signs at ground level are in place and being respected;
- tool belts are used by maintenance employees;
- edge protection and precautions are in place on working platforms;
- those at ground level are wearing head protection, if required.

## *'Suitable and sufficient'*

**2.4** Risk assessments under the *Management Regulations 1999* (and several other Regulations) must be 'suitable and sufficient', but the phrase is not defined in the Regulations themselves. However, the ACOP to the Regulations states that 'The level of risk arising from the work activity should determine the degree of sophistication of the risk assessment'. The ACOP also states that insignificant risks can usually be ignored, as can risks arising from routine activities associated with life in general ('unless the work activity compounds or significantly alters those risks').

In practice, a risk can only be concluded to be insignificant if some attention is paid to it during the risk assessment process and, if there is any scope for doubt, it is prudent to state in the risk assessment record which risks are considered insignificant. Some examples of this are contained in CHAPTER 5: ASSESSMENT RECORDS.

Similarly the risk assessment process should identify which routine activities of life might be compounded or significantly altered by work activities. Going out of doors in winter weather (with its attendant rain, ice, snow or wind) may be considered to be a routine activity. However, the risks may be considerably greater for work activities such as:

- work on electrical equipment situated outdoors;
- driving a fork lift truck in an icy yard;
- agricultural or construction work in a remote location;
- maintenance activities on an exposed part of a manufacturing plant.

**2.5** The ACOP states that increasingly sophisticated risk assessments will be required in higher risk situations but unfortunately provides little in terms of illustrations and examples. (See CHAPER 5: ASSESSMENT RECORDS for examples based on practical experience of risk assessment.)

The ACOP statements can be summarised as:

## Small businesses with few or simple hazards

- A straightforward process based on informed judgement and reference to guidance.
- Obvious hazards and risks can be addressed directly.
- No complicated process or skills required.

## Intermediate cases

- Some areas might require specialist advice, knowledge or techniques.

## Large and hazardous sites

- A much more sophisticated approach will be required, especially for 'complex or novel processes'.
- Other legislation may require detailed safety cases or reports, eg bulk storage or use of hazardous substances, large scale mineral extraction or nuclear plant.

Emphasis is also placed in the ACOP upon the need for risk assessments to consider both workers and members of the public who might be affected by the undertaking. It refers to railway companies needing to take into account rail workers (their own employees and others), passengers and others, such as level crossing users.

Similarly a construction company would need to consider risks to (and from):

- their employees;
- sub-contractors;
- visitors to their sites;
- passers by;
- possible trespassers on sites.

A residential care home should take into account risks to (and from):

- their staff;
- residents;
- visiting medical specialists;
- visitors to residents;
- visiting contractors.

Further guidance on categories of people who may need to be covered in the risk assessment process is provided in CHAPTER 4: CARRYING OUT RISK ASSESSMENTS – SEE 4.5: CONSIDER WHO MIGHT BE AT RISK and 4.8: CHECKLIST OF POSSIBLE RISKS.

## Who should carry out the assessment?

**2.6** *Regulation 3* of the *Management Regulations 1999* requires the employer (or self-employed person) to make the assessment. However, *regulation 7* contains a requirement for employers to have competent health and safety assistance. *Paragraph (1)* of the Regulation states:

> 'Every employer shall, subject to paragraphs (6) and (7), appoint one or more competent persons to assist him in undertaking the measures he needs to take to comply with the requirements and prohibitions imposed upon him by or under the relevant statutory provisions and by Part II of the *Fire Precautions (Workplace) Regulations 1997*.'

The 1999 version of the *Management Regulations* demonstrates a clear preference for the source of health and safety advice to be in the employer's employment, through *paragraph (8)* which states:

> 'where there is a competent person in the employer's employment, that person shall be appointed for the purposes of paragraph (1) in preference to a competent person not in his employment.'

Consequently, employers may appoint someone to carry out risk assessments on their behalf with the *Management Regulations 1999* expressing a preference for an employee over external persons such as health and safety consultants.

*Paragraph (5)* of the Regulation provides a definition of competence as:

> 'a person shall be regarded as competent for the purposes of paragraphs (1) and (8) where he has sufficient training and experience or knowledge and other qualities to enable him properly to assist in undertaking the measures referred to in paragraph (1).'

*Paragraphs (2) and (3)* introduce requirements in respect of co-operation and the adequacy of the health and safety assistance.

> '(2) Where an employer appoints persons in accordance with paragraph (1), he shall make arrangements for ensuring adequate co-operation between them.
>
> (3) The employer shall ensure that the number of persons appointed under paragraph (1), the time available for them to fulfil their functions and the means at their disposal are adequate having regard to the size of his undertaking, the risks to which his employees are exposed and the distribution of those risks throughout the undertaking.'

Employers are also required by *paragraph (4)* to ensure those providing health and safety assistance are given all necessary information about health and safety factors associated with their undertaking and those persons working in it.

It is also open to employers to act as their own source of health and safety assistance and carry out their own risk assessments. *Regulation 3, paragraphs (6)* and *(7)* state:

> '(6) Paragraph (1) shall not apply to a self-employed employer who is not in partnership with any other person where he has sufficient training and experience or knowledge and other

qualities to enable him properly to undertake the measures referred to in that paragraph himself.

(7) Paragraph (1) shall not apply to individuals who are employers and who are together carrying on business in partnership where at least one of the individuals concerned has sufficient training and experience or knowledge and other qualities–

(a) properly to undertake the measures he needs to take to comply with the requirements and prohibitions imposed upon him under the relevant statutory provisions; and

(b) properly to assist his fellow partners in undertaking the measures they need to take to comply with the requirements and prohibitions imposed upon them by or under the relevant statutory provisions.'

The HSE leaflet *INDG 163 Five steps to risk assessment (1998)* states 'If you are a small firm and you are confident you understand what's involved, you can do the assessment yourself (you don't have to be a health and safety expert!).'

The key attributes are having 'sufficient training and experience or knowledge and other qualities' to be able to identify risks and evaluate the effectiveness of precautions to control those risks. Many people running small businesses should have such abilities in relation to their own work activities – this book aims to show them how best to use those abilities.

HSE guidance to *regulation* 7 refers to competence as not necessarily depending on the possession of particular skills or qualifications. It states that simple situations may only require:

- an understanding of relevant current best practice;
- an awareness of the limitations of one's own experience and knowledge; and
- the willingness and ability to supplement existing experience and knowledge, where necessary, by obtaining external help and advice.

*Five steps to risk assessment* suggests that larger firms ask a responsible employee, safety representative or safety officer to become involved in carrying out the risk assessment. However, the same leaflet recognises that help from external sources (such as health and safety consultants) may be necessary. A separate HSE leaflet *INDG 322 Need help on health and safety? (2000)* gives valuable guidance on this important subject. It makes reference to the different types of specialist support which are available from consultancies and also to the various qualifications available and the professional bodies active in the field of health and safety.

The Institution of Occupational Safety and Health ('IOSH') is probably the pre-eminent professional body and will provide employers with guidance on consultancies available. (IOSH, The Grange, Highfield Drive, Wigston, Leicestershire LE18 1NN, tel: 0116 257 3100.)

Neither external consultants nor in-house health and safety specialists are likely to be able to conduct a risk assessment of a work activity without significant contact with those responsible for managing the activity, those who actually carry out the activity and also their health and safety representatives. Further advice on the importance of consultation is provided within CHAPTER 4: CARRYING OUT RISK ASSESSMENTS – SEE 4.11: DISCUSSIONS.

Employers should be sceptical of consultancies and other organisations who offer to provide risk assessment documentation without the involvement of the employer and his staff. Such documents may be successful in identifying risks (particularly in more common work activities) and precautions required to control those risks. However, it is not usually possible to evaluate the effectiveness of the precautions without contact with those involved in the work activity and/or visiting the work location.

## Reviewing risk assessments

**2.7** *Regulation 3, paragraph (3)* requires a risk assessment to be reviewed if:

'(a) there is reason to suspect it is no longer valid;

(b) there has been a significant change in the matters to which it relates; and where as a result of any such review changes to an assessment are required, the employer or self-employed person concerned shall make them.'

The ACOP to the *Management Regulations 1999* states that those carrying out risk assessments 'would not be expected to anticipate risks that were not foreseeable'. However, what is foreseeable can be changed by subsequent events. An accident, a non-injury incident or a case of ill-health may highlight the need for a risk assessment to be reviewed because:

- a previously unforeseen possibility has now occurred;
- the risk of something happening (or the extent of its consequences) is greater than previously thought;
- precautions prove to be less effective than anticipated.

Such information may come from outside the organisation itself – from others involved in the same work activity, through trade or specialist health and safety journals, from the suppliers of equipment or materials or from the Health and Safety Executive or other specialist bodies. Routine monitoring activity (inspections, audits, etc) or consultation with employees may also identify the need for an assessment to be reviewed for the same sort of reasons as identified above. A review of the risk assessment may be required because of significant changes in the work activity – changes to the equipment or materials used, to the environment where the activity takes place, to the system of work used or to the numbers of types of people carrying out the activity.

A review of the risk assessment does not necessarily require a repeat of the whole risk assessment process but it is quite likely to identify the need for increased or changed precautions. However, in some cases the conclusion may be that even if the risks have increased, there are no precautions which are reasonably practicable available to control the risks.

Examples of changes requiring a review of a risk assessment (and the improved precautions which may be necessary) are:

- Larger components are to be processed on a machine tool (these necessitate larger openings in the guard, thus allowing easy access to dangerous parts)–
  - extension tunnels need to be fitted to both sides of the guard,
  - improved mechanical handling apparatus is required.
- Increased storage needs mean that finished products are now stacked in the factory yard–
  - stacks need to be protected from accidental impact from heavy goods vehicles,
  - fork lift truck drivers need to be provided with waterproof clothing.
- Night shift maintenance cover is reduced to one person–
  - improved systems of communication with that person are required, eg portable phones, alarm devices, checks by security staff,
  - improved mechanical handling apparatus is required (for manual handling tasks previously carried out by two people),
  - a second person must be available from another source to assist in certain types of electrical work.

In practice, workplaces and the activities within them are constantly subject to gradual changes and the ACOP states 'it is prudent to plan to review risk assessments at regular intervals'. The frequency of such reviews should depend on the extent and nature of the risks involved and the degree of change likely. In the author's view, all risk assessments should be reviewed at least every five years. Further guidance is provided in CHAPTER 4: CARRYING OUT RISK ASSESSMENTS – SEE 4.20: ASSESSMENT REVIEW.

As the ACOP points out, there are many activities where the nature of the work or the workplace itself changes constantly. Examples of such situations are construction work or peripatetic maintenance or repair work. Here it is possible to carry out 'generic' assessments of the types of risks involved and the types of precautions which should be taken. However, some reliance must be placed upon workers themselves to identify what precautions are appropriate for a given set of circumstances or to deal with unexpected situations. Clearly such workers must be well informed and well trained in order for them to be competent to make what are often called 'dynamic' risk assessments. This concept of dynamic risk assessment is dealt with in more detail in CHAPTER 15: RISK ASSESSMENT RELATED CONCEPTS.

## *Related requirements of the Management Regulations 1999*

**2.8** A number of other requirements of the *Management Regulations 1999* are of considerable importance to the process of risk assessment – they are part of the 'relevant statutory provisions' and the risk assessment must identify the measures necessary to comply with them.

### Principles of prevention to be applied (Regulation 4)

**2.9** *Regulation 4* and *Schedule 1* require preventive and protective measures to be implemented on the basis of specified principles. These principles will be referred to in more detail in CHAPTER 8: IMPLEMENTATION OF PRECAUTIONS.

### Health and safety arrangements (Regulation 5)

**2.10** Employers are required to have appropriate arrangements for the effective planning, organisation, control, monitoring and review of preventive and protective measures. Those employers with five or more employees must record these arrangements. This application of the 'management cycle' to health and safety matters will be covered in some detail in CHAPTER 8: IMPLEMENTATION OF PRECAUTIONS.

## Health surveillance (Regulation 6)

**2.11** Where risks to employees are identified through a risk assessment, *regulation 6* requires that they 'are provided with such health surveillance as is appropriate'. In practice, surveillance is more likely to be necessary to comply with the requirements of more specific Regulations, eg COSHH, Asbestos, Ionising Radiations. However, some types of surveillance may be appropriate to deal with risks not covered elsewhere:

- colour blindness, eg in electricians or train drivers;
- other vision defects, eg vehicle or train drivers;
- blackouts, epilepsy, eg drivers, operators of machinery, those working at heights.

HSE guidance is available on this important area (see *HSG 61 Health surveillance at work (1999)*).

## Health and safety assistance (Regulation 7)

**2.12** The requirements of this Regulation are described at 2.6: WHO SHOULD CARRY OUT THE ASSESSMENT?

## Procedures for serious and imminent danger and for danger areas (Regulation 8)

**2.13** *Regulation 8* requires every employer to 'establish and where necessary give effect to appropriate procedures to be followed in the event of serious and imminent danger to persons at work in his undertaking'. It also refers to the possible need to restrict access to areas 'on grounds of health and safety unless the employee concerned has received adequate health and safety instruction'.

The need for emergency procedures or restricted areas should of course be identified through the process of risk assessment. Situations 'of serious and imminent danger' might be due to fires, bomb threats, escape or release of hazardous substances, out of control processes, personal attack, escape of animals, etc.

The Regulation also requires the nomination of sufficient competent persons to implement evacuation (where this is necessary) and that emergency procedures should:

- 'so far as is practicable, require any persons at work who are exposed to serious and imminent danger to be informed of the nature of the hazard and of the steps taken or to be taken to protect them from it';
- enable such persons 'to stop work and immediately proceed to a place of safety in the event of their being exposed to serious, imminent and unavoidable danger';
- 'require the persons concerned to be prevented from resuming work in any situation where there is still a serious and imminent danger' (save in exceptional cases).

Areas may justify access to them being restricted because of the presence of hazardous substances, unprotected electrical conductors (particularly high voltage), potentially dangerous animals or people etc.

## Contacts with external services (Regulation 9)

**2.14** This regulation states that 'Every employer should ensure that any necessary contacts with emergency services are arranged, particularly as regards first aid, emergency medical care and rescue work'. Quite clearly this links very closely to the emergency procedures required by *regulation 8*. The ACOP to the *Management Regulations 1999* provides further advice on the interface with external services.

## Information for employees (Regulation 10)

**2.15** Employers are required to provide employees with comprehensible and relevant information on:

- the risks to their health and safety identified by the risk assessment;
- the preventive and protective measures;
- emergency procedures.

This relates closely to the training requirements in *regulation 13*. *Regulation 10* also includes specific requirements relating to the employment of children. These are dealt with in some detail in CHAPTER 3: SPECIAL CASES.

## Co-operation and co-ordination (Regulation 11)

**2.16** This Regulation requires employers and self-employed persons sharing a workplace (whether on a temporary or a permanent basis ) to:

- co-operate with each other in respect of health and safety;

- co-ordinate their precautions;
- take all reasonable steps to inform each other about health and safety risks.

Sharing of workplaces may be temporary (such as in short-term construction work) or more permanent (as in a multi-occupancy building). Information may need to be provided to the other occupants about the use of hazardous substances or radioactive materials or in relation to high risk activities, particularly those which may affect the other occupants.

Co-ordination and co-operation are particularly likely to be necessary in relation to fire and other emergency procedures but may be relevant in other areas, eg leaving adequate space or visibility for vehicles used by other to circulate safely. Here, even those who do not have employees working on the premises but have responsibilities for common parts or services will also have an important part to play through their duties under *HASAWA 1974, section 4*.

Once again, the need to provide others with information should be identified through the risk assessment process. In respect of construction work, the requirements of the *Construction (Design and Management) Regulations 1994 ('the CDM Regulations 1994')* and particularly the need for a Health and Safety Plan must also be taken into account (see CHAPTER 15: RISK ASSESSMENT RELATED CONCEPTS).

## Persons working in host employers' or self-employed persons' undertakings (Regulation 12)

**2.17** Requirements are placed on host employers (or self-employed persons) to provide other employers (or self-employed persons) whose employees are working in the host's undertaking with comprehensible information on:

- risks to those visiting employees' health and safety arising out of or in connection with the conduct of the host's undertaking;
- precautions already taken by the host in relation to those visiting employees.

In addition, the host must 'ensure that any person working in his undertaking who is not his employee ... is provided with appropriate instructions and comprehensible information regarding any risks to that person's health and safety which arise out of the conduct' of the host's undertaking. In both cases, this must include information about any evacuation procedures.

Essentially this Regulation identifies three issues which must be addressed during the risk assessment process.

### *Which visiting employees need to be considered?*

Contractors are the obvious answer, but contractors provide a variety of services – cleaning, catering, security, servicing, maintenance, construction, etc. In some cases, workers supplied under a contract agreement may work alongside the host's own employees. Each of these groups will be exposed to different types of risks in relation to the host's undertaking. The Regulation can also be interpreted as applying to members of the emergency services who are exposed to risks (although no mention is made of this in the ACOP or HSE guidance on the Regulations).

### *What types of risk are relevant?*

The Regulation itself places no limit on the risks in respect of which information must be provided. However, the ACOP indicates that the host should be concerned about the more significant or unusual risks associated with the host's activities or premises. The likely state of knowledge and awareness of the visiting employees may also need to be taken into account – an experienced service engineer may only need to be informed about risks peculiar to the host's activities or premises, whereas inexperienced workers supplied under contract are likely to need more comprehensive information.

### *How will the information be communicated?*

The host has duties in respect of both the employer of visiting employees *and* the visiting employees themselves. Information (about risks, precautions and emergency procedures) might be provided to the employer together with the contract order. It might be in the form of a standard contractors' information sheet or handbook or through a document prepared specifically for the contractor in question. Documentation may need to be supported by face to face meetings and in some cases contractors' activities may be controlled through permit to work systems (see CHAPTER 15: RISK ASSESSMENT RELATED CONCEPTS).

Information can be supplied to visiting employees (about risks and emergency procedures) either directly by the host or via their own employer. However, it is the host's duty to ensure it is done. Depending on the nature and extent of the risk, the host may choose to use an informal briefing or more formal induction methods (possibly even accompanied by a test to ensure the information has been assimilated). Again, use could be made of information sheets or contractors' handbooks, although the style and content may need to be different for visiting employees as opposed to their employers. It should be noted that these requirements overlap with some requirements of the *CDM Regulations 1994*, particularly the duties of the 'Principal Contractor' under those Regulations.

Detailed guidance on managing contractors and the *CDM Regulations 1994* is available from the HSE (*Managing contractors. A guide for employers (1997); L54 Managing construction for health and safety. The Construction (Design and Management) Regulations 1994. Approved code of practice (1995); and A guide to managing health and safety in construction (1995)*).

## Capabilities and training (Regulation 13)

**2.18** This Regulation is in three parts – *paragraph (1)* states 'Every employer shall, in entrusting tasks to his employees, take into account their capabilities as regards health and safety'.

The capabilities of employees include not only the training they may have received but also their capacity to put that training into practice. Some tasks may require a high degree of skill in order to be carried out safely. In other situations, employees may be required to make a judgement about the risks involved and choose appropriate precautions, ie carry out a dynamic risk assessment. The employer must identify these types of tasks through the risk assessment process and be satisfied that staff performing them possess necessary skills or are properly equipped to make judgements on risks and precautions.

*Paragraph (2)* requires employers to ensure employees are provided with adequate health and safety training:

(a) on their being recruited into the employer's undertaking; and

(b) on their being exposed to new or increased risks because of–

- a transfer or a change of responsibilities,
- introduction of new work equipment or changes in existing equipment,
- introduction of new technology, or
- a new or changed system of work.

Consequently the risk assessment should identify what should be included in general induction training (eg fire and other emergency procedures, general PPE requirements) and what training is required by employees carrying out specific tasks (eg operating equipment) or working in certain areas (eg high voltage switchrooms). Operating some types of equipment (eg a machine fully enclosed with fixed and interlocked guards) may only justify fairly simple health and safety training, whereas driving a fork lift truck, operating an overhead crane or using a chainsaw will require a much more comprehensive approach.

Employees who are transferred or given new responsibilities are also likely to need training in their new tasks or in relation to their new environment. Changes in equipment, technology or systems of work will necessitate a review of the risk assessment in relation to training needs, as well as other factors.

*Paragraph (3)* of the Regulation states:

> 'The training referred to in paragraph (2) shall–
>
> (a) be repeated periodically where appropriate;
>
> (b) be adapted to take account of new or changed risks to the health and safety of the employees concerned; and
>
> (c) take place during working hours.'

The risk assessment should identify where refresher training may be necessary, eg where competence may decline if tasks are not performed regularly. Reviews of risk assessments may be prompted by changes in the workplace or by feedback from monitoring systems (audits, inspections, accident/incident investigations) and may indicate the need for changes to training programmes.

The ACOP to the Regulations states that 'if it is necessary to arrange training outside an employee's normal hours, this should be treated as an extension of time at work'. This would usually be expected to qualify for time off in lieu or overtime payments. Employers are required by the *Safety Representatives and Safety Committee Regulations 1977*) to consult safety representatives about arrangements for health and safety training. The ACOP emphasises that *HASAWA 1974, section 9* prohibits employers from requiring employees to pay for their own health and safety training.

Most of the other requirements of the *Management Regulations 1999* are of little relevance to the risk assessment process with the important exceptions of:

- risk assessment in respect of new or expectant mothers (*Regulation 16*); and
- protection of young persons (*Regulation 19*).

Both of these special cases are covered in detail in CHAPTER 3: SPECIAL CASES.

## References

### (all HSE publications)

**2.19**



| | | |
|---|---|---|
| 1 | L21: | Management of health and safety at work. Management of Health and Safety at Work Regulations 1999. Approved code of practice (2000) |
| 2 | INDG 163: | Five steps to risk assessment (1998) |
| 3 | INDG 322: | Need help on health and safety? (2000) |
| 4 | HSG 61: | Health surveillance at work (1999) |
| 5 | | Managing contractors. A guide for employers (1997) |
| 6 | L 54: | Managing construction for health and safety. The Construction (Design and Management) Regulations 1994. Approved code of practice (1995) |
| 7 | | A guide to managing health and safety in construction. (1995) |

# 3 Special cases

**3.1** The *Management Regulations 1999* identify two particular types of workers to whom special attention must be given in carrying out risk assessments:

- children and young persons; and
- new and expectant mothers.

The requirements of the Regulations in respect of these categories are dealt with in this chapter.

## Children and young persons

### Introduction

**3.2** Previous Acts and Regulations identified many types of equipment that children and young persons were not allowed to use, or processes or activities that they must not be involved in. Many of these 'prohibitions' were revoked by the *Health and Safety (Young Persons) Regulations 1997*, since incorporated into the *Management Regulations 1999*. (A few 'prohibitions' still remain – several of these are listed later in the chapter at 3.9: PROHIBITIONS ON CHILDREN AND YOUNG PERSONS). The emphasis has now changed to restrictions on the work that children and young persons are allowed to do, based upon the employer's risk assessment.

The *Health and Safety (Training for Employment) Regulations 1990* have the effect of giving students on work experience training programmes and trainees on training for employment programmes the status of 'employees'. The immediate provider of their training is treated as the 'employer'. (There are exceptions for courses at educational establishments, ie universities, colleges, schools etc). Therefore employers have duties in respect of all children and young persons at work in their undertaking – full-time employees, part-time and temporary employees and also students or trainees on work placement with them.

### Definitions

**3.3** The terms 'child' and 'young person' are defined in *Regulation 1(2)* of the *Management Regulations 1999*.

*Child* is defined as a person not over compulsory school age in accordance with:

- *the Education Act 1996, section 8* (for England and Wales); and
- *the Education (Scotland) Act 1980, section 31* (for Scotland).

(In practice this is just under or just over the age of sixteen.)

*Young person* is defined as 'any person who has not attained the age of eighteen'.

Some of the prohibitions remaining from older Health and Safety Regulations use different cut-off ages – where relevant these are referred to later in the chapter at 3.9: PROHIBITIONS ON CHILDREN AND YOUNG PERSONS. Further detail is also provided in HSE guidance *(HS(G) 165 Young people at work. A guide for employers (1997))*.

The hours and types of work that children are allowed to do are subject to prohibitions and restrictions imposed by other (non-health and safety) legislation.

## Requirements of the Management Regulations

**3.4** The general requirements for risk assessments placed on employers by *Regulation 3* of the *Management Regulations 1999* were described in the previous chapter (see 2.1: INTRODUCTION). *Regulation 3, paragraphs (4) and (5)* introduce specific requirements in respect of young persons, ie all under 18s.

> '(4) An employer shall not employ a young person unless he has, in relation to risks to the health and safety of young persons, made or reviewed an assessment in accordance with paragraphs (1) and (5).
>
> (5) In making or reviewing the assessment, an employer who employs or is to employ a young person shall take particular account of–
>
> (a) the inexperience, lack of awareness of risks and immaturity of young persons;
>
> (b) the fitting-out and layout of the workplace and the workstation;
>
> (c) the nature, degree and duration of exposure to physical, biological and chemical agents;
>
> (d) the form, range and use of work equipment and the way in which it is handled;
>
> (e) the organisation of processes and activities;

(f) the extent of the health and safety training provided or to be provided to young persons; and

(g) risks from agents, processes and work listed in the Annex to Council Directive 94/33/EC on the protection of young persons at work.'

The risk assessment in respect of young persons must also take particular note of the requirements of *Regulation 19* which states:

'(1) Every employer shall ensure that young persons employed by him are protected at work from any risks to their health or safety which are a consequence of their lack of experience, or absence of awareness of existing or potential risks or the fact that young persons have not yet fully matured.

(2) Subject to paragraph (3), no employer shall employ a young person for work–

(a) which is beyond his physical or psychological capacity;

(b) involving harmful exposure to agents which are toxic or carcinogenic, cause heritable genetic damage or harm to the unborn child or which in any way chronically affect human health;

(c) involving harmful exposure to radiation;

(d) involving the risk of accidents which it may reasonably be assumed cannot be recognised or avoided by young persons owing to their insufficient attention to safety or lack of experience or training; or

(e) in which there is a risk to health from–

(i) extreme cold or heat,

(ii) noise, or

(iii) vibration;

and in determining whether work will involve harm or risk for the purposes of this paragraph, regard shall be had to the results of the assessment.

(3) Nothing in paragraph (2) shall prevent the employment of a young person who is no longer a child for work–

(a) where it is necessary for his training;

(b) where the young person will be supervised by a competent person; and

(c) where any risk will be reduced to the lowest level that is reasonably practicable.

(4) The provisions contained in the Regulations are without prejudice to–

(a) the provisions contained elsewhere in these Regulations; and

(b) any prohibition or restriction, arising otherwise than by this Regulation, on the employment of any person.'

## Assessing risks to children and young persons

**3.5** A good starting point in assessing risks is to consider the three characteristics associated with young people which are mentioned in both *Regulations 3(5)* and *19(1)*:

- lack of experience;
- lack of awareness of existing or potential risks; and
- immaturity (in both the physical and psychological sense).

All young people share these characteristics but to differing extents – for example, one would have different expectations of a school leaver who had already been playing a prominent role in a family business such as a shop, restaurant or farm, as opposed to a work experience student or trainee with no previous exposure to the world of work. The degrees of physical and psychological maturity of young people also vary hugely.

These three characteristics must then be considered in respect of the risks involved in the employer's work activities and particularly those identified in *Regulations 3(5)* and *19(2)*. As an aid to the risk assessment process, the contents of those regulations (including those risks listed in the Annex to *Council Directive 94/33/EC*) have been consolidated into a single checklist, given below.

## Checklist: Work presenting increased risks for children and young persons

**3.6** This checklist is based upon the *Management of Health and Safety at Work Regulations 1999*, *Regulations 3(5)* and *19(2)* and the *Annex to Council Directive 94/33/EC*. It is intended to assist employers conducting risk assessments in respect of work by children and young persons.

These types of work are not necessarily prohibited, although the requirements of *Regulation 19(2)* must be taken into account. However, such work is likely to require restrictions for most young persons (particularly children) and additional precautions are likely to be required to provide them with adequate protection from risk.

### Excessively physically demanding work

- Manual handling operations where the force required or the repetitive nature of the activity could injure someone whose body is still developing (including production line work).
- Certain types of piecework.

### Excessively psychologically demanding work

- Work with difficult clients or situations where there is a possibility of violence or aggression.
- Difficult emotional situations, eg dealing with death, serious illness or injury.
- Decision-making under stress.

### Harmful exposure to physical agents

- Ionising radiation.
- Non-ionising radiation, eg lasers, UV from electric arc welding, IR from furnaces or burning/welding.
- Risks to health from extreme cold or heat.
- Excessive noise.
- Hand-arm vibration, eg from portable tools.
- Whole-body vibration, eg from off-road vehicles.
- Work in pressurised atmospheres and diving work.

### Harmful exposure to biological or chemical agents

- Toxic or carcinogenic substances (including lead and asbestos).
- Substances causing heritable genetic damage or harming the unborn child.

- Substances chronically affecting human health.
- Other hazardous substances (harmful, corrosive, irritant).

## Work equipment

Where there is an increased risk of injury due to the complexity of precautions required or the level of skill required for safe operation, for example:

- woodworking machines;
- food slicers and other food processing machinery;
- certain types of portable tools such as chainsaws;
- setting of power presses;
- vehicles such as fork lift trucks, mobile cranes, construction vehicles;
- firearms.

## Dangerous processes or activities

- Work with explosives, including fireworks.
- Work with fierce or poisonous animals, eg on farms, in zoos or veterinary work.
- Certain types of electrical work, eg exposure to high voltage or live electrical equipment.
- Handling of highly flammable materials, eg petrol, other flammable liquids, flammable gases.
- Work with pressurised gases.
- Work in large slaughterhouses.
- Holding large quantities of cash or valuables.

## Dangerous workplaces or workstations

- Work at heights, eg on high ladders or other unprotected forms of access.
- Work in confined spaces, particularly where the risks specified in the *Confined Spaces Regulations 1997* are present.
- Work where there is a risk of structural collapse, eg in construction or demolition activities or inside old buildings.

**3.7** The purpose of all risk assessments is to identify what measures the employer needs to take in order to comply with the law. Measures which the employer must consider in order to provide adequate protection for young persons are:

- not exposing the young person to the risk at all;*
- providing additional training;
- providing close supervision by a competent person;
- carrying out additional health surveillance (as required by *Regulation 6* of the *Management Regulations 1999* or other Regulations, eg *COSHH 1999*);
- taking other additional precautions.

* *Regulation 19(2)* means that serious consideration must always be given to whether the risks remaining after control measures have been applied require this option to be taken. More flexibility is allowed by *Regulation 19(3)* in respect of young persons who are no longer children.

In deciding what precautions are required, the employer must consider both young people generally and the characteristics of individual young persons. For example, higher levels of training and/or supervision may be necessary in respect of young people with 'special needs'. Young people should gradually acquire more experience, awareness of risks and maturity, particularly as they pass through formal training programmes within the NVQ system. As this occurs, restrictions on their activities may be progressively removed.

Even when young workers have passed the age of 18, it should be noted that *Regulation 13* of the *Management Regulations 1999* still requires employers to take account of their capabilities in entrusting tasks to them and also to provide them with adequate health and safety training.

## Provision of information

**3.8** *Regulation 10* of the *Management Regulations 1999* contains general requirements for employers to provide all employees with information about risks and associated precautions. It must always be borne in mind that young persons will generally be less aware of risks than more experienced workers. However, important additional requirements in respect of the employment of children are contained in *paragraphs (2)* and *(3)* of the Regulation which state:

'(2) Every employer shall, before employing a child, provide a parent of the child with comprehensible and relevant information on–

(a) the risks to their health and safety identified by risk assessment;

(b) the preventive and protective measures; and

(c) the risks notified to him in accordance with *Regulation 11(1)(c)*.

(3) The reference in *paragraph (2)* to a parent of the child includes–

(a) in England and Wales, a person who has parental responsibility, within the meaning of *section 3* of the *Children Act 1989*, for him; and

(b) in Scotland, a person who has parental rights, within the meaning of *section 8* of the *Law Reform (Parent and Child) (Scotland) Act 1986*, for him.'

This requirement to provide information to parents includes situations where children are on work experience programmes (where they have the status of employees by virtue of the *Health and Safety (Training for Employment) Regulations 1990* and also includes part time or temporary work.

The wide-ranging impact of these provisions is lessened to a certain extent by the introduction of *paragraph (2)* into *Regulation 2* 'Disapplication of these Regulations'. This states:

'(2) Regulations 3(4), (5),10(2) and 19 shall not apply to occasional work or short-term work involving–

(a) domestic service in a private household; or

(b) work regulated as not being harmful, damaging or dangerous to young people in a family undertaking.'

However, the key term 'family undertaking' is not defined in the Regulations. HSE guidance (*HS(G) 165 Young people at work. A guide for employers (1997), page 3*) indicates that this should be interpreted as meaning 'small and medium-sized firms, owned by, and employing members of the same family'. They suggest family members should include 'husbands, wives, fathers, mothers, grandfathers, grandmothers, stepfathers, stepmothers, sons, daughters, grandsons, granddaughters, stepsons, stepdaughters, brothers, sisters, half-brothers and half-sisters'.

As far as is known, this narrow interpretation of 'family undertaking' has not been tested in the courts. Common usage of the term would suggest small and medium-sized businesses controlled and managed by members of the same family but not necessarily only employing family members, as implied by the words used by the HSE.

The HSE guidance accompanying *Regulation 10* allows for the information on the key findings of the risk assessment to be passed on verbally to parents or guardians or even via the child itself (although it acknowledges the potential fallibility of this latter method). However, many would recommend the provision of a written summary – most organisations managing work experience programmes already have standard forms for doing this.

As the HSE acknowledge, the information required by *Regulation 10* to be given to all young persons may be provided either orally or in writing or possibly both. Key items (eg critical restrictions or prohibitions) should be recorded.

Means of providing information might include:

- induction training programmes;
- employee handbooks or rulebooks;
- job descriptions;
- formal operating procedures;
- trainee agreement forms (increasingly common for young persons on formal training programmes, eg modern apprenticeships);
- information forms for parents of work experience students.

The information must be comprehensible – special arrangements may be necessary for young people whose command of English is poor or for those with special needs. The type of information required to be provided will obviously relate to the work activities and the risks involved. The content must be relevant – both to the workplace and the young person. It might include the following types of information:

- general risks present in the workplace
    - eg fork lift trucks are widely used in the warehouse;
- general precautions taken in respect of those risks
    - eg all fork lift drivers are trained to the standard required by the ACOP;
- specific precautions in respect of the young person

- eg the induction tour includes identification of areas where fork lift trucks operate and indication of warning signs;

- restrictions or prohibitions on the young person
  - eg X will not be allowed to drive fork lift trucks or any other vehicles (he will be considered for fork lift truck training after attaining the age of 17);
- supervision arrangements
  - eg X will be supervised by the warehouse foreman (or other persons designated by him);
- PPE (personal protective equipment) requirements
  - eg safety footwear must be worn by all employees working in the warehouse (this is supplied by the company).

Where restrictions or prohibitions are removed (eg after successful completion of training programmes), an appropriate record should be made, either on the original restriction/prohibition or upon the individual's training record.

## Prohibitions on children and young persons

**3.9** These prohibitions were still in place following the introduction of the *Management of Health and Safety at Work Regulations 1999*. However, the HSE continue to modernise legislation and some of these are likely to be revoked.

### Explosives

Under-16s may not enter rooms where explosives are made, or where explosives (or their ingredients) are stored.

Under-18s may only be employed in explosives buildings in the presence of and under the supervision of a person aged 21 or over. [*Explosives Act 1875* as amended by the *Explosives Act 1923*]

Under-18s may not be employed as a driver or attendant of an explosives vehicle and may only enter the vehicle under supervision of someone over 18. (There are exceptions where the risks are slight.) [*Carriage of Explosives by Road Regulations 1996*]

## Ionising radiation

Under-18s may not be designated as 'classified persons'. Dose exposure limits are lower for under-18s. [*Ionising Radiations Regulations 1999*]

## Lead

Various old Regulations and two sections of the *Factories Act 1961 (sessions 74 and 131)* prohibit young persons from working with lead and lead compounds. Some requirements only apply to under-16s or females under 18.

## Carriage of dangerous goods

Under-18s may not supervise road tankers or vehicles carrying dangerous goods nor supervise the unloading of petrol from a road tanker at a petrol filling station. [*Carriage of Dangerous Goods by Road Regulations 1996*]

## Agriculture

Under-13s may not ride on vehicles and machines including tractors, trailers etc. Children (under the minimum school leaving age) may not operate certain machines and tractors carrying out certain operations. [*Agriculture (Avoidance of Accidents to Children)Regulations 1958* and associated ACOP]

## Mines and quarries

Various restrictions exist for under-18s and under-16s relating to the use of winding and rope haulage equipment, locomotives, shunting, quarry vehicles and shot firing. Some restrictions also apply to under-21s and under-22s.

## Shipbuilding and shiprepairing

Under-18s, until they have been employed in a shipyard for six months, may not be employed on staging or in any part of a ship where they are liable to fall more than two metres or into water where there is a risk of drowning. [*Shipbuilding and Shiprepairing Regulations 1960*]

## Docks

Under-18s may not operate powered lifting appliances in dock operations unless undergoing a suitable course of training under proper supervision of a competent person (serving members of HM Forces are exempt). [*Docks Regulations 1988*]

## *New and expectant mothers*

### Introduction

**3.10** Amendments made in 1994 to the previous *Management Regulations* implemented the *EC Directive on Pregnant Workers (92/85/EEC)*, requiring employers in their risk assessments to consider risks to new or expectant mothers. These amendments were subsequently incorporated into the *Management Regulations 1999. Regulation 1* of the *Management Regulations 1999* contains two relevant definitions:

- *New or expectant mother* means an employee who is pregnant, who has given birth within the previous six months, or who is breastfeeding.
- *Given birth* means 'delivered a living child or, after twenty-four weeks of pregnancy, a stillborn child'.

### Requirements of the Management Regulations 1999

**3.11** The requirements for 'Risk Assessment in respect of new and expectant mothers' are contained in *Regulation 16* which states in *paragraph (1)*:

> 'Where–
>
> (a) the persons working in an undertaking include women of child-bearing age; and
>
> (b) the work is of a kind which could involve risk, by reason of her condition, to the health and safety of a new or expectant mothers, or to that of her baby, from any processes or working conditions, or physical, biological or chemical agents, including those specified in Annexes I and II of Council Directive 92/85/EEC on the introduction of measures to encourage improvements in the safety and health at work of pregnant workers and workers who have recently given birth or are breastfeeding;
>
> the assessment required by *Regulation 3(1)* shall also include an assessment of such risk.'

*Regulation 16, paragraph (4)* states that in relation to risks from infectious or contagious diseases an assessment must only be made if the level of risk is in addition to the level of exposure outside the workplace.

The types of risk which are more likely to affect new or expectant mothers are described later in the chapter at 3.12: RISKS TO NEW OR EXPECTANT

MOTHERS. *Regulation 16, paragraphs (2) and (3)* set out the actions employers are required to take if these risks cannot be avoided. *Paragraph (2)* states:

> 'Where, in the case of an individual employee, the taking of any other action the employer is required to take under the relevant statutory provisions would not avoid the risk referred to in paragraph (1) the employer shall, if it is reasonable to do so, and would avoid such risks, alter her working conditions or hours of work.'

Consequently where the risk assessment required under *Regulation 16(1)* shows that control measures would not sufficiently avoid the risks to new or expectant mothers or their babies, the employer must make reasonable alterations to their working conditions or hours of work.

In some cases, restrictions may still allow the employee to substantially continue with her normal work but in others it may be more appropriate to offer her suitable alternative work.

Any alternative work must be:

- suitable and appropriate for the employee to do in the circumstances;
- on terms and conditions which are no less favourable.

*Regulation 16, paragraph (3)* states:

> 'If it is not reasonable to alter the working conditions or hours of work, or if it would not avoid such risk, the employer shall, subject to section 67 of the 1996 Act, suspend the employee from work for so long as is necessary to avoid such risk.'

The '1996 Act' referred to here is the *Employment Rights Act 1996* which provides that any such suspension from work on the above grounds is on full pay. However, payment might not be made if the employee has unreasonably refused an offer of suitable alternative work. Employment continues during such a suspension, counting as continuous employment in respect of seniority, pension rights, etc. Contractual benefits other than pay do not necessarily continue during the suspension. These are a matter for negotiation and agreement between the employer and employee, although employers should not act unlawfully under the *Equal Pay Act 1970* and the *Sex Discrimination Act 1975*. Enforcement of employment rights is through employment tribunals.

*Regulation 17* of the *Management Regulations 1999* deals specifically with night work by new or expectant mothers and states:

'Where–

(a) a new or expectant mother works at night; and

(b) a certificate from a registered medical practitioner or a registered midwife shows that it is necessary for her health or safety that she should not be at work for any period of such work identified in the certificate,

the employer shall, subject to section 46 of the 1978 Act, suspend her from work for so long as is necessary for her health or safety.'

Such suspension (on the same basis as described above) is only necessary if there are risks arising from work. The HSE do not consider there are any risks to pregnant or breastfeeding workers or their children working at night per se. They suggest that any claim from an employee that she cannot work nights should be referred to an occupational health specialist. The HSE's own Employment Medical Advisory Service are likely to have a role to play in such cases.

The requirements placed on employers in respect of altered working conditions or hours of work and suspensions from work only take effect when the employee has formally notified the employer of her condition. *Regulation 18* states:

'(1) Nothing in paragraph (2) or (3) of *Regulation 16* shall require the employer to take any action in relation to an employee until she has notified the employer in writing that she is pregnant, has given birth within the previous six months, or is breastfeeding.

(2) Nothing in paragraph (2) or (3) of *Regulation 16* or in *Regulation 17* shall require the employer to maintain action taken in relation to an employee–

(a) in a case–

(i) to which Regulation 16(2) or (3) relates; and

(ii) where the employee has notified her employer that she is pregnant, where she has failed, within a reasonable time of being requested to do so in writing by her employer, to produce for the employer's inspection a certificate from a registered medical practitioner or a registered midwife showing that she is pregnant;

(b) once the employer knows that she is no longer a new or expectant mother; or

(c) if the employer cannot establish whether she remains a new or expectant mother.'

## Risks to new or expectant mothers

**3.12** The HSE booklet *HS(G) 122 New and expectant mothers at work. A guide for employers (1994)* provides considerable guidance on those risks which may be of particular relevance to new or expectant mothers, including those listed in the *EC Directive on Pregnant Workers (92/85/EEC)*. This guidance is both summarised and augmented below.

## Physical agents

### *Manual handling*

**3.13** Pregnant women are particularly susceptible to risk from manual handling activities as also are those who have recently given birth, especially after a caesarean section. Manual handling assessments (as required by the *Manual Handling Operations Regulations 1992* are dealt with in some detail in CHAPTER 11: ASSESSMENT OF MANUAL HANDLING OPERATIONS.

### *Noise*

The HSE do not consider that there are any specific risks from noise for new or expectant mothers. Compliance with the requirements of the *Noise at Work Regulations 1989* should provide them with sufficient protection.

### *Ionising radiation*

The foetus may be harmed by exposure to ionising radiation, including that from radioactive materials inhaled or ingested by the mother. The *Ionising Radiations Regulations 1999* set an external radiation dose limit for the abdomen of any woman of reproductive capacity and also contain a specific requirement to provide information to female employees who may become pregnant or start breast-feeding. Systems of work should be such as to keep exposure of pregnant women to radiation from all sources as low as reasonably practicable. Contamination of a nursing mother's skin with radioactive substances can create risks for the child and special precautions may be necessary to avoid such a possibility.

Several HSE publications provide detailed guidance on work involving ionising radiation. (See *L 121 Work with ionising radiation. Ionising Radiations Regulations 1999. Approved code of practice and guidance (2000); L 58 The protection of persons against ionising radiation arising from any work activity (1994); HSG 91 A framework for the restriction of occupational exposure to ionising radiation (1992).*)

### Other electromagnetic radiation

The HSE do not consider that new or expectant mothers are at any greater risk from other types of radiation, with the possible exception of over exposure to radio-frequency radiation which could raise the body temperature to harmful levels. Compliance with the exposure standards for electric and magnetic fields published by the National Radiological Protection Board should provide adequate protection.

### Work in compressed air

Although pregnant women may not be at greater risk of developing the 'bends', potentially the foetus could be seriously harmed by gas bubbles in the circulation should this condition arise. There is also evidence that women who have recently given birth have an increased risk of the bends.

The *Work in Compressed Air Regulations 1996, Regulation 16(2)* states:

> ' . . . the compressed air contractor shall ensure that no person works in compressed air where the compressed air contractor has reason to believe that person to be subject to any medical or physical condition which is likely to render that person unfit or unsuitable for such work.'

This would appear to prohibit such work by pregnant women or those who have recently given birth. In their booklet *HS(G)122*, the HSE state that there is no physiological reason why a breastfeeding mother should not work in compressed air although they point out that practical difficulties would exist. HSE booklet *L96 A guide to the Work in Compressed Air Regulations 1996 (1996)* provides detailed guidance on the requirements of the *Work in Compressed Air Regulations 1996.*

### Diving work

The HSE draw attention to the possible effects of pressure on the foetus during underwater diving by pregnant women and state that they should not dive at all.

Under the *Diving at Work Regulations 1997, Regulation 15*, divers must have a certificate of medical fitness to dive and the HSE guidance to doctors issuing such certificates advises that pregnant workers should not dive.

*Regulation 13(1)* states that 'No person shall dive in a diving project– . . . if he knows of anything (including any illness or medical condition) which makes him unfit to dive'.

A series of HSE booklets provide general guidance on different types of diving projects. *(See L 103 Commercial diving projects offshore (1998); L 104 Commercial diving projects inland/inshore (1998); L 105 Recreational diving projects (1998); L 106 Media diving projects (1998); and L 107 Scientific and archaeological diving projects (1998).)*

### *Shock, vibration etc*

Major physical shocks or regular exposure to lesser shocks or low frequency vibration may increase the risk of a miscarriage. Activities involving such risks (eg the use of vehicles off-road) should be avoided by pregnant women.

### *Movement and posture*

Fatigue from standing and other physical work has been associated with miscarriage, premature birth and low birth weight. Ergonomic considerations will increase as the pregnancy advances and these could affect display screen equipment (DSE) workstations (discussed at 3.16: WORKING CONDITIONS, below), work in restricted spaces (eg for some maintenance or cleaning activities), or work on ladders or platforms. Underground mining work is likely to involve movement and posture problems and will also be subject to some of the other 'physical agents' described in this section. Driving for extended periods or travel by air may also present postural problems.

Pregnant women should be allowed to pace their work appropriately, taking longer and more frequent breaks. They may need to be restricted from carrying out certain tasks. Seating may need to be provided for work that is normally done standing and adjustments to DSE and other workstations may be necessary.

### *Physical and mental pressure*

Excessive physical or mental pressure could cause stress and lead to anxiety and raised blood pressure. Workplace stress is a complex issue which has recently been receiving increased attention. Fatigue issues are referred to above but other possible causes of stress may also need to be considered. These might be associated with the workload of individual pregnant employees (eg for those in management or administrative roles), the pressure of decision-making (eg in the health care or financial sectors) or the trauma of certain possible work situations (eg in the emergency services).

### *Extreme cold or heat*

Pregnant women are less tolerant of heat and may be more prone to fainting or heat stress. Although the risk is likely to reduce after birth, dehydration may impair breastfeeding. Exposure to prolonged heat at work, eg at furnaces or ovens should be avoided. Maintenance or cleaning work in hot situations should also be avoided, particularly if this involves use of less secure forms of access such as ladders, where fainting could result in a serious fall.

The HSE do not consider that there are any specific problems from working in extreme cold although obviously appropriate precautions should be taken as for other workers, eg the provision of warm clothing.

## Biological agents

**3.14** Many biological agents in hazard groups 2, 3 and 4 (as categorised by the Advisory Committee on Dangerous Pathogens) can affect the unborn child should the mother be infected during pregnancy. Some agents can cause abortion of the foetus and others can cause physical or neurological damage. Infections may also be passed on to the child during or after birth, eg while breastfeeding.

Agents presenting risks to children include hepatitis B, HIV, herpes, TB, syphilis, chickenpox, typhoid, rubella (german measles), cytomegalovirus and chlamydia in sheep. Most women will be at no more risk from these agents at work than living within the community but the risks are likely to be higher in some work sectors, eg laboratories, health care, the emergency services and those working with animals or animal products.

Details of appropriate control measures for biological agents are contained in *Schedule 9* and an ACOP to the *COSHH Regulations 1999*, published together with other COSHH ACOPs in HSE booklet *L5 General COSHH ACOP, Carcinogens ACOP and Biological Agents ACOP. Control of Substances Hazardous to Health Regulations 1999. Approved codes of practice (1999)*. There is a separate HSE publication on *Infections in the workplace to new and expectant mothers (1997)*. When carrying out a risk assessment in respect of new or expectant mothers, normal containment or hygiene measures may be considered sufficient, but there may be the need for special precautions such as use of vaccines. Where there is a high risk of exposure to a highly infectious biological agent it may be necessary to remove the worker entirely from the high risk environment.

## Chemical agents

### *Substances labelled with certain risk phrases*

**3.15** The *Chemicals (Hazard Information and Packaging for Supply) Regulations 1994* ('CHIP') require many types of hazardous substances to be labelled with specified risk phrases. Several of those are of relevance to new or expectant mothers:

- R40 – possible risk of irreversible effects;
- R45 – may cause cancer;
- R46 – may cause heritable genetic damage;
- R61 – may cause harm to the unborn child;
- R63 – possible risk of harm to the unborn child;
- R64 – may cause harm to breastfed babies.

The *CHIP Regulations 1994* are regularly subject to amendment and employers should be alert for other risk phrases which indicate risks in respect of new or expectant mothers.

Control of such substances at work is already required by the *COSHH Regulations 1998* or the separate Regulations governing lead and asbestos. Risk assessments in relation to pregnant women or those who have recently given birth may indicate that normal control measures are adequate to protect them also. However, additional precautions may be necessary, eg improved hygiene procedures, additional PPE or even restriction from work involving certain substances.

The ACOPs relating to the *COSHH Regulations* (contained in HSE booklet *L5*) together with *HS(G)97 A step by step guide to COSHH assessment (1992)* provide further details of the types of precautions which may be appropriate.

### Mercury and mercury derivatives

The HSE state that exposure to organic mercury compounds can slow the growth of the unborn baby, disrupt the nervous system and cause the mother to be poisoned. They consider there is no clear evidence of adverse effects on the foetus from mercury itself and inorganic mercury compounds. Mercury and its derivatives are subject to the *COSHH Regulations* and normal control measures (see above) may be adequate to protect new or expectant mothers. (See HSE publications *L5* and *HS(G) 97*, as mentioned above; and *EH 17 Mercury and its inorganic equivalent compounds (1996)*; and *MS 12 Mercury: medical guidance notes (1996)*.)

### Antimitotic (cytotoxic) drugs

These drugs (which may be inhaled or absorbed through the skin) can cause genetic damage to sperm and eggs and some can cause cancer. Those workers involved in preparation or administration of such drugs and disposal of chemical or human waste are at greatest risk, eg pharmacists, nurses and other health care workers. Antimitotic drugs can present a significant risk to those of either gender who are trying to conceive a child as well as to new or expectant mothers, and all those working with them should be made aware of the hazards.

The *COSHH Regulations 1994* again apply to the control of these substances (see above). Since there is no known threshold limit for them, exposure must be reduced to as low a level as is reasonably practicable.

### Agents absorbed through the skin

Various chemicals including some pesticides may be absorbed through the skin causing adverse effects. These substances are identified in the tables of occupational exposure limits in HSE booklet *EH40 Occupational exposure limits* (an updated version is published annually), in which some substances are accompanied by an annotation 'Sk'. Many such agents (particularly pesticides which are subject to the *Control of Pesticides Regulations 1986*) will also be identified by product labels.

Effective control of these chemicals is obviously important in respect of all employees (the *COSHH Regulations* applying once again) although risk assessments may reveal the need for additional precautions in respect of new or expectant mothers, eg modified handling methods, additional PPE, or even their restriction from activities involving exposure to such substances.

HSE booklet *L9 Safe use of pesticides for non-agricultural purposes (1998)* contains a further ACOP in relation to COSHH obligations.

### *Carbon Monoxide*

Exposure of pregnant women to carbon monoxide can cause the foetus to be starved of oxygen with the level and duration of exposure both being important factors. There are not felt to be any additional risks from carbon monoxide to mothers who have recently given birth or to breast-fed babies.

Once again, it is important to protect all members of the workforce from high levels of carbon monoxide (the *COSHH Regulations* require it) but it may also be necessary to ensure that pregnant women are not regularly exposed to carbon monoxide at lower levels, eg from use of gas-fired equipment or other processes or activities. HSE Guidance Note *EH43 Carbon monoxide (1998)* provides general guidance on carbon monoxide.

### *Lead and lead derivatives*

High occupational exposure to lead has historically been linked with high incidence of spontaneous abortion, stillbirth and infertility. Decreases in the intellectual performance of children have more recently been attributed to exposure of their mothers to lead. Since lead can enter breast milk, there are potential risks to the child if breastfeeding mothers are exposed to lead.

All women of reproductive capacity are prohibited from working in many lead processing activities. All work involving exposure to lead is subject to the *Control of Lead at Work Regulations 1998*. Even where women of reproductive capacity are allowed to work with lead or its compounds, the blood-lead concentrations contained within the Regulations as an 'action level' and a 'suspension level' are set at half the figures for adult males. This is intended to ensure that women who may become pregnant already have low blood lead levels. Once pregnancy is confirmed, the doctor carrying out medical surveillance (as required by *Regulation 10*) would normally be expected to suspend the woman from work involving significant exposure to lead. There is, however, no specific requirement in the Regulations themselves that this must happen. Detailed guidance on the Regulations is contained in HSE booklet COP 2 Control of lead at work (1998).

## Working conditions

**3.16** HSE guidance in HS(G) 122 in relation to the 'working conditions' referred to in the *Management Regulations 1999, Regulation 16(1)* repeats the HSE's stated position in respect of work with DSE contained in Annex B to the HSE booklet *L26 Display screen equipment work (1992)*. Their view is that radiation from DSE is well below the levels set out in international recommendations and that scientific studies taken as a whole do not demonstrate any link between this work and miscarriages or birth defects.

There is no need for pregnant women to cease working with DSE. However, the HSE recommend that, to avoid problems from stress or anxiety, women are given the opportunity to discuss any concerns with someone who is well informed on the subject.

## Other aspects of pregnancy

**3.17** Although the HSE booklet on new and expectant mothers at work (*HS(G)122*) draws attention to other features of pregnancy which employers may wish to take into account, it suggests that employers have no legal obligation to do so. However, this view has not been tested by the courts and an argument could be advanced that some of these represented 'working conditions' which involve risk to the mother or her baby within the terms of the *Management Regulations 1999, Regulation 16, paragraph (1)(b)*.

The impact of these aspects will vary during the course of the pregnancy and employers are likely to need to keep the situation under review. A modified version of the appendix from the HSE booklet dealing with these 'other aspects' is provided below.

### *Aspects of pregnancy that may affect work*

| *Aspects of pregnancy* | *Factors in work* |
|---|---|
| Morning sickness | Early shift work<br>Exposure to nauseating smells<br>Difficulty in leaving job |
| Backache | Standing for extended periods<br>Posture for some activities<br>Manual handling |
| Varicose veins | Standing/sitting |
| Haemorrhoids | Working in hot conditions/sitting |
| Frequent visits to toilet | Difficulty in leaving job/site of work |
| Increasing size | Use of protective clothing<br>Work in confined areas<br>Manual handling<br>Posture at DSE workstations<br>Dexterity, agility, co-ordination, speed of movement, reach, may also be impaired |
| Tiredness | Overtime<br>Evening work |
| Balance | Problems working on slippery, wet surfaces |
| Comfort | Problems working in tightly fitting workspaces |

## A practical approach to assessing risks

**3.18** Essentially risk assessment in respect of new or expectant mothers must be carried out by an employer if:

- there are women of childbearing age; and
- their work could involve risks to new or expectant mothers or their babies.

Most organisations employ women of childbearing age and, particularly in the case of large businesses, there may be a number of work activities that could create relevant risks. In some cases (eg those involving exposure to hazardous substances or radiation), it may be appropriate to stipulate that women are not allowed to work in certain activities, processes or departments once their pregnancy has been notified and/or for a finite period after they return to work after giving birth.

However, in many workplaces the issues will be far from clear cut – it would be neither necessary nor practical to prohibit pregnant workers from carrying out *any* manual handling or standing up or sitting down or climbing up ladders. Also it is difficult for any employer to identify in advance exactly what steps need to be taken to alter working conditions or hours of work so that risks can be avoided for every female employee who may become pregnant.

A much more practical approach is for the employer to develop a checklist similar to the sample provided at the end of this section. Such a checklist can be prepared by carrying out a review of the organisation's activities in order to identify risks which are present which *may* be of relevance in relation to new or expectant mothers. The risks described in the previous part of this chapter provide a good starting point from which a workplace-specific checklist can be developed. In some workplaces it may be appropriate to develop more than one such checklist (eg for production, maintenance and administration) because the profiles of risks are different.

Such a checklist should be completed by a suitable employer's representative (a personnel or health and safety specialist or the pregnant woman's manager perhaps) together with the pregnant woman herself. The checklist is intended to provoke discussion about the employee's possible exposure to the risks the employer has identified so that any necessary additional precautions (or changes to work practices) can be agreed. There is the opportunity to identify whether any further review of the situation is necessary. The process would be repeated once the mother returned to work after giving birth.

The sample checklist provided is for a firm of developers. Many of their female staff would only be exposed to risks in the office but some might visit actual or potential development sites where they may be exposed to different types of risks (difficult or dangerous access, contamination). Some female staff may be involved in work outside office hours and also travel extensively, sometimes to destinations abroad.

XYZ Development
New and expectant mothers at work

## Risk assessment checklist

| **Name of employee:** | **Work location:** | |
|---|---|---|
| **Risk type** | **Possible risk situations** | **Work practice changes/additional precautions agreed** |
| Manual handling | • Handling stationery or printed materials<br>• Work in archives or stores<br>• Moving office equipment, furniture, exhibition stands | |
| Posture and movement | • Unsatisfactory position at DSE workstation<br>• Cramped working position<br>• Standing for lengthy periods<br>• Excessive use of stairs necessary<br>• Access to difficult locations (eg ladder work)<br>• Risks of slips or falls (eg on site)<br>• Excessive travel (particularly by car or air) | |
| Physical and mental pressure | • Overall workload/deadlines<br>• Difficult decision making<br>• Attendance at meetings at unsuitable hours<br>• Dealing with aggressive or aggrieved persons | |
| Biological and chemical agents | • Contamination on sites/unusual workplaces<br>• Work abroad (diseases, inoculations) | |
| Other issues | • Lack of toilet facilities/rest areas | |

Signature (for XYZ Development): Date: Signature (new/expectant mother): Date for further review (if any):

(This form should be completed when the pregnancy is first notified and when the new mother returns to work.)

## *Reference*

**3.19**

### (All HSE publications)

| | | |
|---|---|---|
| 1 | HS(G) 165: | Young people at work. A guide for employers (1997) |
| 2 | HS(G) 122: | New and expectant mothers at work. A guide for employers (1994) |
| 3 | L 121: | Work with ionising radiation. *Ionising Radiations Regulations 1999* Approved code of practice and guidance (2000) |
| 4 | L 58: | The protection of persons against ionising radiation arising from any work activity (1994) |
| 5 | HSG 91: | A framework for the restriction of occupational exposure to ionising radiation (1992) |
| 6 | L 96: | A guide to the Work in *Compressed Air Regulations 1996* (1996) |
| 7 | L 103: | Commercial diving projects offshore (1998) |
| 8 | L 104: | Commercial diving projects inland/inshore (1998) |
| 9 | L 105: | Recreational diving projects (1998) |
| 10 | L 106: | Media diving projects (1998) |
| 11 | L 107: | Scientific and archaeological diving projects (1998) |
| 12 | L 5: | General COSHH ACOP, carcinogens ACOP and biological agents ACOP. *Control of Substances Hazardous to Health Regulations 1999. Approved codes of practice (1999)* |
| 13 | | Infections in the workplace to new and expectant mothers (1997) |
| 14 | HS(G) 97: | A step by step guide to COSHH assessment (1992) |
| 15 | EH 17: | Mercury and its inorganic divalent compounds (1996) |
| 16 | MS 12: | Mercury: medical guidance notes (1996) |
| 17 | EH 40: | Occupational exposure limits (published annually) |
| 18 | L 9: | Safe use of pesticides for non-agricultural purposes (1991) |
| 19 | EH 43: | Carbon monoxide (1998) |
| 20 | COP 2: | Control of lead at work (1998) |
| 21 | L 26: | Display screen equipment work (1992) |

# 4 Carrying out risk assessments



## *Planning and preparation*

**4.1** Taking some time to plan and prepare for risk assessments should always pay dividends – both in saving time later on and in ensuring the assessment is more effective. The important aspects of this phase are set out below.

## Who will carry out the assessments?

**4.2** Decisions need to be taken about who will be involved in the risk assessment team. CHAPTER 2: WHAT THE MANAGEMENT REGULATIONS REQUIRE refers in some detail to the requirements of the *Management Regulations 1999* and particularly *Regulation 7* and its requirements for employers to appoint competent health and safety assistance. In that chapter, reference was made to the key attributes of having sufficient training and experience or knowledge together with other qualities, in order to be able to identify risks and evaluate the effectiveness of precautions to control those risks.

As the HSE acknowledge in their guidance on risk assessment, in small businesses the employer or a senior manager may be quite capable of carrying out the risk assessment. Some organisations, both large and small, employ consultants to co-ordinate or carry out their risk assessment programme. Other employers create risk assessment teams who might be drawn from:

- managers;
- engineers and other specialists;
- supervisors or team leaders;
- health and safety specialists;
- safety representatives; and
- ordinary employees.

Whether the assessments are to be carried out by an individual or by a team, others will need to be involved during the process. Managers, supervisors, employees, specialists, etc will all need to be talked to about the risks involved in their work and the precautions that are (or should be) taken.

A good combination is often to have an 'insider' and an 'outsider' working together. The 'insider' should be familiar with the work activity being assessed – the risks involved, the possible variations in the activity, the precautions available and their effectiveness, and also whether what is being observed is typical. The 'outsider' is better able to question the status quo, to suggest possible risks that may have been overlooked, to put forward alternative precautions which may not have been considered and to bring to bear their knowledge and experience of similar situations elsewhere.

The 'outsider' role is often filled by a health and safety specialist (this is where employing an experienced consultant can be beneficial) although managers or safety representatives from other departments can also play the role effectively. The 'insider' is likely to be a manager, supervisor or safety representative from the department or section being assessed.

## How will the assessments be organised?

**4.3** In a small workplace it may be possible to carry out a risk assessment as a single exercise but in larger organisations it will usually be necessary to split the assessment up into manageable units. If done correctly, this should mean that assessment of each unit should not take an inordinate amount of time and also allows the selection of the people best able to assess an individual unit on a 'horses for courses' basis. Division of work activities into assessment units might be on the basis of:

- department or sections;
- buildings or rooms;
- parts of processes;
- product lines; and
- services provided.

As an illustration, a garage might be divided into:

- servicing and repair workshop;
- body repair shop;
- parts department;
- car sales and administration; and
- petrol and retail sales.

In dividing workplaces into units like this, it is important to take account of aspects which may be common to all assessment units, eg fire precautions, electrical supply, access roads, the impact of work activities on neighbours and others.

Where workplaces to be assessed have similarities to each other (eg groups of garages, retail chains or networks of offices), then use of the concept of a 'model risk assessment' may be appropriate. This is dealt with in more detail in CHAPTER 6: MODEL RISK ASSESSMENTS.

## Gathering documents

**4.4** There is a wide range of documents which might be of value during the risk assessment process. Some of these are likely to be internal documents whilst others will be reference material from the HSE and other external sources. Internal documents of relevance could include:

### *Previous risk assessments*

There has been a legal requirement for risk assessment since the beginning of 1993. Even if previous assessments are considered to be inadequate or well out of date, they should be able to provide at least some useful information.

### *Specific risk assessments*

Risk assessments carried out to comply with specific Regulations (eg COSHH or Noise) may also be useful. There may be an overlap with the more general risk assessment (eg eye protection against a corrosive substance may also protect against other risks) and the validity of the specific risk assessments may also be reviewed as part of the exercise.

### *Operating procedures*

Good operating procedures should also incorporate health and safety considerations – the risks involved and the precautions required. Examples of this approach are provided in CHAPTER 5: ASSESSMENT RECORDS. Existing procedures may already do this to some extent and should be reviewed as part of the assessment process.

### *Safety handbooks etc*

Many organisations produce safety handbooks or lists of safety rules in order to inform employees about risks and precautions. The awareness which should be created by such handbooks can be an important precaution in its own right and the detailed contents of the handbook can be useful in the risk assessment.

### *Training programmes and records*

Checking the adequacy of employee training in health and safety should be an important part of risk assessment. The health and safety content of induction programmes and operator training should be reviewed, as should whether employees have actually received the training that they should have.

### *Accident/incident records*

Work activities that have caused accidents or near misses in the past obviously involve potential risks which need to be evaluated. Accident and incident statistics and investigation report forms should be reviewed. Even in smaller workplaces without formal investigation systems, a study of the Accident Book is likely to be worthwhile.

### *Health and safety inspection reports*

In organisations which have formal inspection systems, a review of the report forms is likely to reveal regular problems which are being identified or the occasional major problem with high risk potential (The need for regular health and safety inspections may also be one of the recommendations made as a result of the risk assessment).

Amongst external documents which could be of relevance during risk assessments are:

### *Regulations and approved codes of practice*

Risk assessment involves an evaluation of compliance with legal requirements and therefore an awareness of the legislation applying to the workplace in question is essential. HSE approved codes of practice (ACOPs) which accompany Regulations can be referred to in court and almost have the same legal status as the Regulations themselves – the onus is on accused persons or organisations to show that compliance with the law was achieved by other equally satisfactory means.

### *HSE guidance*

The HSE publishes a wide range of booklets and leaflets providing guidance on health and safety topics. Some of these relate to the specific requirements of Regulations, others deal with specific types of risks whilst some publications deal with sectors of work activity.

All of these can be of considerable value in identifying which risks the HSE regard as significant and in providing benchmarks against which precautions can be measured. The guidance on specific types of workplaces (which includes engineering workshops, motor vehicle repair, warehousing, kitchens and food preparation, golf courses, horse riding establishments and many others) should be an essential basis for those carrying out assessments in those sectors.

HSE Books (PO Box 1999, Sudbury, Suffolk CO10 2WA, tel: 01787 881165, fax: 01787 313995, website: www.hsebooks.co.uk) regularly publishes a detailed catalogue of HSE publications. Their booklet *Essentials of Health and Safety at Work* provides an excellent starting point for those in small businesses needing guidance or carrying out risk assessment. The booklet also contains a useful reference section to other HSE publications which may be of relevance.

### *Trade information*

Many trade associations and similar organisations publish their own codes of practice and guidance on health and safety topics. Whilst these do not have the same legal significance as HSE publications, they nevertheless provide useful information on what others involved in similar work activities consider to be significant risks and appropriate precautions.

### *Information from manufacturers and suppliers*

*HASAWA 1974, section 6* places duties on manufacturers and suppliers to provide adequate information so that their products can be used in a safe manner. Such information might be in the form of a handbook associated with a piece of work equipment or a data sheet for a hazardous substance (relevant not only in a COSHH assessment but also in a general risk assessment if the substance is flammable or explosive). The information should identify the risks associated with the product and the precautions recommended by the manufacturer or supplier. It will be for those carrying out the risk assessment to determine what is appropriate in the circumstances of the product's use.

### *General reference books*

There are many reference books which may be useful during the risk assessment process. Some, such as this handbook, provide guidance on how the risk assessment should be undertaken, whilst others provide technical advice on specific topics such as electrical safety, fire safety or machine guarding.

## Consider who might be at risk

**4.5** The risk assessment process must take account of all those who may be at risk from the work activities – both employees and others. It is important that all of these are identified.

### *Employees*

Different categories of employees to take into account might include:

- production workers;
- maintenance workers;
- administrative staff;
- security officers;
- cleaners;
- delivery drivers;
- sales representatives;
- others working away from the premises; and
- temporary employees.

Some of these employees may merit special considerations:

- children and young persons (see CHAPTER 3: SPECIAL CASES);
- women of childbearing age, ie potential new or expectant mothers (see CHAPTER 3: SPECIAL CASES);
- employees with disabilities;
- people working alone;
- those working at night or weekends; and
- inexperienced staff.

### *Contractors and their staff*

Most organisations utilise the services of contractors and their use has increased in recent years. The relationship between the host and the contractor will vary according to the nature of the services the contractor provides. These might include:

- construction or engineering projects;
- routine maintenance or repair;
- hire of plant and operators;
- support services, eg catering, cleaning, security, transport;
- professional services, eg architects, engineers, trainers; and
- supply of temporary staff.

Even though contractors have duties to carry out risk assessments in respect of their own staff, host organisations also have duties towards contractors' employees (as described in CHAPTER 1: INTRODUCTION and CHAPTER 2: WHAT THE MANAGEMENT REGULATIONS REQUIRE). Their duties will normally be greater in respect of temporary staff working alongside their own employees than for contractors providing specialist skills or services. However, even in the latter case, risks associated with facilities, equipment or materials supplied by the host, or created by the host's activities must be taken into account.

### *Others at risk*

Other people that might be put at risk by the organisation's activities will depend upon the nature and location of those activities. Groups of people to be considered include:

- volunteer workers;
- co-occupants of premises;
- occupants of neighbouring premises;
- drivers making deliveries;
- visitors (both individuals and groups);
- passers-by;
- users of neighbouring roads;
- trespassers;

- customers or service users; and
- residents eg in the care or hospitality sectors.

## Identify the issues to be addressed

**4.6** The issues which will need to be addressed during the risk assessment process should be identified. This may be done in respect of the assessment overall or separately for each of the assessment units. Essentially this is a brain-storming process – based upon the knowledge and experience of those carrying out the assessment and the information gathered from the sources described earlier. In effect, this will create an initial list of headings and sub-headings for the eventual record of the risk assessment, although in practice this list is likely to be amended along the way. The sample assessment records contained in the next chapter will demonstrate how such a list can be built up for typical workplaces.

These headings are likely to consist of the more common types of risk. eg fire, vehicles, work at heights, together with some specialised types of risk associated with the work activities such as violence, lasers or working in remote locations. A checklist of possible risks to be considered during risk assessments is provided at 4.8: CHECKLIST OF POSSIBLE RISKS, below. This includes some of the risks which have specific Regulations associated with them.

In some situations, particular notes may also be made to check on the effectiveness of the precautions which should be in place to control the risks, eg standards of machine guarding, compliance with PPE requirements or the quality and extent of training.

## Variations in work activities

**4.7** Consideration should also be given at this stage to possible variations in work activities which may create new risks or increase existing risks. Such variations might involve:

- fluctuations in production or workload demands;
- reallocation of staff to meet changing workloads;
- seasonal variations in work activities;
- abnormal weather conditions;
- alternative work practices forced by equipment breakdown/unavailability;
- urgent or 'one-off' repair work;

- work carried out in unusual locations; and
- the difference in work between days, nights or weekends.

Further variations may emerge later on in the assessment process.

## Checklist of possible risks

**4.8** The checklist on pages 74-75 is intended to assist in identifying which issues need to be addressed during risk assessments. In some cases, the headings and/or sub-headings might be used in the form shown, in other cases it may be more appropriate to combine them or modify the titles. (This is illustrated by practical examples in CHAPTER 5: ASSESSMENT RECORDS.)

Please turn to pages 74-75 for the checklist of possible risks.

## *Making the risk assessment*

**4.9** Good planning and preparation can reduce the time spent in actually making the risk assessment as well as enabling that time to be used much more productively. However, it is important that time is spent in work locations, seeing how work is actually carried out (as opposed to how it should be carried out).

### Observation

**4.10** Observation of the work location, work equipment and work practices is an essential part of the risk assessment process. Where there are known to be variations in work activities, a sufficient range of these should be observed to be able to form a judgement on the extent of the risks and the adequacy of precautions. Typical of evaluations which can be made through observations are:

- effectiveness of fixed guards;
- suitability and condition of access equipment;
- compliance with PPE requirements;
- observance of specified operating procedures or working practices;
- compliance with speed limits;
- standards of housekeeping and storage;
- acceptability of physical working conditions;
- suitability of manual handling practices;
- standards of lighting;
- suitability and availability of fire evacuation routes;
- locations and suitability of fire fighting equipment;
- availability of other emergency equipment;
- configurations of DSE workstations; and
- effectiveness of perimeter fencing.

These are only examples – the potential list is endless. However, by concentrating on the issues previously identified, it is possible to narrow down observations to those that are relevant for that area or that activity.

It should also be borne in mind that work practices may change once

## Checklist of possible risks

- Work equipment
  - Process machinery
  - Other machines
  - Powered tools
  - Hand tools
  - Knives/blades
  - Fork lift trucks
  - Cranes
  - Lifts
  - Hoists
  - Lifting equipment
  - Vehicles
- Access
  - Vehicle routes
  - Rail traffic
  - Pedestrian access
  - Work at heights
  - Ladders and stepladders
  - Scaffolding
  - Mobile elevating work platforms
  - Falling objects
  - Glazing
- Work activity
  - Burning or welding
  - Entry into confined spaces
  - Electrical work
  - Excessive fatigue or stress
  - Handling cash/valuables
  - Use of compressed gases
  - Molten metal
- Services/power sources
  - Electrical installation
  - Compressed air
  - Steam
  - Hydraulics
  - Other pressure systems
  - Buried services
  - Overhead services
- Storage
  - Shelving and racking
  - Stacking
  - Silos and tanks
  - Waste
- Fire (see CHAPTER 14: FIRE RISK ASSESSMENTS)
  - Flammable liquids
  - Flammable gases
  - Storage of flammables
  - Hot work

- External factors
  - Violence or aggression
  - Robbery
  - Large crowds
  - Animals
  - Clients' activities

- Other factors
  - Vibration
  - Lasers
  - Ultra violet/Infra red radiation
  - Work related upper limb disorder

- Work locations
  - Heat
  - Cold
  - Severe weather
  - Deep water
  - Tides
  - Remote locations
  - Work alone
  - Homeworking
  - Poor hygiene
  - Infestations
  - Work abroad
  - Work in domestic property
  - Client's premises
  - Site security

*Risks/issues subject to separate assessment requirements*

Noise (see CHAPTER 10: NOISE ASSESSMENTS)
Manual handling (see CHAPTER 11: ASSESSMENT OF MANUAL HANDLING OPERATIONS)
Display screen equipment workstations (see CHAPTER 12: ASSESSMENT OF DSE WORKSTATIONS)
PPE needs (see CHAPTER 13: ASSESSMENT OF PPE REQUIREMENTS)
Lead
Asbestos
Genetic manipulation
Genetically modified organisms
Conformity of machinery
Major accident hazards (COMAH)
Ionising radiation

*Risks to (or from) others*

Contractors
Volunteer workers
Co-occupants of premises
Neighbouring occupants
Delivery drivers
Visiting groups or individuals
Passers-by
Users of neighbouring roads
Trespassers
Customers or service users
Residents

workers realise they are under observation. Initial or undetected observation of working practices may be the most revealing.

## Discussions

**4.11** Discussions with people carrying out work activities, their safety representatives and those responsible for supervising or managing them are also an essential part of risk assessment. Amongst aspects of the work that might be discussed are:

- possible variations in the work activities;
- problems that workers encounter;
- risks involved in the work, especially those that concern workers involved;
- workers' views of the effectiveness of the precautions available;
- the reasons some precautions are not utilised;
- suggestions for improving health and safety standards;
- the quality and manner of the training staff have received; and
- workpeople's awareness of emergency procedures.

These discussions should utilise open-ended questions such as:

- How do you get the large items onto the shelf?
- What happens if the fork lift truck breaks down?
- How do you carry out the task in high winds?
- What if no-one else is available to help?
- Why don't people adjust the guard correctly?
- How were you trained to carry out the task?
- How do you think the task could be done more safely?
- What do you do if the alarm goes off?

In evaluating the answers to such questions, it should always be borne in mind that those answering may well have different agendas to those carrying out the risk assessment.

## Tests

**4.12** In some situations, it may be appropriate to test the effectiveness of safety precautions. Examples of this are:

- the efficiency of interlocked guards or trip devices;
- stability of guard rails;
- security of locked enclosures;
- audibility of alarms or warning devices;
- suitability of access to remote workplaces, eg crane cabs, roofs; and
- whether lights or extraction fans operate when switched on.

In making any such tests, care must be taken by those carrying out the assessment not to endanger themselves or others, nor to disrupt normal activities. Suffering a fall as a result of an unstable hand rail or causing the premises to be evacuated through an injudicious test of an alarm button is not recommended!

## Further investigations

**4.13** Frequently, further investigations will need to be made before the assessment can be concluded. Such investigations may involve detailed checks on standards or records, or enquiries into how non-routine situations are dealt with. Examples of further checks or enquiries which might be appropriate are:

- detailed requirements of published standards, eg design of guards, thickness of glass;
- specifications of equipment or materials used, eg PPE design, substance data sheets;
- requirements contained in fire certificates;
- contents of operating procedures;
- maintenance or test records;
- contents of training programmes;
- training records;
- equipment not operating during the initial assessment;
- activities not in progress at the time of the assessment visit;

- contents of locked rooms or enclosures;
- intended responses to alarms;
- availability of equipment for non-routine activities; and
- experience of problems or malfunctions.

Once again, the potential list is endless although lines of further enquiry should be indicated by the observations and discussions during the initial phase of the assessment.

## Notes

**4.14** Rough notes should be made throughout the assessment process. It will be on these notes that the eventual assessment record will be based. It will seldom be possible to complete an assessment record 'on the run' during the assessment itself. The notes should relate to anything likely to be of relevance, such as:

- risks discounted as insignificant;
- more detail on risks known to be present;
- additional risks identified during the assessment;
- risks which are being controlled effectively;
- descriptions of precautions which are in place and effective;
- precautions which do not appear to be effective;
- alternative precautions which might be considered;
- problems identified or concerns expressed by others; and
- related procedures, records or other documents.

Such notes could be made on a clipboard or in a notebook, although some may be more comfortable using a hand-held computer or portable voice recorder. Subsequent analysis of the contents of a voice recorder to produce the assessment record may prove difficult however.

## Assessment records

**4.15** This phase of the risk assessment process concludes with the preparation of the assessment records. It may be preferable to record the findings in draft form initially, with a revised version being produced once the assessment has been reviewed more widely and/or recommended actions have been completed.

### *Decide on the record format*

Many different formats are possible as can be seen in CHAPTER 5: ASSESSMENT RECORDS. Decisions need to be made on such questions as:

- Should separate records be prepared for different departments/ sections/activities?
- Will a 'generic' assessment record need to be supported by 'dynamic' risk assessments in the field?
- Is a 'model' assessment record appropriate in this case?
- Should some or all of the assessment record be integrated into documented operating procedures?

### *Identify the section headings to be used*

During the preparatory phase of the assessment, a list of risks and other issues to be addressed in each assessment unit was prepared as an aide memoire. This list will now need to be converted into section headings for the assessment records. As a result of the assessment, some of the headings may have been sub-divided into different headings whilst others may have been merged.

### *Prepare the assessment records*

The rough notes taken during the assessment itself are extremely unlikely to be in a suitable order to link into the section headings to be used. The author has found it extremely useful to give each intended section heading a number and then work through all of the notes inserting the relevant section number (or numbers) alongside each note, usually using a different coloured pen. A similar approach can be taken with computer-based records which could then be reshuffled together under their section headings.

Conversion of rough notes into formal assessment records can then take place more easily, although the process is still likely to be time consuming. Preparing the records will normally require at least half of the time which was spent in the workplace carrying out the assessment and sometimes might even take more time. It is wise not to allow too long to elapse between assessing in the workplace and preparation of the assessment record. Notes will seem much more intelligible and memory will often be able to 'colour in' between the notes.

### *Identify the recommendations*

The assessment will almost inevitably result in recommendations for improvements and these must be identified. As can be seen in CHAPTER 5: ASSESSMENT RECORDS, some assessment record formats incorporate sections in which recommendations can be included, but in other cases separate lists will need to be prepared. The use of risk rating matrices (see CHAPTER 7: SPECIALISED RISK ASSESSMENT TECHNIQUES) may assist in the prioritisation of recommendations.

## *After the assessment*

**4.16** Whilst the recording of the risk assessment is an important legal requirement, it is even more important that the recommendations for improvement identified during the assessment are actually implemented. This is likely to involve several stages.

### Review of the recommendations

**4.17** In many organisations, the effective implementation of the recommendations is likely to involve others outside (and probably senior to) the risk assessment team. An appropriate group should be brought together to review the assessment findings and particularly the recommendations for improvements. The reasoning behind the recommendations can be explained and various alternative ways of controlling risks can be evaluated.

Changes to the assessment findings or recommendations may be made at this stage but the risk assessment team should not allow themselves to be browbeaten into making alterations that they do not feel can be justified. Similarly, they should not hold back on making recommendations they consider are necessary because they believe that senior management will not implement them. Once appointed to carry out risk assessments, the assessment team should carry out their duties to the best of their abilities in identifying what precautions are necessary in order to comply with the law – the responsibility for achieving compliance rests with their employer.

Some recommendations may need to be costed in respect of the capital expenditure or staff time required to implement them. It is unlikely that all recommendations will be able to be implemented immediately – there may be a significant lead time for the delivery of parts or the provision of specialist services from external sources. The risk assessment team should play an active part in costing and prioritisation issues.

## Implementation of the action plan

**4.18** Once costings and prioritisation have been agreed, the recommendations should be converted into an action plan with individuals clearly allocated responsibility for each element of the plan, within a defined timescale. Some members of the risk assessment team (particularly health and safety specialists) may have responsibility for implementing parts of the plan. In some cases, those given responsibilities may need guidance from the risk assessment team on the reasoning behind their recommendations or on the control measures the team believe are more likely to be successful.

## Recommendation follow-up

**4.19** Even in well-intentioned organisations, recommendations for improvement which have been fully justified and accepted are still not implemented. It is essential that the risk assessment process includes a follow-up of the recommendations made. Some of the recording formats provided in CHAPTER 5: ASSESSMENT RECORDS include reference to this.

As well as establishing that the improvements have actually been carried out, consideration should also be given to whether any unexpected risks have inadvertently been created, eg new eye protection may have reduced peripheral vision or a manual handling aid may have been introduced without staff being trained in how to use it correctly.

Once the follow-up has been carried out, the assessment record should be annotated or revised to take account of the changes made. In a minority of cases, a further follow-up may be appropriate to assess the position once changes have had time to 'bed in'.

If recommendations have not been implemented, there is a clear need for the situation to be referred back to senior management for them to take action to overcome whatever are the obstacles to progress. Particularly in larger organisations, the risk assessment team may prefer to do this via a more formal report.

## Assessment review

**4.20** Detailed reference was made in CHAPTER 2: WHAT THE MANAGEMENT REGULATIONS REQUIRE to the circumstances under which the *Management Regulations 1999* and the associated ACOP state that assessments must be reviewed. The ACOP also states that 'it is prudent to plan to review risk assessments at regular intervals'.

At this stage in the assessment process, it may be appropriate to determine how regular those intervals ought to be. The frequency should relate to the extent and nature of the risks involved and the likelihood of creeping changes (as opposed to a major change which would automatically justify a review). Frequencies of review might, for example, be established as:

| | |
|---|---|
| Construction or related activities | Every year |
| Activities of home care workers | Every two years |
| Industrial production processes | Every three years |
| Administrational activities | Every five years |

It should be emphasised that these are suggested frequencies for review of the assessments. The review may conclude that the risks are unchanged, the precautions are still effective and that no revision of the assessments is necessary. The process of conducting regular reviews of assessments and, where appropriate, making revisions may be aided by the application of document control systems of the type used to achieve compliance with ISO 9000 and similar standards.

## *References*

### (HSE publications.)

1 Essentials of health and safety at work (1994)
2 HSG 183 5 steps to risk assessment: Case studies (1998)

# 5 Assessment records

**In this chapter:**



## *Introduction*

**5.1** *Regulation 3(6)* of the *Management Regulations 1999* states:

> 'Where the employer employs five or more employees, he shall record–
>
> (a) the significant findings of the assessment; and
>
> (b) any group of his employees identified by it as being especially at risk.'

The accompanying ACOP refers to the record as representing 'an effective statement of hazards and risks which then leads management to take the relevant actions to protect health and safety'. It goes on to state that the record must be retrievable for use by management, safety representatives, other employee representatives or visiting inspectors. The need for linkages between the risk assessment, the record of health and safety arrangements (required by *Regulation 5* of the *Management Regulations 1999*) and the health and safety policy is also identified. The ACOP allows for assessment records to be kept electronically as an alternative to being in written form.

## Contents of assessment records

**5.2** The essential content of any risk assessment record should be:

- hazards or risks associated with the work activity;
- any employees identified as especially at risk;
- precautions which are (or should be) in place to control the risks (with comments on their effectiveness); and
- improvements identified as being necessary to comply with the law.Other important details to include are:
- name of the employer;
- address of the work location or base;
- names and signatures of those carrying out the assessment;
- date of the assessment; and
- date for next review of the assessment.

(These might be provided as a introductory sheet.)

## Sample assessment format

**5.3** The sample risk assessment form shown on the opposite page contains specific sections for most of the contents referred to above. Groups of employees (or others) especially at risk can be included in the 'Risks identified' column, whilst the name and address of the employer could be overprinted on each sheet or provided at the front of a risk assessment file or manual. It includes a space for cross-references, eg to company procedures or training programmes, to other relevant risk assessments or to relevant HSE publications. The content of the form is not too dissimilar to that provided in the HSE's *Five steps to risk assessment* leaflet, but the layout is felt to be more user friendly.

## Illustrative assessments

**5.4** In the following pages of this chapter, the risk assessment methodology described in CHAPTER 4: CARRYING OUT RISK ASSESSMENTS is used to provide illustrations of how the process can be applied in a variety of workplaces or activities.

For each work situation:

- relevant risks or issues to be addressed are listed (utilising the checklist in 4.8: CHECKLIST OF POSSIBLE RISKS);
- one of those risks or issues is selected;
- relevant Regulations, references and other key assessment points relating to that risk or issue are identified; and
- an illustration of how the completed assessment record might look is provided.

In some cases, the sample risk assessment format has been used, but in others the 'Recommendations' column has been omitted (any recommendations would be listed separately).

Later in the chapter, other possible formats are illustrated, demonstrating how risk assessments might be recorded in alternative documents. (See 5.5: ALTERNATIVE ASSESSMENT RECORD FORMATS.)

| **Risk assessment** | | |
|---|---|---|
| Reference number: | Risk topic/issue: | Sheet _____ of _____ |
| Cross references: | | |
| **Risks identified** | **Precautions in place** | **Recommended improvements** |
| | | |
| **Signature(s)** | **Name(s)** | **Date** |
| **Dates for recommendation follow up** | | **Next routine review** |

On the following pages you will find illustrative risk assessments for the following places of work:

## *Estate agent's office*

Relevant risk topics are likely to include:

- *electrical equipment* – in the office and kitchen;
- *fire* (see CHAPTER 14: FIRE RISK ASSESSMENTS) – general risks only, no special risks;
- *access* – pedestrian access into and around the office;
- *manual handling* (see CHAPTER 11: ASSESSMENT OF MANUAL HANDLING OPERATIONS) – of stationery, printed materials, records;
- *display screen equipment* (see CHAPTER 12: ASSESSMENT OF DSE WORKSTATIONS) – used at workstations in the office;
- *hazardous substances* (see CHAPTER 9: COSHH ASSESSMENTS) – cleaning materials and office supplies;
- *lone working* – staff working alone in the office; and
- *personal safety outside the office* – visiting occupied and unoccupied property, with and without clients.

A sample assessment record for *electrical equipment* is provided opposite.

In conducting this risk assessment:

- the requirements of the *Electricity at Work Regulations 1989* must be complied with;
- the following HSE leaflets are likely to be relevant–
  - *INDG 236 Maintaining portable electrical equipment in offices and other low-risk environments*,
  - *INDG 173 Office wise (this deals with office equipment and other office-related issues)*; and
- particular attention should be paid to–
  - the apparent condition of the electrical equipment,
  - inspection and maintenance arrangements,
  - the electrical isolator and distribution panel, and
  - any safety/guarding issues associated with the equipment.

## Acorn Estate Agents, Newtown

| Risk assessment | | |
|---|---|---|
| Reference number: 1 | Risk topic/issue: Electrical equipment | Sheet 1 of 1 |
| Cross references: **HSE leaflets IND(G) 236 and 173 Risk assessment 3 (Access)** | | |
| **Risks identified** | **Precautions in place** | **Recommended improvements** |
| Unsafe electrical equipment can present risk to staff and clients. | | |
| Electrical supply system and fixed equipment (electrical heaters, water heater, socket outlets). | The isolator and distribution board (with earth leakage protection) are in the storeroom.<br>The distribution board is clearly labelled.<br>All electrical repair and maintenance work is carried out by a reliable, competent electrical contractor. | Ensure cleaning materials do not block access to the isolator or panel. |
| Mobile and portable equipment including fridge, photocopier, computer equipment, shredder, fans. | Staff are encouraged to report immediately any defects in sockets, plugs, cables, connections etc.<br>Electrical equipment is checked during quarterly office health and safety inspections.<br>Equipment is inspected and/or tested by electrical contractors every two years.<br>Photocopier maintained under contract. | Some personal equipment (eg kettles, radio) is in use. This should be forbidden unless the equipment has been tested and/or inspected by a competent person. |
| The photocopier, shredder and computer printers contain in-running nips and other dangerous parts. | Access to these dangerous parts prevented by a combination of fixed guards and interlocked guards. | Staff should be warned about:<br>● hot drums when cleaning photocopier blockages;<br>● risks to tie wearers when using the shredder. |
| **Signature(s)** K Stephenson, R Lewis<br>**Dates for recommendation follow up**<br>February 1999 | **Name(s)** K Stephenson, R Lewis<br>**Next routine review** November 2003 | **Date** 4/11/98 |

## Supermarket

Relevant risk topics are likely to include:

- *food processing machinery* – in the delicatessen;
- *knives* – delicatessen and butchery;
- *fork lift trucks* – warehousing areas;
- *vehicle traffic* – delivery vehicles, customer and staff vehicles;
- *vehicle unloading* – in the goods inward area;
- *pedestrian access* – external to and inside the store;
- *glazed areas* – store windows, display cabinets;
- *electrical installation* – the power system within the store;
- *electrical equipment* – including tills, cleaning equipment, office equipment;
- *shelving* – in the store;
- *racking* – in warehouse areas;
- *refrigerators* – in the store and warehouse;
- *fire* – general risks only, precautions must take account of customers;
- *aggression* – eg from unhappy customers;
- *possible robbery* – the supermarket will hold large quantities of cash;
- *WRULD* – for checkout operators;
- *hazardous substances* – cleaning materials, office supplies;
- *manual handling* – eg shelf stacking, movement of trolleys;
- *display screen equipment* – used at workstations in the office;
- *PPE requirements* – throughout the supermarket; and
- *use of contractors* – for maintenance and repair work.

A sample risk assessment record for ***vehicle traffic*** is provided opposite.

In conducting this risk assessment:

- the requirements of the *Workplace (Health, Safety and Welfare) Regulations 1992* must be complied with;
- HSE booklet *HS(G) 136 Workplace Transport Safety* is likely to be relevant; and
- particular attention should be paid to–
  - signage and road markings,
  - observation of vehicle movements and speeds, and
  - conditions during busy periods and hours of darkness.

## ACME Supermarkets, Oldborough

| Risk assessment | | |
|---|---|---|
| Reference number: 4 | Risk topic/issue: Vehicle traffic | Sheet 1 of 1 |
| Cross references: Cross references: HSE booklet IND(G) 136 Risk assessments 5 (vehicle unloading) and 6 (pedestrian access) | | |
| **Risks identified** | **Precautions in place** | **Recommended improvements** |
| Vehicles making deliveries to the 'Goods inward' bay present risks to each other and to any pedestrians on the access road. | Prominent 10 mph signs are in place on the roadway. The speed limit is enforced effectively.<br>Signs prohibit use of the road by pedestrians and customer or staff vehicles. | |
| There are also risks to other road users as they leave and rejoin the main road. | There are give way signs and road markings at the junction with the main road.<br>Vehicles are parked in a holding area prior to backing up to the 'Goods Inward' bay. | Reposition the advertising sign which partly blocks visibility on rejoining the main road. |
| | Movement of vehicles is controlled by a designated member of the supermarket staff.<br>The area is well lit by roadside lamps and floodlights on the side of the building. | Provide this designated staff member with a high visibility waterproof jacket. |
| Customer and staff vehicles circulating in the car park area present risks to each other and to pedestrians in the area. | The access road around the car park is one way and well indicated by signs.<br>The entrance and exit are well separated from each other and the goods access road. | |
| There are also risks to other road users at the entrance from and access back into the main road. | There are prominent 15 mph signs around the roadways (some vehicles exceed this speed).<br>There are give way markings and signs at all roadway junctions. | Provide clearly marked speed ramps at suitable locations. |
| | Parking bays are well marked.<br>Pedestrian crossing points are clearly marked and signed.<br>The area is well lit by lighting towers which are protected at the base. | The surface of some bays in the southwest corner of the car park should be repaired. |
| | Security staff inspect and, where necessary, salt roadways in icy or snowy weather. | Include the goods access road, Goods inward bay and car park in routine safety inspections. |
| **Signature(s)** T Burke, G Hare<br>**Dates for recommendation follow up** January 1999 | **Name(s)** T Burke, G Hare<br>**Next routine review** October 2001 | **Date** 12/10/98 |

## Motor vehicle repair workshop

Relevant risk topics are likely to include:

- *tools and equipment* – bench machinery, portable powered tools, hand tools;
- *vehicle hoists* – extending to include engine or gearbox lifters, if appropriate;
- *access* – for vehicles and pedestrians;
- *burning and welding* – storage and use of oxyacetylene equipment;
- *electrical installation* – the power system within the workshop;
- *compressed air* – the compressor and air receiver;
- *shelving, racking, etc* – storage of parts and tools;
- *oil tanks* – inside and outside the workshop;
- *fire* – precautions within the workshop, including control of flammable liquids;
- *vehicle recovery work* – if this is applicable;
- *hazardous substances* – engine fumes, valeting work, battery acid, parts cleaning etc;
- *manual handling* – of parts and materials; and
- *PPE requirements* –in the workshop and parts department (if separate).

(This list does not take account of risks associated with body repair work, the parts department, petrol and other sales, car sales showrooms or administrative areas).

A sample assessment record for *tools and equipment* is provided opposite.

In conducting this risk assessment:

- the requirements of the *Provision and Use of Work Equipment Regulations 1998)*('PUWER') and the *Electricity at Work Regulations 1989* must be complied with;
- HSE booklet *HS(G)67 Health and safety in motor vehicle repair* is likely to be relevant; and
- particular attention should be paid to–
  - the power sources used for portable equipment,
  - potential for trailing cables and hoses,
  - physical condition of equipment and its manner of use, and
  - inspection and maintenance arrangements.

## Goodfellows Garage, Tupton

| Risk assessment | | |
|---|---|---|
| Reference number: 1 | Risk topic/issue: Tools and equipment | Sheet 1 of 1 |
| Cross references: HSE Booklet HS(G)67 Risk assessments 3 (access), 5 (electrical installation) and 6 (compressed air) | | |
| **Risks identified** | **Precautions in place** | **Recommended improvements** |
| The equipment below could represent a risk to any member of the workshop staff. | | |
| 30 tonne hydraulic press. | No guards. Slow moving. Apprentices directly supervised until competent to use alone. | Re-secure the floor mountings which have worked loose. |
| Bench mounted drilling machine. | Adjustable chuck guard in place. | |
| Bench mounted grinder/wire brush. | Standard partial enclosing guards for both.<br>Tool rest for grinding wheel.<br>Spindle speed clearly marked.<br>Technician trained to mount grinding wheels.<br>Goggles available on shelf above bench. | Tool rest requires adjusting closer to the wheel. |
| Portable drilling machines. | Air powered or battery operated machines.<br>All technicians provided with safety spectacles. | |
| Portable hand lamps. | Low voltage, totally enclosed type.<br>Compressed air and electric power from suspended supply unit at each servicing bay (minimising tripping hazards). | Replace lamp found with cracked enclosure. |
| Hand tools (both supplied by the company and belonging to technicians). | Staff are expected to check the condition of all equipment before use.<br>(All equipment was in satisfactory condition apart from the exceptions noted).<br>The manager inspects the workshop and the equipment in it every three months.<br>All electrical equipment is inspected and tested (where appropriate) annually by a competent electrical contractor. | Remind technicians that defective equipment must not be used, quoting the above examples. |
| **Signature(s)** A Goodfellow<br>**Dates for recommendation follow up** March 2000 | **Name(s)** A Goodfellow | **Date** 2/2/2000<br>**Next routine review** February 2003 |

## Newspaper publisher

A large workplace like this would need to be divided into assessment units (see CHAPTER 4: CARRYING OUT RISK ASSESSMENTS), which might consist of:

- *common facilities and services* – eg fire, electrical supply, lifts, vehicle traffic;
- *reel handling and stands* – supply of reels of newsprint to the press area;
- *platemaking* – equipment and chemicals used to produce printing plates;
- *printing press* – press machinery, solvents, noise, etc;
- *despatch* – inserting equipment, newspaper stacking, strapping and loading;
- *circulation and transport* – distribution and other vehicles, fuel, waste disposal;
- *maintenance* – workshops, garage, maintenance activities; and
- *offices* – editorial and administrative areas.

Selecting the reel handling and stands unit, risk topics are likely to include:

- *fork lift trucks* – used to unload, transport and stack reels;
- *reel storage* – stability of stacks, access issues;
- *reel handling equipment* – hoists, conveyors and the reel stands feeding the press;
- *wrappings and waste* – removal of wrappings, storage and disposal of waste paper etc; and
- *noise and dust* – from the operation of the reel stands and nearby press.

A sample assessment record for *reel handling equipment* is provided opposite.

In conducting this risk assessment:

- the requirements of the *Provision and Use of Work Equipment Regulations 1998* ('PUWER'), the *Lifting Operation and Lifting Equipment Regulations 1998* and the *Manual Handling Operations Regulations 1992* must be complied with;
- reference may need to be made to *BS 5304:1988 Safety of machinery* or to other standards for conveyors or specialist handling equipment; and
- particular attention should be paid to–
  - guarding standards and the possible presence of unguarded dangerous parts,
  - any need for manual handling of the reels,
  - training issues relating to the above, and
  - statutory examination records (for the hoist).

## Grimtown News

| Risk assessment | | |
|---|---|---|
| Reference number: B3 | Risk topic/issue: Reel handling and stands – reel handling equipment | Sheet 1 of 1 |
| Cross references: Risk assessments B1 (forklift trucks), B2 (reel storage), B5 (Noise and dust) | | |
| **Risks identified** | **Precautions in place** | **Recommended improvements** |
| The equipment below presents risks to all staff working in the area. | | |
| *Reel hoist* – Carries reel down from the reels store to the reel stand basement. It is fed by forklift trucks and feeds onto the roller conveyor system. | Slow moving hoist protected by a substantial mesh guard.<br>No need for access within the hoist enclosure.<br>Sign states 'Do not ride on hoist'.<br>Gap between base of hoist and roller conveyor (no shear trap).<br>Statutory examinations by Insurance Engineers (kept by Works Engineer). | Replace this sign by one complying with the *Safety Signs Regulations*). |
| *Roller conveyor* –This is in a T formation and consists of powered and free running rollers with a turntable at the junction. Reels are transferred to holding bays or floor-based trolleys by fork lift truck. | All drives for the conveyor are fully enclosed and there are no in-running nips. The conveyor is protected by kerbs from fork lift damage.<br>Signs prohibit climbing on the conveyor system. | Replace these signs as above. |
| *Floor-based trolleys* –This system carries reels right up to the transfer carriages which load them onto the reel stands. | Reels can be easily moved by one person using the trolley system. Reels can safely be rolled across the floor onto the trolleys if the correct technique is used. | Include formal training on correct techniques in the induction programme for new staff in the area. |
| Some reels must be transferred manually from the holding bays onto the trolleys. | Two persons are required to move the transfer carriages up to the reel stands. | |
| *Reel stands* –The reel stands rotate mechanically ensuring a constant web feed to the press.<br>The rotating drive shaft for the reel stands is approximately 4 metres above ground level. | There are no accessible in-running nips. Operatives do not need to approach the rotating reels.<br>This shaft is considered to be 'safe by position' for normal operating purposes. | Ensure a safe system of work for maintenance work near the shaft, eg by using a permit to work procedure. |
| **Signature(s)** M Betts S Brown<br>**Dates for recommendation follow up** June 2000 | **Name(s)** M Betts, S Brown<br>**Next routine review** March 2002 | **Date** 26/3/00 |

## *Installation of burglar alarms and closed circuit TV*

Relevant risk topics for this type of work are likely to include:

- *tools and equipment* – portable powered equipment and hand tools;
- *use of lifting equipment* – to raise alarms and cameras into position;
- *work at heights* – installing, maintaining or repairing equipment;
- *electrical work* – making connections into existing systems, testing faults;
- *site-related risks* – eg construction sites, industrial or commercial premises, domestic property;
- *manual handling* – loading, unloading, transporting and installing equipment; and
- *PPE requirements* – for a variety of work activities and work locations.

A sample assessment record for *work at heights* is provided opposite. (As can be seen, *this is only partially complete*. The parts dealing with tower scaffolds, scaffolding and mobile elevating work platforms would be on additional sheets).

This generic assessment would need to be supported by dynamic risk assessments of each project. This would be done initially by the sales staff as described and possibly included in a method statement. Technicians would also be expected to carry out a dynamic assessment before commencing work. Further reference to dynamic risk assessment is contained in CHAPTER 15: RISK ASSESSMENT RELATED CONCEPTS.

The record only refers to the risks identified and the *expected* precautions. Any improvements recommended or situations where precautions fell short of those expected would be referred to in a separate document.

In conducting this risk assessment:

- the requirements of the *Construction (Health, Safety and Welfare) Regulations 1996* and the *Workplace (Health, Safety and Welfare) Regulations 1992* must be complied with;
- HSE booklet *HS(G)150 Health and safety in construction* is likely to be relevant; and
- particular attention should be paid to–
  - actual working practices on site,
  - standards of training (of technicians and sales staff),
  - completed pre-installation survey forms,
  - the standard and availability of access equipment,
  - problem situations experienced by technicians.

## XYZ Security

<table>
<tr><th colspan="2">Risk assessment</th></tr>
<tr><td>Reference number: 3</td><td>Risk topic/issue: Work at heights — Sheet 1 of 3</td></tr>
<tr><td colspan="2">Cross references: Risk assessment 2 (use of lifting equipment), 5 (site related risks) and 6 (manual handling). HSE booklet HS(G) 150</td></tr>
<tr><th>Risks identified</th><th>Expected precautions</th></tr>
<tr><td>Introduction<br>Much installation, maintenance and repair work involves working at heights. XYZ technicians are primarily at risk but others may be at risk from falling objects.<br><br>The degree risk and type of access equipment required will be influenced by:<br>● the location and height of the work positions;<br>● the extent of manual handling involved;<br>● ground conditions;<br>● weather conditions;<br>● vehicle and pedestrian traffic below;<br>● the duration of the work; and<br>● the possibility of objects falling.</td><td>For new installations, sales staff are expected to complete a pre-installation survey form identifying the access equipment required and any special factors associated with the project. For all types of work, the technician must assess whether the access equipment available is satisfactory before starting work. Technicians and sales staff have received relevant training (records available).<br>Access equipment used will normally be one of the following:<br>● extension ladders or stepladders (carried on technicians vehicles);<br>● tower scaffolding (available from the main stores);<br>● scaffolding (erected and inspected by contractors); or<br>● mobile elevating work platforms (hired from specialists).<br><br>Site health and safety inspections are carried out by the Health and Safety Officer and Contracts Manager.</td></tr>
<tr><td>Extension ladders and stepladders<br>Ladders may fall or staff may fall from ladders due to poor working practices.<br><br>Ladders may be damaged or deteriorate.<br><br>Ladders may be hit by passing vehicles.</td><td>Technicians have all received training in ladder use (records available).<br>New technicians will be trained during their induction programme.<br>Technicians' handbook includes a section on ladder safety.<br>Technicians should inspect ladders before using.<br>The storekeeper inspects all ladders every three months (records available).<br>Technicians should ensure barriers or warning signs are put in place where necessary.</td></tr>
<tr><td colspan="2">Signature(s) K Crook    Name(s) K Crook    Date 31/5/00<br>Date for next routine review May 2002</td></tr>
</table>

## Out of school childcare group

Such a group would need to assess risks to its staff and to children in its care, both on its own premises and in outside activities. Relevant risk topics are likely to include:

- *equipment* – cleaning, kitchen equipment, TVs and videos, play equipment;
- *premises and facilities* – internal and external access, electrical installation;
- *control of children* – supervision, permitted play areas, attendance records;
- *fire* – precautions and emergency procedures;
- *external activities* – walks, local visits, special excursions;
- *personal safety* – controlling access to premises, suspicious prowlers, aggressive parents;
- *hazardous substances* – cleaning materials;
- *manual handling* – movement of furniture and equipment; and
- *accidents etc* – dealing with accidents, illness, infectious diseases.

A sample assessment record for *external activities* is provided opposite. The record only refers to the risks identified and the *expected* precautions. In effect, staff will need to carry out a dynamic risk assessment prior to any external activities taking place. This is likely to be more formal in the case of special excursions. Any improvements recommended (eg a checklist for special excursions) would be referred to in a separate document.

In conducting this risk assessment:

- there are no specific Regulations applying, although note must be taken of general obligations to safeguard staff and children;
- there is no specific HSE guidance (although guidance from education, local authority or childcare partnership sources may be available); and
- particular attention should be paid to–
    - observing at least one external activity taking place,
    - discussing potential problems and solutions with staff.

## Funkids, Beachville

<table>
<tr><th colspan="3">Risk assessment</th></tr>
<tr><td>Reference number: 5</td><td>Risk topic/issue: External activities</td><td>Sheet 1 of 1</td></tr>
<tr><td colspan="3">Cross references: Risks assessments 6 (personal safety) and 3 (control of children)</td></tr>
<tr><th>Risks identified</th><th colspan="2">Expected precautions</th></tr>
<tr><td>General<br>Any external visit of activity can create additional or different types of risks to children, whether by putting them closer to risk situations (eg roads or water) or increasing the difficulties in controlling them.</td><td colspan="2">External visits and activities have many benefits both for children and staff.<br>Risks can be minimised with a little thought and planning.<br>Staffing levels must be considered – at least two staff must go with the children making the visit and at least two must stay if any children are to remain on Club premises. The numbers and capabilities of the children making the visit must be taken into account.<br>A mobile telephone should normally be taken by the staff member in charge of the external activity.</td></tr>
<tr><td>Local visits<br>Local visits may be made to:<br>• parks, woodland or play areas;<br>• the beach;<br>• sports centres or swimming pools; and<br>• shops etc.</td><td colspan="2">Activities must be chosen that relate to the ages and capabilities of the children involved. Some activities may require the children to be told to bring appropriate clothing or equipment with them, eg towels and swimming costumes.<br>Weather conditions must be assessed before the visit is allowed to go ahead.<br>Travel routes should be planned to utilise footpaths as much as possible and to avoid road crossings, especially those on busy roads without controlled crossing points.<br>Consideration may need to be given to the need for wheelchair access.<br>Rules for walking should be clearly established and communicated to the children. These will normally involve a staff member at the front and the rear of the group.<br>If public transport is to be used, care must be taken to avoid the group being split up.</td></tr>
<tr><td>Special excursions<br>Occasional visits may be made to major attractions or facilities which are further afield.</td><td colspan="2">Locations and activities must be chosen that relate to the ages and capabilities of the children involved.<br>Staffing levels should normally be at least at a level of 1:4.<br>Volunteer assistance, eg from parents may be necessary.<br>Transport must be booked from a reputable source (public transport should be avoided if possible). Coaches or minibuses must have seatbelts suitable for children and arrangements for wheelchair access may be necessary.<br>Refreshment arrangements must be planned in advance – either by requiring the children to bring food and drink with them or by pre-booking refreshments at the visit location.<br>Children must be required to bring suitable bad weather clothing if the visit involves significant time outdoors.<br>Parents should be advised in writing of when the group is expected to return.</td></tr>
<tr><td>Signature(s) C Sands A Castle<br>Date for next routine review April 2002</td><td>Name(s) C Sands, A Castle</td><td>Date 27/4/00</td></tr>
</table>

## *Alternative assessment record formats*

**5.5** Providing it contains all the essential ingredients, a risk assessment can be recorded in alternative formats to those used so far in this chapter. The remaining illustrations utilise:

- an employees' guide;
- a contractors' manual; and
- a standard operating procedure.

### Employees' guides or handbooks

**5.6** This format can be particularly useful when staff are working away from their employer's base. The example opposite is adapted from a guide prepared for engineers involved in *installing and maintaining specialist garage equipment* such as vehicle hoists, lubrication systems, vehicle washes etc. The topics covered include:

- legal requirements;
- liaising with the customer;
- manual handling;
- access;
- electrical work;
- decommissioning equipment;
- personal protective equipment;
- portable tools;
- compressed air;
- hazardous substances;
- asbestos;
- waste disposal;
- fire safety;
- compressed gases; and
- accidents and first aid.

The guide was prepared following visits to a number of the company's installation sites with an experienced engineer. A draft version was launched at a training event attended by all the engineers. As a result, a number of amendments were suggested by the engineers and these were included in the final version. The guide provides a useful basis for the induction of new engineers joining the company.

The example illustrated is the section dealing with *fire safety*. As can be seen, although this is a generic risk assessment providing guidance to engineers, they will still need to carry out a dynamic risk assessment before starting work at a location.

## *Garage equipment engineers' health and safety guide*

Section 13 Fire safety

(a) The main risks

The main fire risks on site will be associated with hot work (eg welding or burning) especially if this has to be carried out close to flammable liquids. Care will particularly be necessary in the vicinity of:

- paint spray booths;
- highly flammable liquid stores;

oil stores or tanks.

Where highly flammable liquids are being used (eg in spray booths), the use of any electrical equipment in the area may also introduce a source of ignition.

(b) Precautions required

Engineers should always make themselves aware of fire evacuation routes, fire assembly points and the locations of fire alarm points and fire extinguishers on arrival in the premises for the first time.

The level of fire precautions necessary for high risk activities or locations should be discussed with the customer before the work starts.

Precautions necessary might include:

- suspension of paint spraying operations;
- removal of flammable liquid containers and other combustible materials form the area;*
- provision of suitable fire extinguishers close to the work; and
- provision of a 'fire watcher' by the customer.

* Where combustible materials cannot be moved an adequate distance from hot work they should be covered with overlapping sheets of non-flammable material or protected by non-flammable screens.

Should an engineer be unhappy with the customer's response he should contact the Operations Manager for further instructions.

## Contractors' manuals

**5.7** Many manufacturers and suppliers of equipment are conscious of the importance of ensuring that sub-contractors who install their products do so with due regard to health and safety. This concern is not purely altruistic but is partly borne out of pressure from clients and/or principal contractors who are mindful of their own obligations under the *CDM Regulations 1994*. Installation contractors are often only small companies without risk assessment documentation of their own – some are too small for recording of risk assessments to be a legal requirement.

The demands for risk assessment documentation from clients or principal contractors can quite legitimately be met by the manufacturer or supplier preparing a generic risk assessment relating to the installation of their product in the form of an installation contractors' manual or guide. However, such a manual would need to be supported by some sort of an assessment relating to the requirements of a specific project – as referred to in the illustration earlier in the chapter relating to the installation of burglar alarms and closed circuit TV. There would also need to be a monitoring system in place to ensure that contractors complied with the requirements of the manual, probably through a system of spot checks by the manufacturer or supplier.

The example opposite is taken from such a manual relating to the *installation of communication and alarm equipment inside residential property*, the majority of which would be occupied during installation. The topics covered in the manual included:

- *residents and the public* – how they should be protected;
- *services* – electricity, telecommunications, gas, water, sewage;
- *asbestos* – likely to be present in older property;
- *personal protective equipment* – requirements for sites generally and for specific activities;
- *electrical work* – when working on or connecting into existing supplies;
- *work equipment* – use of power tools;
- *work at heights* – in stairways, lobbies, lofts;
- *fire* – general precautions;
- *hazardous substances* – sealants, adhesives, electrical cleaners;
- *manual handling* – particularly movement of heavy control panels; and
- *first aid and accidents*.

The illustrative example provided has been slightly adapted from the section relating to *residents and the public.*

**Installation contractors' manual**

Section 1 Residents and the public

*Possible Risks*

Installation work is often carried out within buildings where residents are still present. Other members of the public may visit the buildings and pass through or close to the installation site.

The nature of our products means that residents are often elderly, frail and lacking in mobility.

Visitors may also include young children who will be unaware of risks that might be obvious to adults and such children may also be unable to understand warning signs.

Precautions:

- prior to work starting, there should be communication with affected residents about the nature of the work, its likely duration and any impact on them – particularly in respect of access;
- every effort should be made to maintain clear pedestrian access through application of good housekeeping standards and careful choice of storage locations;
- vehicles should be parked sensibly, leaving access clear for residents' and other vehicles, particularly those used by the emergency services;
- at some locations it may be necessary to bring equipment onto site using a vehicle and then park the vehicle off site;
- where special access risks are created, eg by excavations in roadways or footpaths or blockages of staircases or corridors, use of barriers and warning signs should be made;
- every effort should be made to avoid leaving uncovered excavations or blocked access routes for extended periods, particularly overnight and at weekends; and
- staff carrying out installation work must keep close control over the equipment and materials they are using, particularly if these might be dangerous to children etc.

## Standard operating procedures

**5.8** In work activities, there is often a tendency to place issues such as production, quality of product and health and safety into separate compartments, each covered by separate procedures or rules. This often makes life difficult at shop floor level where a single integrated standard operating procedure is not only much less confusing but also can be an invaluable training aid.

A risk assessment approach should be taken in the development of such procedures, with the risks and the appropriate precautions being identified at each stage of the manufacturing process. The example opposite has been extracted and adapted from a procedure for the *manufacture of pre-stressed concrete beams*.

Whilst the existence of a procedure of this type would not totally eliminate the need for other risk assessments, the process was so much at the heart of this small company's operations that the amount of other risk assessment documentation was greatly reduced. Risk assessments similar to those described earlier in the chapter were prepared for (see 5.4: ILLUSTRATIVE ASSESSMENTS):

- *fork lift trucks and lifting equipment* – operator training, maintenance, statutory examinations;
- *beam stacking and storage* – general rules and precautions;
- *hazardous substances* – extremely limited use;
- *fire* – a low risk in this environment;
- *noise* – from saws and other process equipment;
- *work equipment* – guarding of saws, fitting of cutting discs, operator training; and
- *PPE requirements* – including more detail on specifications of PPE types.

The procedure emphasises the precautions which must be taken at each stage in the process without necessarily going into the same level of detail on the risks involved. However, in many cases the risks are fairly self evident, especially for those familiar with industrial equipment such as Stihl saws. In some situations though, it is important to emphasise risks which may be less apparent, eg the risk of stack collapse. Operatives are more likely to take precautions if they understand the reasons why such precautions are necessary.

| Manufacturing and health and safety procedure | | |
|---|---|---|
| **Activity** | | **Key health and safety points** |
| **2** | **Removal of cast beams** | |
| 2.1 | Attach the appropriate lifting beam to the forks of the fork lift truck. | The fork lift truck must only be driven by licensed drivers. |
| 2.2 | Locate the hooks of the lifting beam into the lifting eyes cast into the concrete beams. | |
| 2.3 | Raise the lifting beam a few centimetres using the fork lift truck. | The fork lift truck driver should beware of excessive resistance.<br>It may be necessary to take remedial action if beams are sticking in the moulds (The supervisor should be consulted in such cases) |
| 2.4 | An operative must then stand on the moulds and cut out the spacers and wires using a Stihl saw or electric saw. Spacers must be placed in the 'wheelie bin' provided. | Only trained operatives may use the Stihl saw or electric saw.<br>The saw guard must be in position.<br>Care must be taken standing on the moulds and using the saw.<br>The operative must wear:<br>• eye protection (a face visor or goggles);<br>• safety footwear;<br>• hearing protection (muffs or plugs);<br>• a dust mask; and<br>• suitable gloves.<br>(others working in the immediate vicinity must wear similar protection) |
| 2.5 | Lift out the row of beams using the fork lift truck. | |
| 2.6 | Place the beams on the designated stack. | Care must be taken to ensure that the stack is stable.<br>No stacks must be more than ten beams high. |
| 2.7 | At the same time, an operative at the rear of the stack places wooden spacers below the beams and removes the lifting beam hooks from the lifting eyes. | This operative must remain alert for possible stack collapse.<br>Care must be taken in positioning his hand to avoid trapping.<br>Suitable gloves and safety footwear must be worn. |

# 6 Model risk assessments

**In this chapter:**



## *Introduction*

**6.1** The concept of a model risk assessment is referred to in the ACOP to the *Management Regulations 1999* which states 'Employers who control a number of similar workplaces containing similar activities may produce a 'model' risk assessment reflecting the core hazards and risks associated with these activities'. The ACOP also refers to their development by trade associations, employers' bodies or other organisations concerned with a particular activity.

This chapter contains examples of model risk assessments used in office environments and in the motor vehicle trade, and the author has also seen the technique used successfully in the retail sector and in residential care homes.

## *Implementation and adaptation*

**6.2** The issue of a model risk assessment by a major employer or trade association will achieve very little if its findings are not implemented at local level and the assessment adapted to match local circumstances. The ACOP states that employers or managers at each workplace must:

- satisfy themselves that the 'model' is appropriate to their type of work; and
- adapt the 'model' to the detail of their own actual work situations, including any extension necessary to cover hazards and risks not referred to in the 'model'.

The examples provided in this chapter all contain a column headed 'local arrangements' in which each location is expected to provide details of how they implement the precautions identified as being necessary. This approach works particularly well when used in conjunction with an auditing programme. For example, the auditor can identify from the document who has been made responsible for maintenance and testing of the fire alarm and therefore knows who to approach to examine the relevant records. The records may demonstrate full compliance with the required standards or alternatively that precautions fall a long way short of those intended.

The existence of such an auditing programme should be an integral part of the 'management cycle' required by the *Management Regulations 1999, Regulation 5* (as described in more detail in CHAPTER 8: IMPLEMENTATION OF PRECAUTIONS). The audit constitutes part of the 'monitor' stage of the management cycle. This and the 'review' stage of the cycle can be particularly embarrassing for local managers who have simply placed the model risk assessment on a shelf.

## Sample model assessments

**6.3** The remainder of this chapter provides examples of work situations where model risk assessments have been developed successfully, together with sample extracts from those model assessments.

### Offices

The examples provided on the next two pages are modified extracts from a model risk assessment developed for the offices occupied by a regional development agency.

Topics covered by the assessment included:

- *fire*;
- *accidents and other emergencies* – including first aid arrangements, guidance on bomb threats;
- *visitors and contractors* – access control, contractor selection and management;
- *access* – inside and outside the offices;
- *office and kitchen equipment* – including lifts;
- *services*;
- *hazardous substances* – predominantly office supplies and cleaning materials;
- *manual handling* – stationery, archived records etc; and
- *display screen equipment* – arrangements for eye tests and workstation assessments.

A separate section of the risk assessment documents provides generic assessments relating to the activities of agency staff away from their office, including:

- *personal safety issues* – general guidance;
- *personal protective equipment* – guidance on PPE which may be required for foreseeable risks;
- *managed workspace and estates* – the agency's role as landlord and managing agent;
- *unoccupied sites* – under the agency's ownership or control;
- *home working* – an increasing practice in many organisations; and
- *work abroad* – medical issues and risks which may be greater in foreign countries.

Given the varied activities of the agency and its staff, these generic assessments must be supported by further dynamic assessments – a concept developed further in CHAPTER 15: RISK ASSESSMENT RELATED CONCEPTS.

The first example contains the subsections dealing with *fire alarms and emergency lighting* (other subsections deal with fire certificates, fire evacuation routes, evacuation procedures, evacuation drills, fire fighting equipment and fire prevention. Forms for recording tests, drills etc are provided at the end of the section).

The second example is the section relating to services. As can be seen, it is primarily concerned with arrangements for maintenance and repairs. The agency has established procedures for regular health and safety inspections which should be able to identify where repairs are necessary. Some offices, eg those with electrical heating and no air conditioning would identify some subsections as 'not applicable'.

# 1 Fire

| Details of risks | Expected precautions | Local arrangements |
| --- | --- | --- |
| | *1.3 FIRE ALARMS* | |
| A fire could break out at any time within the Agency's own offices, elsewhere in shared buildings or within adjacent property. | Arrangements must be in place to ensure that electrical fire alarm systems are checked by specialist companies at least once per year. | Alarm maintained by: |
| The Agency's own staff would be at risk, together with any visitors or contractors present on the premises.<br><br>Agency activities would not normally create any abnormal fire risk but work by contractors may do – see section 3 of the risk assessment. | The fire alarm system must be tested regularly, using different call points in rotation. Where a frequency is not specified in the fire certificate, tests must be carried out at least weekly.<br><br>Records must be kept of the date of the test, the call point(s) used and the condition of the alarm.<br>(A suitable record form is provided at the end of section 1). | Alarm tested and records kept by: |
| | *1.4 EMERGENCY LIGHTING* | |
| (This general description of risks is contained in the first part of this section) | Offices will normally be provided with emergency lighting and arrangements must be in place to ensure that this is checked by a specialist company at least once per year. | Emergency lighting maintained by: |
| | The emergency lighting must be tested regularly. Where a frequency is not specified in the fire certificate, tests must be carried out at least every six months. Records of the date of each test must be kept which include the date and details of any faults found. (A suitable record form is provided at the end of Section 1). | Emergency lighting tested and records kept by: |

# 6 Services

| Details of risks | Expected precautions | Local arrangements |
|---|---|---|
| | *6.1 FIXED ELECTRICAL INSTALLATION* | |
| The fixed electrical installation, any gas supplies and any central heating or hot water boilers all present possible risks to agency staff and others on the premises. | • The fixed electrical installation (distribution boards, isolators, circuit-breakers or fuses, cables and conduits and socket outlets) in each office must be inspected by a competent person (eg an electrician) *at least every 4 years.*<br>• Distribution boards, isolators, circuit-breakers and fuses should be labelled as appropriate.<br>• Access to isolator switches should be kept readily available (where it is important to keep isolators secure, keys to locked rooms or cupboards should be kept in glass-fronted boxes or otherwise available for emergency access). | Inspection of the electrical installation is carried out by: |
| | *6.2 GAS INSTALLATION & EQUIPMENT*<br>• Locations with gas installations and equipment must ensure that this is checked by a CORGI registered installer at least every year. Any repairs must be carried out promptly, also by a CORGI registered installer. In some offices maintenance will be the responsibility of the landlord. | Maintenance and repairs of gas equipment are carried out by: |
| | *6.3 BOILERS*<br>• Arrangements must be in place for regular maintenance and, where necessary, repairs of central heating or hot water boilers by a competent organisation. In some offices maintenance will be the responsibility of the landlord.<br>• An adequate number of staff must be able to operate the controls of boilers and related equipment. | Boiler maintenance and repairs are carried out by: |
| | *6.4 AIR CONDITIONING EQUIPMENT* | |
| Cooling water systems associated with air conditioning equipment may contain significant quantities of legionella bacteria creating a risk to agency staff and others, including neighbours. | • Arrangements must be in place for regular maintenance and, where necessary, repairs of air conditioning equipment by a competent organisation. This may require chemical dosing to control the formation of legionella bacteria. In some offices maintenance will be the responsibility of the landlord. | Maintenance and repairs of the air conditioning equipment are carried out by: |

## *Motor trade*

The remaining examples of model assessments are from a manual issued by a national network of garage dealerships. The manual contained the company's health and safety policy and the sections of model risk assessments relating to:

- *general topics*, eg fire, electrical installation, site security;
- *service workshops*;
- *parts departments*;
- *showrooms and administrative areas*;
- *bodyshops*; and
- *petrol storage and sales*.

The last two sections only applied to a minority of the company's locations.

The first two examples are both adapted from the *service workshops* section and are parts of the subsections dealing with *hazardous substances* and *lifting equipment*. General guidance is provided on risks and the precautions expected and then the dealership must insert details relating to their own arrangements for inspections, maintenance, statutory examinations and training.

A further example is provided which has been adapted from the section for dealerships with *bodyshops*. This provides details on the risks associated with the use of *radioactive anti-static devices* (which are only used by a limited number of body repair workshops). The assessment identifies the precautions which are necessary in the use of such units and directs users towards complying with some of the detailed requirements of the relevant Regulations.

# B9 Hazardous substances

| Details of risks | Expected precautions | Local arrangements |
|---|---|---|
| | *B 9.4 COMMON EXPOSURES TO HAZARDOUS SUBSTANCES*<br>(Use of hazardous substances in body shops is covered in section E of the manual).<br>*Vehicle exhaust emissions* | |
| Vehicle exhausts contain a variety of hazardous gases. | Workshops should normally be equipped with exhaust extraction systems or have very good standards of general ventilation. Workshop management is expected to ensure that extraction systems are used by staff where appropriate. The system must be inspected and tested by a competent person at least every 14 months with inspection reports kept on file. | The extraction system is inspected and tested by:<br><br>Inspection reports are kept by: |
| | *Welding and burning* | |
| All types of burning and welding work produce hazardous gases and fumes. | Only limited amounts of welding and burning work are normally carried out in servicing workshops. Where extraction facilities have not been provided, this work must be carried out in a well ventilated area and preferably in the open air.<br>PPE must be worn as described in section B11 of the manual.<br>Use of respiratory protection will not normally be necessary. | |
| | *Parts cleaning* | |
| Exposure of the skin to cleaning solvents can lead to dermatitis. Some cleaning solvents also create a significant inhalation risk. | Each branch must have a proprietary self-contained parts cleaning unit which is regularly serviced and maintained.<br>Parts should be cleaned by brush wherever possible. Suitable impermeable gloves must be provided for cleaning work. | The parts cleaning unit is serviced and maintained by: |

Further parts of this sub-section deal with:

- battery acid;
- anti-freeze;
- valeting chemicals;
- brake linings (possible asbestos risk);
- air conditioning units (fluorocarbon gases); and
- aerosols.

# B12 Lifting equipment

| Details of risks | Expected precautions | Local arrangements |
|---|---|---|
| | *B 12.1 TESTING & EXAMINATION* | |
| | All lifting equipment must have a declaration of conformity or a report of a thorough examination specifying its safe working load, (provided by the suppliers or manufacturers) before it is taken into use. Every item of lifting equipment must carry a clear identifying reference number (or letter). | |
| The condition of lifting equipment may deteriorate due to damage, misuse, the environment or wear and tear. | Lifting equipment must continue to be thoroughly examined by a competent person (usually an insurance company engineer) throughout its lifespan.<br>The statutory examination periods are normally:<br>6 months for accessories for lifting such as chains, ropes and lifting tackle (including fabric and wire rope slings, shackles, eye bolts etc.)<br>12 months for other lifting equipment (including vehicle hoists, fork lift trucks, chain blocks, electric hoist blocks and engine lifters). | Thorough examinations are carried out by: |
| | | Examination reports are kept by: |
| | *B 12.2 USE OF LIFTING EQUIPMENT* | |
| Inadequately trained staff may operate lifting equipment incorrectly or be unaware of good lifting and slinging practice. | Fork lift trucks may only be operated by persons who have been trained in accordance with the HSE Approved code of practice (ACOP).<br>All staff involved in using lifting equipment must be provided with appropriate in-house training and suitable records of training should always be kept. | The following persons have been trained to ACOP standard in fork lift truck operation: |
| Equipment may have been damaged since the last time it was used. | Staff should always check the condition of lifting equipment prior to using it. Equipment in poor condition must be taken out of use (Where lifting equipment is scrapped, its reference number should be recorded so that it is removed from the 'thorough examination' inventory.) | |
| Overloading of lifting equipment could result in its sudden dramatic failure or in hidden damage. | The weights of the load to be lifted should be established (either by reference to manuals or a realistic estimate).<br>The safe working load of all items of lifting equipment being used must be adequate for the load. | Lifting equipment training records are kept by: |

(Further guidance on good lifting practice is provided in the remainder of this sub-section.)

# E7 Radioactive anti-static devices

| Details of risks | Expected precautions | Local arrangements |
|---|---|---|
| | *E 7.1 INTRODUCTION* | |
| Some body shops use radioactive sources in compressed air blow down guns to reduce the problems caused by static electricity.<br>(Suppliers of this equipment will usually give specialist assistance in compliance with the relevant Regulations). | Any dealership keeping such radioactive sources must be registered with the Environment Agency (EA) and keep a copy of the registration on file. | The Environment Agency registration is kept by: |
| | The Health and Safety Executive must be notified prior to use of the radioactive source commencing. (In most cases, the suppliers will arrange for EA registration and HSE notification on behalf of the dealership.) | The HSE have been notified by: |
| | A competent member of staff must be appointed as a radiation protection supervisor (RPS). The RPS must be aware of the contents of this section of the manual and relevant information from the supplier, particularly in respect of methods of use of the unit and the actions necessary in case of its damage or loss. | The radiation protection supervisor is: |
| | Instructions relating to the use of the unit and actions in case of damage or loss must be prominently displayed in the area where it is used. A record must also be kept of the unit's location. (Some suppliers provide a wall chart for these purposes). | Instructions about the unit are displayed: |

## E7 Radioactive anti-static devices

| Details of risks | Expected precautions | Local arrangements |
|---|---|---|
| | E 7.2 USE OF THE UNIT | |
| | When the ionising gun is not in use it must be detached from the air line and locked in a storage box. (Any spare cartridge must also be locked in the box). | The lockable storage box is kept: |
| | The unit must only be used for its intended purpose. The unit must not be modified, cleaned or disposed of. The foil surface must not be damaged and the nozzle must not be probed with wire or any other pointed instrument. | |
| | Suppliers' requirements for returning cartridges to them must be complied with. | |
| | The unit must not be moved to another location without consulting the supplier (further EA registration and HSE notification may be required).<br>The unit should be checked regularly for signs of damage or deterioration. | |
| | *E 7.3 DAMAGE TO OR LOSS OF THE UNIT* | |
| The unit may be damaged by fire, mechanical impact, exposure to corrosive materials etc. It may also be lost or stolen. | All cases of damage or loss or suspicions of its loss or theft must be reported immediately to the RPS. | |
| | The RPS is responsible, where necessary, for notifying the suppliers and following their advice. Notification to the EA and/or HSE may also be required. (If the RPS cannot be contacted, advice should be obtained from the suppliers directly.) | The home telephone number of the RPS and the suppliers' emergency number are displayed: |
| Fire in the area of the unit. | The Fire Brigade must be informed of the unit's presence. | |
| Fire, mechanical damage or corrosion affecting the unit. | Access to the area must be prevented and advice sought from the suppliers or any other competent source. | |
| Mechanical or corrosive damage to the foil may release small quantities of radioactive material. | Anyone who has touched the gun, or any object in the immediate area, should wash their hands thoroughly. Further contact should be avoided until competent advice has been obtained. | |

# 7 Specialised risk assessment techniques

**In this chapter:**



## *Introduction*

**7.1** The *Management Regulations 1992* resulted in a variety of risk assessment techniques being developed, many of which involved the use of risk rating or quantitative assessment techniques. However, the ACOPs accompanying both the 1992 and the 1999 regulations have emphasised that the degree of sophistication of the risk assessment should be determined by the level of risk arising from the work activity. The 1999 ACOP provides further detail on this point:

*Small businesses* presenting few or simple hazards:

- 'risk assessment can be a very straightforward process based on informal judgement and reference to appropriate guidance'.

*Intermediate cases*:

- risk assessment will need to be more sophisticated;
- specialised advice may be required in some cases; and
- some specialist analytical techniques may be required eg measuring air quality and assessing its impact.

*Large and hazardous sites:*

- require the most developed and sophisticated risk assessments, particularly where there are complex or novel processes;
- for sites using or storing bulk hazardous substances, large scale mineral extraction or nuclear plant, risk assessment will be a significant part of the safety case or report and may incorporate such techniques as quantified risk assessment; and
- the *Control of Major Accident Hazard Regulations 1999* ('COMAH') and other statutory requirements (eg in the nuclear industry) may require more specific and detailed assessment techniques.

## Risk rating matrices

**7.2** Many different risk rating matrices have been developed as an aid to the risk assessment process. Several examples are put forward below whilst the pros and cons of this type of approach are set out later in the section (see 7.3: ADVANTAGES and 7.4: DISAVANTAGES).

Most matrices utilise a simple combination of the likelihood of a hazard having an adverse effect and the severity of the consequences if it did. Some use numbers to produce a risk rating, as in the example below:

| *Risk assessment matrix* | | | *Likelihood of adverse effect* | | |
|---|---|---|---|---|---|
| | | | *Unlikely* | *Possible* | *Frequent* |
| | | | 1 | 2 | 3 |
| Severity of consequences | Minor | 1 | 1 | 2 | 3 |
| | Moderate | 2 | 2 | 4 | 6 |
| | Severe | 3 | 3 | 6 | 9 |

The numbers can be replaced by descriptions of the level of risk as shown in the next example:

| *Risk assessment matrix* | | *Likelihood of adverse effect* | | |
|---|---|---|---|---|
| | | *Unlikely* | *Possible* | *Frequent* |
| Severity of consequences | Minor | Low | Low | Medium |
| | Moderate | Low | Medium | High |
| | Severe | Medium | High | Very high |

A more complex version of this approach was provided in a supplement to the May 1993 issue of *The Safety & Health Practitioner*, the magazine of the Institution of Occupational Safety & Health. This approach requires firstly the identification of the worst likely outcome in respect of each hazard ie:

- a fatality;
- major injury or permanent disability (including permanent ill health);
- minor injury; or
- no injury.

Next a judgement must be made of the probability or likelihood of harm occurring, based on the following table:

| *Probability/likelihood* | *Description* |
|---|---|
| Likely/frequent | Occurs repeatedly/event only to be expected. |
| Probable | Not surprised. Will occur several times. |
| Possible | Could occur sometimes. |
| Remote | Unlikely, though conceivable. |
| Improbable | So unlikely that probability is close to zero. |

Decisions on what actions (if any) should be taken can then be made by reference to the matrix below:

| | *Likely* | Probable | Possible | Remote | Improbable |
|---|---|---|---|---|---|
| Fatal | 1st | 2nd | 2nd | 3rd | |
| Major injury/ permanent disability | 2nd | 2nd | 3rd | | |
| Minor injury | 3rd | 3rd | | | |
| No injury | | | | | |

KEY:

| | |
|---|---|
| | 1st rank actions |
| | 2nd rank actions |
| | 3rd rank actions |
| | Acceptable risk – no action |

Alternative versions of this matrix approach further divide the severity of the consequences into two components:

- the severity of the injury – eg fatal/serious, moderate, minor; and
- the number of people who could be harmed – eg many, more than one, one.

## Advantages

**7.3** Advocates of risk rating using these types of matrices put forward the following arguments in its favour:

- it ensures that both severity and likelihood are considered;
- some subjectivity is removed from the process; and
- it helps in determining priorities for improvements.

## Disadvantages

**7.4** Detractors (including the author) feel that the approach is pseudo-scientific and unnecessary:

- its application to every hazard associated with each individual activity or situation can be very time consuming;
- much time can be spent debating risk values, rather than evaluating the effectiveness of controls; and
- some quick and simple measures to improve the control of lesser risks may be overlooked whilst attention is focused on higher-scored risks.

As more organisations gain in experience of actually conducting risk assessments in practice, opinion seems to be swinging against the use of risk rating matrices and more in favour of the approach described in CHAPTER 4:CARRYING OUT RISK ASSESSMENTS. HSG publication *HSG 183 5 steps to risk assessment: case studies (1998)* does not utilise the matrix approach.

## More sophisticated approaches

**7.5** The ACOP recognises that more sophisticated approaches to risk assessment must be taken in high risk situations. Many such situations are controlled by the *COMAH Regulations 1999* and HSE guidance on the regulations (*HSG 190 Preparing safety reports. Control of Major Accident Hazard Regulations 1999 (1999)*) refers to several techniques which may be used, including:

- *HAZOP*

Hazard and operating studies (HAZOP) were first used by ICI in the 1960s to identify hazards, particularly during the design of chemical plants. The HAZOP approach is described more fully later in the chapter (see 7.6: HAZOP).

- *FMEA*

Failure mode and effects analysis (FMEA) is a technique which can be used to calculate the possibility of failure of components in a piece of equipment or a system and thus calculate the possibility of failure of the equipment or system as a whole.

- *Event tree analysis*

This technique starts from a possible component failure and is intended to identify possible resulting hazards. It is used for rather more complex systems than FMEA.

- *Fault tree analysis*

Fault trees start from a hazardous outcome and then work downwards to identify the potential causes of such an outcome and the possibilities of these causes occurring. It is a 'top down' approach as opposed to event tree analysis which involves analysis from the bottom up.

Detailed descriptions of these techniques is outside the scope of this handbook but is available in other more specialised publications (see *Safety, reliability and risk management. An integrated approach. S J Cox and NRS Tait, Butterworth Heinemann (1998)*).

The HSE and other organisations have commissioned studies into quantified risk assessment (QRA). In the Foreword to one such paper relating particularly to the nuclear industry (HSE publication *Quantified risk assessment: its input to decision making (1989)*), the HSE state

> 'QRA is an element that cannot be ignored in decision-making about risk since it is the only discipline capable, however imperfectly, of enabling a number to be applied and comparisons of a sort to be made, other than of a purely qualitative kind. This said, the numerical element must be viewed with great caution and treated as only one parameter in an essentially judgemental exercise. Moreover, since any judgement upon risk is distributional, risks being caused to some as an outcome of the activity of others, it is therefore essentially political in the widest sense of the word.'

Much the same can be said in respect of attempts to quantify risk at far more basic levels.

## HAZOP

**7.6** As stated previously, HAZOP is a technique that can be used to identify potential hazards and to introduce appropriate precautions to control those hazards. It is particularly useful when designing chemical plants and similar installations, although it can be applied to existing plants. It is best used by a multi-disciplinary team involving persons with expertise in design, commissioning, operations, maintenance and health and safety functions.

The technique identifies hazards through the application of guide words to individual elements of the proposed design. The HAZOP team brainstorms how each guide word might apply to the element under review, identifying deviations from the intended performance, possible causes of these deviations and potential consequences of the deviation. Where a significant risk is identified as a result, actions are specified which should reduce the risk to an acceptable level. These actions may involve modifications to the design, making changes at the installation location, introducing maintenance or inspection routines or adopting specified precautions during operation.

The accompanying table shows how the HAZOP guidewords can be used to identify deviations and is followed by an example of a completed HAZOP worksheet.

## HAZOP: Guide words for the generation of process deviations

| Guide word | Possible deviations |
|---|---|
| *None* | No liquid flow.<br>No electric current.<br>No pressure.<br>Reverse flow.<br>Operational sequence omitted. |
| *More of or (Less of)* | Quantitative increase (or decrease) in any parameter, eg flow, pressure, temperature, electric current, viscosity, volume, weight, dimension. |
| *Part of* | Only some of the design intention is achieved, eg a change in chemical composition, incomplete reaction. |
| *More than* | Something else is present eg impurities in a raw material, gas is present in a liquid (or liquid in a gas). |
| *Other* | What else can happen?<br>● instrumentation failure;<br>● sampling activities;<br>● corrosion of components;<br>● reliefs activating, eg blow-off valve;<br>● service failure, eg cooling water, compressed air;<br>● maintenance activities; or<br>● static electricity generated/ discharged. |

## *HAZOP Worksheet*

| **Project** | New manufacturing facility – Flixwood | | | | |
|---|---|---|---|---|---|
| **Section** | Solvent pumps and supply pipelines | | | Sheet 1 of 3 | |
| Brief description of function | Supply of solvent from the tank farm to the manufacturing building | | | **Date reviewed** | 14 Aug 2000 |
| | | | | **Date agreed by team** | 21 Aug 2000 |
| **Guideword** | **Deviation** | **Possible causes** | **Consequences** | **Action required** | **Responsibility** |
| *More of* | Increased flow. | Higher solvent pressure during start-up. | High turning moment on dog-leg pipe.<br>Possibility of rupture. | Check whether pipe can stand start-up pressure. | Design engineer |
| *None* | No flow. | Pump seal leak. | Major leakage in pump area, possibility of fire. | Reliable pump seals already selected. | |
| | | | | Consider need for remotely operated isolation valve. | Design engineer |
| | | | | Provide suitable fire fighting equipment in area. | Operations |
| | | Pipeline failure due to impact damage. | Major leakage next to road, high risk of fire. | Protect pipeline with crash barriers. | Design engineer |

## References

**7.7**


| | | |
|---|---|---|
| 1 | HSG 183: | 5 steps to risk assessment: case studies, HSE (1998) |
| 2 | HSG 190: | Preparing safety reports. Control of Major Accident Hazard Regulations 1999, HSE (1999) |
| 3 | | Safety, reliability and risk management. An integrated approach. SJ Cox and NRS Tait, Butterworth Heinemann (1998) ISBN: 0 7506 4016 2 |
| 4 | | Quantified risk assessment: Its input to decision making, HSE (1989) |

# 8 Implementation of precautions

**In this chapter:**

## Introduction

**8.1** The time spent in conducting risk assessments of any type can be regarded as wasted unless the precautions identified as being necessary are actually implemented. Much of this chapter is concerned with the management actions which should be taken to ensure effective implementation – the 'management cycle'. However, firstly a change introduced by the *1999 Management Regulations* will be examined, ie that certain principles of prevention must be applied.

## Principles of prevention

**8.2** *Regulation 4* of the *Management Regulations 1999* states:

> 'Where an employer implements any preventive and protective measures he shall do so on the basis of the principles specified in Schedule 1 to these Regulations'.

Schedule 1 specifies the general principles of prevention set out in *Article 6(2)* of *European Council Directive 89/391/EEC*. These are:

(a) avoiding risks;

(b) evaluating the risks which cannot be avoided;

(c) combating the risks at source;

(d) adapting the work to the individual, especially as regards the design of workplaces, the choice of work equipment and the choice of working and production methods, with a view, in particular, to alleviating monotonous work and work at a predetermined work-rate and to reducing their effect on health;

(e) adapting to technical progress;

(f) replacing the dangerous by the non-dangerous or the less dangerous;

(g) developing a coherent overall prevention policy which covers technology, organisation of work, working conditions, social relationships and the influence of factors relating to the working environment;

(h) giving collective protective measures priority over individual protective measures; and

(i) giving appropriate instructions to employees.

These principles – particularly avoiding risks, combating risks at source and giving collective protection priority over individual protective measures – have been accepted for many years in health and safety. In some UK Regulations a hierarchical approach is required. For instance in the *COSHH Regulations* (see CHAPTER 9: COSHH ASSESSMENTS) exposure of employees to hazardous substances must be prevented where reasonably practicable. If this is not the case, exposure must be adequately controlled – by measures other than the provision of personal protective equipment, so far as is reasonably practicable ie there is a clear order of preference:

1 prevention of exposure;

2 adequate control, other than by PPE;

3 adequate control through PPE.

A similar approach is taken in *Regulation 11* of the *Provision and Use of Work Equipment Regulations 1998* ('PUWER'). This requires effective measures to be taken to prevent access to any dangerous part of machinery (or any rotating stock bar) or to stop its movement before any part of a person enters a danger zone. In this case the following measures must be adopted 'where and to the extent that it is practicable to do so' in this order of preference:

1 fixed enclosing guards;

2 other guards or protection devices eg interlocked guards, photo-electric beams;

3 protection appliances eg jigs, holders or push-sticks; and

4 provision of information, instruction, training and supervision.

Note that this hierarchy must be more strictly applied than in the *COSHH Regulations* since the qualifying term used is 'practicable' as opposed to 'reasonably practicable'.

Whilst the *HSE Guidance to Regulation 4* of the *Management Regulations 1999* clearly indicates a preference for a similar hierarchical approach to be taken, it also accepts that this will not always be possible. In paragraph 31 the guidance states: 'These are general principles rather than prescriptive requirements. They should, however, be applied wherever it is reasonable to do so. Experience suggests that, in the majority of cases, adopting good practice will be enough to ensure risks are reduced sufficiently.'

## The management cycle

**8.3** *Regulation 5* of the *Management Regulations 1999* requires employers to take effective steps to implement the precautions identified by the risk assessment as being necessary – the theory must be translated into practice in the workplace. *Paragraph (1)* of *Regulation 5* states:

> 'Every employer shall make and give effect to such arrangements as are appropriate, having regard to the nature of his activities and the size of his undertaking for the effective planning, organising, control, monitoring and review of the preventive and protective measures.'

*Paragraph (2) of Regulation 5* requires employers with five or more employees to record these arrangements.

Such a 'management cycle' has long been applied to other areas of business activity, such as finance, but relatively few employers have utilised it in relation to health and safety. Managers have often stated their good intentions but have not always set up the organisational structure and control to implement those intentions and have failed to monitor what is actually happening in the workplace.

The cycle can be applied to an employer's overall approach to health and safety:

- Plan – through the statement of intent within the health and safety policy;
- Organise – by allocating responsibilities for implementing the policy and making the necessary resources available;
- Control – through application of relevant management systems and techniques and the use of performance standards;
- Monitor – through health and safety audits and inspections; and
- Review – in health and safety committee and management meetings.

The cycle can also be applied in other ways to ensure that systems or procedures are implemented effectively (this is illustrated in relation to health and safety inspections later in the chapter). It can also be applied to specific types of precautions such as the provision of guarding for dangerous parts of machinery.

- Plan by stated objectives eg compliance with legislation (eg PUWER 1998) or related European or British standards;

- Organise – through having staff competent to interpret and apply such standards;
- Control – by procedures for selecting new equipment or modifying existing equipment and arrangements for supervisory staff to ensure that guards are used as appropriate;
- Monitor – through the health and safety inspection programme; and
- Review – via problem solving or other meetings which result in actions such as redesign of guards or the re-training of supervisors or employees.

In the remainder of this chapter each of the five stages of the management cycle will be examined in more detail. It should perhaps be emphasised that the various elements which make up health and safety management programmes can straddle more than one stage of the management cycle. Whilst a health and safety committee will *review* the effectiveness of health and safety measures, its members should also be expected to *monitor* precautions – both through formal inspection programmes and by informal observations during their daily work. The ACOP to the *Management Regulations* states that whilst more complex health and safety management systems may be appropriate for large complicated organisations, the principles of good health and safety management are the same, irrespective of an organisation's size. It refers to the key elements of effective systems as contained in '*Successful health and safety management*' (REF. 1) and *BS 8800* (REF. 2).

## Planning

### Health and safety policy statement

**8.4** *Section 2(3)* of *HASAWA 1974* requires all employers with five or more employees to have a written statement of their health and safety policy. This should have three components – a statement of intent, responsibilities within the organisation for implementing the policy and the arrangements for implementing the policy. All of these form part of the planning process:

- Statement of intent – where does the organisation plan to be on health and safety?
- Responsibilities – who should be made responsible for implementing actions within the organisation? (equipping people to carry out those responsibilities is considered later under 'organisation'); and

- Arrangements – what procedures and mechanisms need to be established to deliver the desired standards? (the nature of such procedures is considered later under 'control').

## Annual health and safety plans

**8.5** Whilst many organisations achieve good health and safety standards, none are perfect – the minority that think they are perfect are deluding themselves! All employers should seek constant improvement in their management systems and should also recognise that they must take account of changes taking place both externally (new Regulations, changes in ACOPs and HSE guidance) and internally (new equipment, processes, materials and organisational restructuring). Many employers now choose to prepare an annual health and safety plan to achieve desired improvements or cope with changes. Such plans should of course be accompanied by identification of responsibilities, timescales and resources for their implementation.

## Development of performance standards

**8.6** Objectives contained in policy statements or annual health and safety plans relating to improved accident performance are just wishful thinking unless the actions intended to achieve the improvement are properly identified. These actions must be:

- Measurable – a defined activity to be carried out by a specific date or to a specified frequency; and
- Realistic – capable of being achieved by those responsible within the timescale specified, taking into account the availability of resources and other prevailing circumstances.

Such standards can be built into annual plans

> eg – Refresher training in manual handling (to a specified syllabus) will be delivered to all warehouse staff by the safety officer during the second quarter.

They can also be incorporated into procedures or systems

> eg – All new employees and transferees will receive health and safety induction training (of a specified content) from their manager or supervisor during their first day in their new department.

A health and safety inspection will be carried out in each department every month by a supervisor and a safety representative.

### Risk assessments

**8.7** The importance of planning the risk assessment programme was stressed in CHAPTER 4: CARRYING OUT RISK ASSESSMENTS. Once the initial programme has been completed, planning of how assessments are to be reviewed and revised must also take place.

## *Organisation*

### Responsibilities for implementation

**8.8** Where individuals are allocated responsibility for implementing elements of the health and safety programme they must be capable of accepting such responsibilities. This applies whether the responsibilities result from the health and safety policy, an annual health and safety plan or a need to carry out risk assessments. For example:

- A newly appointed supervisor is likely to need training on relevant health and safety legislation and his responsibilities under it, together with procedures such as permits to work, accident investigation or emergency evacuation that he must now implement;
- A safety officer may need training in instructional techniques, even before delivering training on a subject he is already familiar with, such as manual handling; and
- A risk assessment team is likely to require training both on the legal background to their work and on assessment techniques before embarking on their programme.

### Communication and consultation

**8.9** The value of health and safety committees in respect of monitoring and review will be stressed later. However, such a committee or an alternative means of consulting employees must first be established. Employers have legal duties to consult employees or their representatives imposed on them by the *Safety Representatives and Safety Committees Regulations 1977* (REF. 3) and the *Health and Safety (Consultation with Employees) Regulations 1996* (REF. 4). Essential health and safety information must also be communicated to employees whether through induction programmes, safety handbooks, newsletters, notice boards, briefing sessions. All of these activities require organisational effort on the part of the employer.

### Advice and information

**8.10** Employers have a duty imposed on them through *Regulation 7* of the *Management Regulations 1999* to have competent health and safety assistance (see CHAPTER 2: WHAT THE MANAGEMENT REGULATIONS REQUIRE). The employer may decide to carry out this role himself, appoint one or more employees to provide the assistance or engage the services of an external consultancy. If the latter course is adopted the employer will still need to organise the selection of a suitable consultancy (REF. 5). Alternatively the employer or the appointed employee(s) will require an appropriate level of training in order to fulfil the role. There will also be a need for ongoing information to ensure the organisation keeps abreast of developments in health and safety – this might be provided through specialist magazines, information update subscription services (REF. 6) or the internet.

## *Control*

### Procedures and systems

**8.11** Control is often established through the creation of formal procedures and systems for delivering key elements of the health and safety programme. Such procedures will provide detail of the 'arrangements' parts of the health and safety policy. The need for procedures will depend upon the size and complexity of the organisation and topics might include:

- Health and Safety Inspections;
- Accident and Incident Investigation;
- Fire Evacuation;
- Other Emergencies eg bomb threats, hazardous substance leaks;
- Medical Screening;
- Permits to Work;
- Selection, Purchase and Issue of PPE;
- Purchase of New Equipment;
- Engineering Projects;
- Selection and Management of Contractors;
- First Aid.

These would be in addition to any operational or production procedures which might include significant health and safety content (as in the example provided at the end of CHAPTER 5: ASSESSMENT RECORDS).

## Training programmes

**8.12** Control can also be established through specifying the content of training programmes throughout the organisation. Such training may relate to:

- Induction – a defined programme for new employees (inc. temps) and transferees;
- Processes – utilising the type of procedure at the end of CHAPTER 5: ASSESSMENT RECORDS;
- Procedures – eg accident investigation, permit to work issue/receipt;
- Equipment – eg driving fork lift trucks, operating cranes;
- Activities – eg manual handling, entering confined spaces, working at heights;
- Status – eg programmes for newly appointed supervisors;
- Changes in legislation – updating of specialists or senior managers;
- Health and safety awareness – for managers, supervisors or employees generally.

In many cases the detailed health and safety content of training programmes can be derived from a process of risk assessment. This is particularly the case in respect of induction training. It is a relatively simple process to extract the key pieces of information a new employee needs by using the risk assessment for the department or section in question. Some training will need to be accompanied by testing in order to confirm that the employee has achieved a desired level of understanding or skill.

## Supervision

**8.13** Good standards of supervision are also essential in achieving control of what happens in the workplace. Supervisors have an important role to play in:

- Communicating and consulting with employees;
- Delivering induction and operator training;
- Implementing procedures;

- Enforcing standards eg PPE requirements, speed limits;
- Identifying deficiencies in procedures (or the need for new ones).

This latter task is part of the important assistance that supervisors can provide in the monitoring of health and safety standards.

## *Monitoring*

### Health and safety inspections

**8.14** Conducting regular health and safety inspections is an important means of ensuring that standards are monitored systematically. It is important that inspections take account of the way people are working rather than just paying attention to equipment and premises. It is well established that 'unsafe acts' (eg non-compliance with PPE standards, speeding, removing guards, cutting corners on procedures) are a much more common cause of accidents than 'unsafe conditions'. Indeed many unsafe conditions (eg missing guards, damaged equipment, blocked fire exits) result from earlier unsafe acts.

Where trade unions are formally recognised by employers, union-appointed safety representatives have a right to carry out inspections at least every three months of areas where their members work. (REF. 3) Many employers arrange for supervisors or managers to carry out inspections jointly with these safety representatives and many more consider it good practice to involve employees in inspections, even when there is no formal recognition of a union.

Whilst those carrying out inspections should be alert for any possible problems, there will inevitably be some issues which are of more importance in specific workplaces. Inspection checklists can be derived from risk assessment records which highlight these important issues. These might relate to:

- compliance with PPE requirements;
- maintenance of fire exit routes or self-closing fire doors;
- presence of or adjustment of guards;
- manual handling practices;
- housekeeping standards or condition of floors;
- driving standards.

An example of an inspection checklist relating to an office environment is provided later in the chapter. This is accompanied by a sheet which can be used to track action points resulting from the inspection.

The management cycle can be applied to the implementation of a health and safety inspection programme:

- Plan
  - a statement of intent to carry out regular inspections and involve employee representatives;
- Organise
  - provide training in inspection technique for those who are involved;
  - identify areas to be inspected eg by splitting a large workplace into inspection units;
  - define the frequencies for inspections to take place (these may vary between areas with different levels of risk);
  - identify who is responsible for making the inspections; eg the supervisor and safety representative jointly;
  - provide area specific inspection checklists;
  - establish a mechanism for allocating responsibility for remedial actions.
- Control
  - develop a procedure defining all the above arrangements;
  - provide reminders for inspection participants;
  - ensure participants have time available to carry out inspections.
- Monitor
  - check that inspections are being made as scheduled;
  - review the quality of inspection reports;
  - check whether remedial actions are being implemented.
- Review
  - reasons for any shortcomings in the system eg failure to carry out inspections due to sickness absence or pressure of other duties, ineffective communication of remedial actions required;
  - identify means of overcoming these differences.

| MIDSHIRES DEVELOPMENT AGENCY<br>OFFICE HEALTH AND SAFETY INSPECTION<br>Office Location: Inspection by:<br>Date: | | |
|---|---|---|
| Risk Topic | Specific items | Comments |
| 1. FIRE | Evacuation routes available<br>SC doors not wedged open<br>Alarm tests taking place<br>Extinguishers in position | |
| 2. ACCIDENTS etc | First aid equipment | |
| 3. VISITORS AND CONTRACTORS | Signing in/out arrangements<br>Control of contractors | |
| 4. ACCESS (INTERNAL AND EXTERNAL) | Corridors, walkways clear<br>Access to shelves, cupboards etc.<br>External footpaths, roadways | |
| 5. OFFICE AND KITCHEN EQUIPMENT | Condition of equipment<br>Cables, plugs, sockets etc. | |
| 6. SERVICES | Fixed electrical installation<br>Access to isolators, switches etc. | |
| 7. HAZARDOUS SUBSTANCES | Control of cleaning materials<br>Gloves available/used | |
| 8. MANUAL HANDLING | Archives, stationery storage<br>Access to shelves | |
| 9. DISPLAY SCREEN EQUIPMENT | DSE Workstations | |
| 10. OTHER ITEMS | | |

DETAIL ACTION POINTS OVERLEAF

HEALTH AND SAFETY INSPECTION ACTION POINTS

Date of inspection:

⋆ **Priority Code: A** – Urgent; **B** – Important; **C** – Routine

| Ref | Action Point | Priority Code ⋆ | Action By | Details of Progress | Initials |
|---|---|---|---|---|---|
| | | | | | |

## Health and safety audits

**8.15** The terms audits and inspections are often used interchangeably but in health and safety terminology they have gradually developed to have distinct meanings.

- *Health and safety inspection* – a check of physical working conditions, equipment, working practices and behaviour of employees (and others), usually carried out over a relatively short period of time.
- *Health and safety audit* – a much more detailed and comprehensive evaluation of management systems. This is likely to involve checking on policies and procedures, examining records, interviewing employees and carrying out some sample inspections – to determine whether the systems are working in practice.

Several commercial health and safety auditing systems are available including DNV's International Safety Rating System (ISRS), the British Safety Council's 5 Star Audit and HASTAM's CHASE. However, these may have limitations for some organisations either because they are products of another country's health and safety culture or they do not deal with all of the aspects of health and safety management appropriate to the organisation in question. As a result many organisations have developed their own bespoke auditing systems.

Another important consideration is whether the audit is to be purely qualitative or quantitative as well. Quantification can aid in comparing performances between different locations or in measuring progress (or deterioration). However, there is a danger of the emphasis of the audit switching to points chasing or quibbling about the auditor's judgement rather than focussing on the systematic evaluation of safety management systems.

The best auditing systems are those which place only limited reliance on the individual auditor's judgement. The questions within the audit should preferably be capable of being answered with a simple yes or no and should by their nature be indicative of what is required in a correctly functioning safety management system. Such systems, if properly applied, can be used just as productively for self audits as by external auditors. In either case the auditor should require confirmatory evidence that a system is in place and working, rather than accepting unsubstantiated assurances.

Topics which may be appropriate for health and safety auditing are:

- Risk Assessments;
- Operating Procedures;

- Emergency Procedures;
- Training;
- Occupational Health;
- Inspections and Audits (in-house);
- Accident and Incident Investigation;
- Control of Contractors;
- Communication with Employees;
- Engineering and Purchasing Controls.

Health and safety related procedures can also be included within audits carried out of procedures generally as part of ISO 9000 control systems.

## Other monitoring techniques

**8.16** Informal monitoring of health and safety standards may be carried out by managers, health and safety specialists or safety representatives. Other more specialised techniques include:

- *Safety surveys* – a detailed examination of a specific part of a management system (eg quality of accident investigation reports) or a specific activity or item of equipment (eg use of ladders).
- *Safety sampling* – a detailed inspection of a small work area.
- *Safety tours* – a walk through evaluation of a workplace to form a general impression of standards (often conducted by a senior manager).
- *Safety observations* – a detailed observation of the work methods and equipment used in carrying out a specific task.
- *Compliance surveys* – a check on a readily observable aspect of employee behaviour eg compliance with speed limits or a PPE requirement.

## Accident and incident investigation

**8.17** Whilst inspections and audits provide pro-active means of monitoring health and safety performance, the investigation of accidents and incidents constitutes an important reactive monitoring technique.

## Accident ratio studies

**8.18** Heinrich and others have studied the relationship between major injury, minor injury and non injury accidents. Heinrich's data showed that for every major or lost time injury there were 29 minor injuries and 300 non-injury incidents. Other researchers (Bird in the USA and Tye/Pearson in the UK) have demonstrated similar ratios (REF. 1). As an illustration, if a man slips on a patch of spilled oil, he may be unhurt, he may damage clothing or equipment, he may break his arm or he may fracture his skull and die. As the studies show, most of the time the man is lucky and the consequences of his accident are small. However, the potential for injury should always be considered – effective accident prevention and loss control should concentrate on the causes of the accident. The reasons for the spilled oil should be sought and remedied in order to remove the potential for a serious accident.

## Causes of accidents

**8.19** (For brevity, the term accidents is also intended to embrace non-injury incidents)

Most accidents have multiple causes, with several circumstances combining to produce an unwanted result. Frank Bird in his book '*Practical Loss Control Leadership*' also developed Heinrich's domino model of loss causation, which consists of five toppling dominoes:

- The final domino to fall represents a *loss* (eg personal injury, equipment damage etc);
- This is due to a specific *incident* (eg a slip on a patch of oil), represented by the fourth domino;
- The incident has *immediate causes* (eg a leaky vehicle or a failure to clear up the spill), which is the third domino;
- Behind the immediate causes is the second domino – *basic causes* (eg inadequate maintenance, lack of oil absorbent materials, absence of clean up procedures);
- These immediate causes are symptomatic of a *lack of control* – the first domino. A well managed workplace has well regulated maintenance procedures, an adequate supply of materials etc. If the business is correctly managed the first domino will not topple onto the others and there will be no resultant loss.

## Purpose of investigation

**8.20** The purpose of accident and incident investigation systems should always be to identify shortcomings in the management of health and safety. Organisations should learn from the large numbers of non-injury incidents and minor accidents which the accident ratio studies demonstrate are occurring and utilise them to prevent future accidents, possibly with more serious consequences in terms of injury or damage.

Whilst there is also a need to investigate in order to submit reports under RIDDOR or in order to provide information in relation to future compensation claims, investigation procedures which are driven purely by RIDDOR and insurance company needs will not be successful in reducing accidents. The objective should always be never to waste an accident.

### *Investigation procedures*

Larger organisations should have a formal procedure for investigating accidents and incidents while smaller employers should at least have clearly established local arrangements.

These should include the following elements:

- What should be investigated–
  - Whether a particular set of circumstances causes an 'Accident', damage to plant or materials, a 'Dangerous Occurrence' or just a near miss, may be a matter of chance,
  - Significant injuries and damage incidents must always be thoroughly investigated, but so also should many minor accidents or near misses especially those with potentially more serious consequences.
- The purpose of investigation–

  Investigation should be concerned with:
  - Finding out *what* happened – notification under RIDDOR may be necessary and accurate facts need to be recorded in case of possible compensation claims,
  - Finding out *why* it happened – immediate causes eg faulty equipment, unsafe methods, and basic causes eg inadequate maintenance, lack of training or supervision,
  - *Preventing* it happening again – getting things fixed, improving

procedures, changing employees' behaviour or attitudes - or arranging for others to do so,

  - Procedures should emphasise each of these aspects.

- Investigation timescale–
  - Investigations should normally start as soon as possible after the incident and a minimum timescale for submission of at least an interim report should be set.
- Responsibility for investigation–
  - This will normally rest with front-line supervision although senior managers or specialists may well become involved in more serious or complex incidents.
- Reports and remedial action–
  - It must be clearly established who is to receive and review reports and who is to allocate responsibility for and follow up the necessary remedial action – the most important step in the procedure from the accident prevention viewpoint.

### *Investigation technique*

Good investigation technique should involve the following elements:

- Observing–
  - Looking at the scene and the surrounding area (not being an armchair investigator).
- Interviewing–
  - The injured person and/or witnesses (preferably separately),
  - At the scene if possible,
  - Noting down beforehand some key questions to be answered,
  - Asking open-ended questions in a friendly manner,
  - Keeping an open mind.
- Involving others–
  - Seeking advice from specialists (engineers, chemists) or others who may be able to contribute.

- Drawing Conclusions–
  - On what happened, why it happened and how it might be prevented from happening again.
- Reporting–
  - See below.
- Taking action–
  - The Investigator should take whatever action he or she is able to and press others to act on recommendations made.

### *Investigation reports*

- Report forms should be designed to contain all the relevant details of the accident or incident–
  - who or what was involved,
  - details of any injury or damage,
  - the date and time,
  - the name and signature of the person investigating.
- Sufficient space should be allocated to record–
  - *what* happened – a descriptive report,
  - the investigator's conclusions as to *why* it happened, including both immediate and basic causes,
  - recommendations to *prevent* it happening again.

A sample investigation report form is provided later within this chapter. (It should be noted that some organisations require reports to be submitted to Departmental Managers before or in addition to health and safety specialists).

# ACCIDENT & INCIDENT INVESTIGATION REPORT

Department | Section
Person involved | Surname | First name(s)
Status of person | Employee [ ] | Visitor [ ] | Member of Public [ ]
*(tick as appropriate)* | Temp. [ ] | Contractor [ ] | Other (state) [ ]

| Date | Time | Location |
|---|---|---|

Details of any injuries (inc. first aid treatment) or damage

Description of incident – What Happened

A sketch or photo may be helpful. Continue on a separate sheet if necessary.

Contributory causes – Why you think it happened

What action has been taken (or will be taken) to prevent similar incidents

Person submitting report | Name | Position | Date

**FOR COMPLETION BY THE HEALTH AND SAFETY OFFICER**
Further action required/Progress of remedial action/Other comments

Action was completed on | Name

## Review

### Health and safety committees

**8.21** In large and medium sized organisations the establishment of an effective joint health and safety committee should constitute an important part of the employer's health and safety programme, not just in reviewing the management of health and safety but in providing a forum for:

- Consultation on the existence of risks and the effectiveness of precautions;
- Sharing knowledge and experience;
- Providing different perspectives on health and safety issues;
- Giving greater awareness of what is happening within the workplace;
- Achieving wider ownership and commitment.

#### *Composition of the committee*

**8.22** The composition of the Committee should be a matter for local agreement, whether or not a Committee has been formally requested by union Safety Representatives (REF. 3). Care should be taken that the Committee has a good balance of representation without becoming too large.

Membership should include:

- Managers and supervisors;
- Health and safety specialists;
- Other specialists eg engineers, chemists;
- Employee representatives.

The employee representatives will often be union Safety Representatives (or other elected representatives), but this need not automatically be the case – other individuals may also be able to contribute.

#### *Committee activities*

**8.23** An effective Committee can assist the employer at all the stages of the safety management cycle (Plan, Organise, Control, Monitor, Review). Committees are normally active in the following areas:

- reviewing accident and incident reports;
- overseeing the health and safety inspection programme;
- monitoring remedial actions resulting from both of the above;
- reviewing health and safety audits;
- reviewing accident statistics;
- reviewing occupational hygiene survey results;
- planning health and safety initiatives;
- reviewing new and existing procedures and arrangements;
- monitoring the effectiveness of health and safety training;
- reviewing communications from and actions of inspectors (HSE/ local authority);
- providing feedback on the suitability of PPE;
- assisting in communications and publicity.

### *Conduct of meetings*

**8.24** The principles behind holding effective Safety Committee meetings are little different from those governing other meetings:

- there must be a designated Chairperson–
  - (often a senior manager, although this is not essential).
- someone must be responsible for taking minutes;
- meetings must be held at an agreed frequency–
  - (often monthly, although 2 or 3 monthly may be appropriate for smaller organisations).
- meeting dates must be planned well in advance–
  - (cancellations or postponements should be avoided).
- a detailed agenda should be circulated to members well in advance;
- votes should be avoided (the Committee should primarily be a consultation and review body, ultimate responsibility rests with the employer);

- minutes should be circulated to members soon after meetings;
- responsibility for implementing actions should be clearly identified;
- Committee activities should be widely publicised–
  - (eg minutes on notice boards, extracts in newsletters).

## Management meetings

**8.25** The review of standards of health and safety management may also take place within separate management meetings. Some members of management and health and safety specialists may feel less constrained in such an environment. They may be rather more frank in their appraisal than in a joint forum. Many of the topics appropriate for joint committees will also be appropriate for management meetings. Developing annual health and safety action plans which have the full commitment of the management team and reviewing their subsequent progress are important management activities.

## A continuous cycle

**8.26** The management cycle should be regarded as continuous, not linear. The review of deficiencies, whether in a joint Health and Safety Committee or a management only meeting should eventually result in plans for rectifying the deficiencies and the whole cycle should start again.

# *References*

**8.27**


| | | |
|---|---|---|
| 1 | HSG 65: | Successful Health and Safety Management (HSE 1997) |
| 2 | BS 8800:1996 | Guide to occupational health and safety management systems British Standards Institute 1996 |
| 3 | L 87: | Safety representatives and safety committees (HSE 1996) |
| 4 | L 95: | A guide to the *Health and Safety (Consultation with Employees) Regulations 1996* (HSE 1996) |
| 5 | INDG 322: | Need help on health and safety? – free HSE leaflet 2000 |
| 6 | | Tolley's Health and Safety at Work Looseleaf |

# 9 COSHH assessments

Information, instruction and training (*Regulation 12*)
Review of assessments (*Regulation 6*)

**Some pitfalls**

The data sheet library
Armchair assessments
Overkill
Not seeing the wood for the trees
Slaves to record systems

**References**

## *Introduction*

**9.1** The *Control of Substances Hazardous to Health Regulations* (COSHH) were first introduced in 1988 but have been amended several times since, with the latest changes in 1999. They are the principal Regulations affecting the use of hazardous substances, although there are separate Regulations dealing with asbestos and lead. The Regulations follow general principles which can be applied to most occupational health risks:

- *Assess the risk* – What substances are in use, in what ways and to what extent.
- *Eliminate the risk* – If possible, stop using the hazardous substance or replace it by a less hazardous one eg substitute solvent-based paints by water-based ones.
- *Provide controls* – Control at source eg by enclosure or local exhaust ventilation (LEV) is preferable, although it may be necessary to rely on personal protective equipment (PPE).
- *Maintain the controls* – Control measures eg LEV and PPE must be checked regularly and maintained in good condition.
- *Monitor* – Check on working conditions and working practices regularly. Atmospheric sampling or health surveillance may be necessary.
- *Inform Employees* – About the risks from substances they are using, the precautions they should be following, how to use LEV and PPE etc.

## *How substances cause harm*

**9.2** Before carrying out assessments under the *COSHH Regulations* it is necessary to have an understanding of how hazardous substances can harm the body.

### Entry routes

**9.3** Hazardous substances may be present in different forms such as:

- Solids.
- Dusts.
- Smoke.
- Fumes.
- Liquids.
- Mists and aerosols.
- Vapour.
- Gas.

These can cause harm to the body by three main entry routes:

- *Inhalation* – the hazardous substance may damage the lungs or some other part of the respiratory system. Inhalation also allows substances to enter the bloodstream and thus affect other parts of the body.
- *Ingestion* – accidental ingestion is always possible, especially if containers are not correctly labelled. Eating, drinking and smoking in the workplace introduce risks of small quantities of hazardous substances being inadvertently ingested.
- *The Skin* – substances can damage the skin (or eyes) through their corrosive or irritant effects. Some solvents can enter the body by absorption through the skin. Entry through cracks or cuts in the skin must also be considered.

### Harmful effects

**9.4** The detailed consideration of how hazardous substances can harm the body is a matter for more specialist text-books. However, the list below illustrates the wide range of problems which may be caused.

- Respiratory problems–
  - *Pneumoconiosis* – eg asbestosis, silicosis, byssinosis, siderosis,

   - *Respiratory irritation* – caused by inhaling acid or alkali gases or mists,
   - *Asthma* – sensitisation of the respiratory system can be caused by many substances eg isocyanates, flour, grain, hay, animal fur, wood dusts,
   - *Respiratory cancers* – eg from certain chemicals, asbestos, pitch and tar,
   - *Metal fume fever* – flu-like condition caused by zinc fumes.

- Poisoning – acute (short-term) or chronic (long-term) poisoning may be caused by–
   - *Metals and their compounds* – eg lead, manganese, mercury, beryllium, cadmium,
   - *Organic chemicals* – affecting the nervous system, the liver, the kidneys or the gastro-intestinal system,
   - *Inorganic chemicals* – as above plus asphyxiant effects eg from carbon monoxide.

- Skin conditions–
   - Dermatitis
      - caused by primary irritants eg damage to skin tissue by acids or alkalis or removal of natural oils by solvents, detergents etc.
      - due to sensitising agents eg isocyanates, solvents, food-stuffs,
   - *Skin cancer* – caused by pitch, tar, soot, mineral oils etc.

- Biological problems – from contact with animals, birds, fish (including their carcasses and products) or with micro-organisms from other sources–
   - *Livestock diseases* – eg anthrax or brucellosis,
   - *Allergic alveolitis* – from mould or fungal spores present in grain etc,
   - *Viral hepatitis* – usually from contact with blood or blood products,
   - *Legionnaire's disease* – caused by inhaling airborne water droplets containing the legionella bacteria,
   - *Leptospirosis* – Weil's disease, from contact with urine from small mammals eg rats.

Information on the harmful effects associated with individual products should be available on the packaging or in a data sheet provided by the manufacturer or supplier.

## The COSHH Regulations summarised

**9.5** The definition of '*substance hazardous to health*' is contained in *Regulation 2(1)* of the Regulations and includes:

- substances designated as very toxic, toxic, corrosive, harmful or irritant under product labelling legislation (these substances should be labelled with the standard orange and black symbols);
- substances for which a Maximum Exposure Limit is specified (in *Schedule 1* to the *COSHH Regulations*);
- substances for which the Health and Safety Commission has approved an Occupational Exposure Standard;
- biological agents (micro-organisms, cell cultures or human endoparasites);
- dust of any kind, at a substantial concentration in air;
- any other substance creating comparable hazards.

Given this widely drawn definition, in any cases of doubt it is advisable to treat the *COSHH Regulations* as applying.

The Regulations place duties on employers in relation to their employees and also on employees themselves (*Regulation 8*). The self-employed have duties as if they were both employer and employee. *Regulation 3(1)* extends the employer's duties 'so far as is reasonably practicable' to 'any other person, whether at work or not, who may be affected by the work carried on'. Consideration must be given to:

- contractors, visitors or joint occupants;
- neighbours and passers-by;
- members of the public – in public places and buildings.

Some of these (eg children) cannot be expected to behave in the same way as employees or contractors. An early prosecution under the *COSHH Regulations* was of a doctor's surgery when a young child gained access to an insecure cleaner's cupboard and drank the contents of a bottle of carbolic acid, suffering serious ill effects.

The main requirements of the Regulations are summarised below. Most will be explained in more detail later. Full details of the Regulations and associated ACOPs are provided in a single HSE booklet (REF. 1).

- *Prohibitions relating to certain substances (Regulation 4)* – the manufacture, use, importation and supply of certain substances is prohibited (further details are contained in *Schedule 2* to the Regulations).
- *Application of Regulations 6 to 12 (Regulation 5)* – exceptions are made from the application of these Regulations where other more specific Regulations are in place. These relate to lead, asbestos, radioactive, explosive or flammable properties of substances, substances at high or low temperatures or high pressure, substances administered in medical treatment and public health or environmental issues.
- *Assessment (Regulation 6)* – an assessment of health risks must be made to identify steps necessary to comply with the Regulations.
- *Prevention or control of exposure (Regulation 7)* – this must be achieved through elimination or substitution or the provision of adequate controls eg enclosure, LEV, ventilation, systems of work, PPE.
- *Use of control measures etc (Regulation 8)* – employees must make 'full and proper use of control measures, PPE etc', and employers 'take all reasonable steps' to ensure they do.
- *Maintenance, examination and test (Regulation 9)* – control measures, including PPE, must be maintained in an efficient state.
- *Monitoring exposure at the workplace (Regulation 10)* – workplace monitoring may be necessary to ensure adequate control or protect health.
- *Health surveillance (Regulation 11)* – this may be required in some circumstances.
- *Information, instruction and training (Regulation 12)* – must be provided for persons exposed to hazardous substances.

## Planning and preparing for the assessment

### What the Regulations require

**9.6** *Regulation 6* of the *COSHH Regulations 1999* states:

'(1) An employer shall not carry on any work which is liable to expose any employees to any substance hazardous to health unless he has made a suitable and sufficient assessment of the risks created by that work to the health of those employees and of steps that need to be taken to meet the requirements of these Regulations.

(2) The assessment required by paragraph (1) shall be reviewed regularly and forthwith if

(a) there is reason to suspect that the assessment is no longer valid; or

(b) there has been a significant change in the work to which the assessment relates and, where as a result of the review, changes in the assessment are required, those changes shall be made'.

In making assessments, it should be noted that *Regulation 3(1)* also requires employees to take account, so far as is reasonably practicable, of others who may be affected by the work eg visitors, contractors, customers, passers-by and members of the emergency services.

Essentially there are four aspects to be considered during the assessment:

- Identification of risks to the health of employees or others.
- Consideration of whether it is reasonably practicable to prevent exposure to hazardous substances creating risks.
- If prevention is not reasonably practicable, identification of the measures necessary to achieve adequate control of exposure, as required by *Regulation* 7 (these control measures are described in greater detail later in the chapter).
- Identification of other measures necessary to comply with *Regulation 8* to *12*–
  - use of control measures,
  - maintenance, examination and test of control measures etc,
  - monitoring of exposure at the workplace,
  - health surveillance,
  - provision of information, instruction and training.

(All of these are described more fully later in the chapter.)

The assessment must be 'suitable and sufficient'. Paragraph 17 of the ACOP accompanying the Regulations (REF. 1) states 'An assessment can be considered sufficient and suitable if the detail and expertise with which it is carried out are commensurate with the nature and degree of risk arising from the work, as well as the complexity and variability of the process.'

This is demonstrated by the sample assessment records provided later in the chapter. A COSHH assessment in an office environment will be a straightforward matter, not requiring any specialist skills. However, an assessment in a manufacturing plant handling large quantities of chemicals will be a much more complex affair.

The planning and preparation for a COSHH assessment should follow a similar pattern to that described in CHAPTER 4: CARRYING OUT RISK ASSESSMENTS for general risk assessments. Some of those principles are repeated below and additional guidance specific to COSHH assessments is also provided.

## Who will carry out the assessments?

**9.7** As described in CHAPTER 4: CARRYING OUT RISK ASSESSMENTS, *Regulation 7* of the *Management Regulations 1999* requires employers to appoint a competent person or persons to assist them in complying with their duties – which include carrying out COSHH assessments. *Regulation 12(3)* of the *COSHH Regulations* themselves also states:

> 'Every employer shall ensure that any person (whether or not his employee) who carries out any work in connection with the employer's duties under these Regulations has the necessary information, instruction and training.'

As with general risk assessments the degree of knowledge and experience required will depend upon the circumstances. An assessment in a workplace containing a few straightforward uses of hazardous substances may be carried out by someone without any specialist qualifications or experience but with the capability to understand and apply the principles contained in this chapter. However, higher risk situations with much more complex and significant use of hazardous substances are likely to require multi-disciplinary teams, some of whom have more specialist knowledge and experience. Possible candidates for such a team might be:

- health and safety officers;
- occupational hygienists;
- occupational health nurses;
- physicians with occupational health experience;
- chemical or process engineers;

- ventilation engineers.

As with general risk assessments, the combination of an 'insider' (a manager, supervisor or engineer from the department concerned) working together with an 'outsider' (a health and safety specialist) is often beneficial.

In some situations an in-house team or individual with little or no specialist qualification or experience may be able to carry out the majority of its COSHH assessments. They can then identify those areas where more specialised assistance is required to come to a conclusion or where occupational hygiene surveys are necessary before a decision can be made.

## How will the assessments be organised?

**9.8** Larger workplaces will usually need to be divided into manageable assessment units which might be based on:

- departments or sections;
- buildings or rooms;
- process lines;
- activities or services.

Where an assessment team is used, those individuals most suited for a particular situation can be selected to assess that unit. As an example a small paint manufacturing plant might be divided into units as follows:

- Raw material storage – including any tank farms and drum storage areas.
- Manufacturing – possibly split into different product lines or buildings.
- Container filling – if carried out separately from process lines.
- Product storage – warehouses and container storage areas.
- Maintenance – including maintenance activities in process areas and use of hazardous substances in maintenance work.
- Administration/miscellaneous.

## Gathering information

**9.9** Identification of substances present – all hazardous substances must be taken into account during the assessments and as many of these as possible should be identified before the assessment takes place.

- Raw materials and the contents of stores
- Process materials–
  - intermediate compounds,
  - products,
  - waste and by-products,
  - emissions from the process,
- Buildings and the work environment,
  - surface treatments,
  - pollution or contaminants,
  - bird droppings, animal faeces etc.

Hazards associated with substances – Information should be gathered on the hazardous substances identified. Potential sources include:

- Manufacturers' or suppliers' data sheets.
- Information on containers or packaging (including the symbols required by the *CHIP Regulations*).
- HSE publications (references 2 to 23 indicate the range of information available – the HSE catalogue includes far more).
- Reference books and technical literature.
- Direct enquiries to specialists or suppliers.

This information should primarily concern the hazards associated with the substance but note should also be taken of recommendations on control methods. However, caution should be exercised in this latter respect, particularly in relation to information from suppliers. The substance's actual circumstances of use may constitute a greater or lesser degree of risk than the supplier anticipated – it is for the assessor(s) to determine what control measures are necessary in each situation.

### *Previous assessments, surveys etc*

**9.10** Even if previous COSHH assessments were inadequate or are now out of date, they may still contain information of value in the assessment process. The results of previous occupational hygiene surveys (eg dust, gas or vapour concentrations) are also likely to be useful as will the collective results of any health surveillance work which has previously been carried out.

### *Existing control measures*

**9.11** Existing control measures may be described in operating procedures, health and safety rule books or listings of PPE requirements or may be referred to within training programmes. In some cases it may be appropriate to seek detailed specification information in relation to control measures eg design flow rates for ventilation equipment or performance standards for PPE such as respiratory protection or gloves. (Some of this information may be sought during the assessment itself or prior to the preparation of the assessment record).

## *Prevention or control of exposure*

**9.12** Before commencing the assessment itself it is important to have an understanding of what the Regulations require in terms of prevention or control and also the range of control measures available.

### Hierarchy of measures

**9.13** *Regulation 7 of the COSHH Regulations* sets out a clear hierarchy of measures which must be taken to prevent or control exposure to hazardous substances. It states:

> '(1) Every employer shall ensure that the exposure of his employees to substances hazardous to health is either prevented or, where this is not reasonably practicable, adequately controlled.
>
> (2) So far as is reasonably practicable, the prevention or adequate control of exposure of employees to a substance hazardous to health, except to a carcinogen or biological agent, shall be secured by measures other than the provision of personal protective equipment.
>
> (4) Where the measures taken in accordance with paragraph (2) or (3), as the case may be, do not prevent, or provide adequate control of, exposure to substances hazardous to health to which those paragraphs apply, then, in addition to taking those measures, the employer shall provide those employees with such suitable personal protective equipment as will adequately control their exposure to those substances.'

(Paragraph (3) contains specific requirements relating to carcinogens which will be referred to later).

Thus a clear order of preference is established:

- prevention of exposure;
- adequate control measures other than by PPE;
- adequate control through PPE.

## Prevention of exposure

**9.14** The first preference should always be to prevent exposure to hazardous substances.

Means available include:

- Changing work methods eg cleaning items using ultrasonic techniques or high pressure water jets rather than with solvents.
- Using non-hazardous (or less hazardous) alternatives eg replacing solvent-based paints or inks by water-based ones (or ones utilising less hazardous solvents).
- Using less-hazardous forms of substances eg substituting powdered materials by granules or pellets, using hazardous substances in a more dilute form.
- Modifying processes eg eliminating production of hazardous by-products, waste or emissions by altering process parameters such as temperature or pressure.

Exposure must be prevented 'so far as is reasonably practicable' – a definition of this qualifying phrase is provided in CHAPTER 1: INTRODUCTION. The level of risk will be determined by the type and severity of the hazards associated with a substance and its circumstances of use.

Factors weighing against prevention of exposure being reasonably practicable might be the costs associated with using alternative methods or materials, the detrimental effect of alternatives on the product or additional risks introduced by the alternatives.

For example:

- ultrasonic cleaning may not achieve the desired results;
- use of high pressure water can introduce additional risks;
- water-based paints may increase problems of corrosion;
- alternative solvents may be more highly flammable.

Nevertheless this option can often prove reasonable practicable – much progress has been made in recent years in the substitution of hazardous materials.

## Control measures, other than PPE

**9.15** This option must be considered where prevention is not reasonably practicable. Both *paragraphs (1)* and *(2)* of *Regulation* 7 refer to 'adequate control'. Further definition of what constitutes 'adequate control' is provided by *paragraphs (6), (7) and (11)* of the Regulation.

> '(6) Where there is exposure to a substance for which a maximum exposure limit has been approved, the control of exposure shall, so far as the inhalation of that substance is concerned, only be treated as being adequate if the level of exposure is reduced so far as is reasonably practicable and in any case below the maximum exposure limit.
>
> (7) Without prejudice to the generality of paragraph (1), where there is exposure to a substance for which an occupational exposure standard has been approved, the control of exposure shall, so far as the inhalation of that substance is concerned, be treated as being adequate if–
>
> (a) that occupational exposure standard is not exceeded; or
>
> (b) where that occupational exposure standard is exceeded, the employer identifies the reasons for the standard being exceeded and takes appropriate action to remedy the situation as soon as is reasonably practicable.
>
> (11) In this Regulation, "adequate" means adequate having regard only to the nature of the substance and the nature and degree of exposure to substances hazardous to health and "adequately" shall be construed accordingly.'

Where a Maximum Exposure Limit (MEL) has been approved the level of exposure must be reduced so far as is reasonably practicable *as well as always* being kept below the MEL at all times. Slightly more latitude is given in respect of substances where an Occupational Exposure Standard (OES) has been approved. Should the OES be exceeded employers must identify the reasons and remedy the situation as soon as is reasonably practicable. Listings of MELs and OESs are published by the HSE (REF. 24).

In some cases it will be relatively easy to make a judgement as to whether exposure is controlled to levels well within the MEL or OES but in other situations it may be necessary to carry out an occupational hygiene survey or even arrange for periodic or ongoing monitoring of exposure. The techniques for doing this are described later in the chapter.

Whilst *paragraph (3)* of *Regulation* 7 only applies to carcinogens it provides a good summary of control measures which might be appropriate for other hazardous substances. These are:

- Total enclosure of process and handling systems;
- Plant, processes and systems of work which minimise the generation of, or suppress and contain, spills, leaks, dust, fumes and vapours. (This often involves a combination of partial enclosure and the use of local exhaust ventilation (LEV). The design of LEV is a subject in its own right – see reference 25);
- Limitation of the quantities of hazardous substances in workplaces.
- Minimising the numbers of persons exposed to hazardous substances.
- Prohibition of eating, drinking and smoking in areas of potential contamination.
- Provision of adequate washing facilities.
- Regular cleaning of walls and surfaces.
- Use of signs to indicate areas of potential contamination.
- Safe storage, handling and disposal of hazardous substances.
- Use of closed and clearly labelled containers.

## Control using PPE

**9.16** Control using PPE should be the third preference, where prevention or adequate control of exposure by other means are not reasonably practicable. This might be the case where:

- the scale of use of hazardous substances is very small;
- adequate control by other means is not technically feasible;
- control by other means is excessively expensive or difficult in relation to the level of risk;
- PPE is utilised as a temporary measure pending the implementation of adequate control by other means;
- employees are dealing with emergency situations;
- infrequent maintenance activities are carried out.

Personal protective equipment (PPE) necessary to control risks from hazardous substances might be:

- respiratory protective equipment (RPE) – SEE REF 26;
- protective clothing;
- hand or arm protection (usually gloves);
- eye protection;
- protective footwear;

General guidance on the selection of PPE is provided in the HSE booklet on the *Personal Protective Equipment at Work Regulations 1992* (REF. 27). The PPE selected must be appropriate for the type of hazardous substances involved. *Paragraphs (5)* and *(8)* of *Regulation 7* of the *COSHH Regulations* stipulate that PPE must comply with certain defined standards.

> '(5) Any personal protective equipment provided by an employer in pursuance of this Regulation shall comply with any provision in the *Personal Protective Equipment (EC Directive) Regulations 1992* which is applicable to that item of personal protective equipment.
>
> (8) Where respiratory protective equipment is provided in pursuance of this Regulation, then it shall–
>
> (a) be suitable for the purpose; and
>
> (b) comply with paragraph (5) or, where no requirement is imposed by virtue of that paragraph, be of a type approved or shall conform to a standard approved, in either case, by the Executive.'

## Carcinogens and biological agents

**9.17** The detailed wording of *paragraph (3)* of *Regulation 6*, which relates solely to carcinogens, in effect places an additional step in the hierarchy of measures for their control. For carcinogens the hierarchy becomes:

- prevention of exposure;
- total enclosure of process and handling systems;
- adequate control measurers, other than PPE (as described earlier);
- adequate control through PPE.

*Paragraph (9)* introduces additional requirements in relation to failure of control measures for carcinogens.

> '(9) In the event of the failure of a control measure which might result in the escape of carcinogens into the workplace, the employer shall ensure that–
>
> (a) only those persons who are responsible for the carrying out of repairs and other necessary work are permitted in the affected area and they are provided with suitable respiratory protective equipment and protective clothing; and
>
> (b) employees and other persons who may be affected are informed of the failure forthwith.'

*Paragraph (10)* of *Regulation 6* requires exposure to biological agents to be prevented or adequately controlled by measures detailed in *Schedule 3* to the *COSHH Regulations*.

Separate ACOPs relating to carcinogens and biological agents accompany the general COSHH ACOP in the HSE booklet containing the *COSHH Regulations* (REF. 1).

## Making the assessment

**9.18** As was the case for general risk assessments, time spent in making COSHH assessments can both be reduced and made more productive by good planning and preparation. Nevertheless, observations of workplaces and work activities must still be an integral part of the COSHH assessment process.

### Observations

**9.19** Sufficient observations must be made to arrive at a conclusion on the adequacy of control measures for exposures to all the hazardous substances in the workplace – be they raw materials, products, by-products, waste, emissions etc. This should include the manner and extent to which employees (and others) are exposed and an evaluation of the equipment and working practices intended to achieve their control.

Aspects to be considered include:

- are specified procedures being followed?
- does local exhaust ventilation or general ventilation appear effective?

- is PPE being used correctly?
- is there evidence of leakage, spillage or dust accumulation?
- what equipment is available for cleaning?
- are dusts, fumes or strong smells evident in the atmosphere?
- are there any restrictions relating to eating, drinking or smoking?
- what arrangements are there for storage, cleaning or maintenance of PPE?
- are there special arrangements for washing, showering or changing clothing?
- what arrangements are in place for storage and disposal of waste?
- is there potential for major spillages or leaks?
- what emergency containment equipment or PPE is available?

Obviously this list could be extended significantly and some of the aspects could be broken down into further sub-components.

## Discussions

**9.20** It is also important to talk to those working with hazardous substances, their safety representatives and those managing or supervising their work. Assessors' questions might relate to working practices, awareness of risks or precautions, the effectiveness of precautions or experience of problems. Questions might include:

- why is the task done that way?
- are the present work practices typical?
- how effective is the LEV/general ventilation?
- what happens if it ever breaks down?
- what types of work require PPE to be used?
- are there any problems with the PPE?
- have workers experienced any health problems?
- how often is the workplace cleaned?
- what methods are used for cleaning?
- how is waste disposed of?
- is there any possibility of leaks or emergencies arising?
- what would happen in such a case?
- what are the arrangements for washing/cleaning/maintaining PPE?

Once again the potential list of questions is endless and there can be many variations on the above themes.

## Further tests and investigations

**9.21** Assessment in the workplace may reveal the need for further tests to take place before the assessment can be concluded. The tests may be in the form of occupational hygiene surveys – usually to measure the airborne levels of dust, fume, vapour or gas and compare them with the relevant MEL or OES. Techniques available for such survey work are described later in this chapter. Alternatively there may be a need to measure the effectiveness of local exhaust ventilation or general ventilation – this too is referred to later in the chapter.

Further investigations may also be necessary into matters such as:

- hazards associated with substances not previously identified during the preparatory phase of the assessment;
- the specifications for PPE found to be in use during the course of the assessment;
- the feasibility of alternative work methods ( eg preventing exposure) or alternative methods of control to those observed.

## Preparation of assessment records

**9.22** The guidance on note taking and the preparation of assessment records contained in CHAPTER 4: CARRYING OUT RISK ASSESSMENTS of the handbook is equally relevant to COSHH Assessments. Several examples of completed assessment records are provided on the succeeding pages, although it should be stressed that (as for general risk assessments) no single record format will automatically cater for all types of workplaces or working activities. The essential components which must be included in COSHH assessment records are:

- the work activities involving risks from hazardous substances;
- information as to the hazardous substances involved;
- control measures which are (or should be) in place;
- improvements identified as being necessary.

The COSHH ACOP does state that assessments need not be recorded in the simplest and most obvious cases which can be easily repeated and explained at any time. However, it suggests that in most cases assessments will need to be recorded and kept readily accessible to those who may need to know the results. Employees or their representatives should be informed of the results of COSHH assessments.

## *Sample assessment records*

**9.23**

**ACORN ESTATE AGENTS, NEWTOWN**

RISK ASSESSMENT

| REFERENCE NUMBER: 6 | RISK TOPIC/ISSUE:HAZARDOUS SUBSTANCES | SHEET 1 of 1 |
|---|---|---|
| CROSS REFERENCES: | | |
| **RISKS IDENTIFIED** | **PRECAUTIONS IN PLACE** | **RECOMMENDED IMPROVEMENTS** |
| The substances listed below could present risks to both staff and clients.<br><br>OFFICE MATERIALS<br>*With warning symbols*<br>Old correction fluid (Harmful)<br>New correction fluid (Flammable)<br>Spray adhesive (Harmful)<br><br>*Without warning symbols*<br>Photocopier and printer toners<br>Various felt tip pens (solvent based) | Office supplies are kept in a cupboard in a part of the office not normally accessible to clients.<br><br>Generally substances are only used in very small quantities for short periods presenting no significant risk.<br><br>If the spray adhesive is used for more than a couple of minutes, a nearby window is opened which provides adequate ventilation.<br><br>The photocopier is used in well ventilated areas and there are no noticeable ozone smells, even on long copying runs. | Provide disposable gloves for cleaning significant spillages of photocopier or printer toner. |
| CLEANING MATERIALS<br>*With warning symbols*<br>Thick bleach (Irritant)<br>Polish stripper (Irritant)<br>Acid descaler (Corrosive)<br><br>*Without warning symbols*<br>Furniture polish<br>Floor polish<br>Window and glass cleaner | The cleaner's cupboard is kept locked except when substances are being removed.<br><br>Suitable gloves are provided (and worn) for handling the irritant and corrosive substances in concentrated form.<br><br>The cleaner is aware of the risks of mixing bleach with other substances eg the acid descaler. | Investigate replacing the thick bleach by a more dilute solution.<br><br>Ensure the relief cleaner is also made aware of these risks. |
| SIGNATURE(S): *K Stephenson, R Lewis* | NAME(S): *K Stephenson, R Lewis* | DATE *4/11/98* |
| DATES FOR RECOMMENDATION FOLLOW UP: *December 1998* | | NEXT ROUTINE REVIEW: *November 2003* |

## TIMREK Engineering

COSHH assessment

### Main risks

1. Electric arc welding, mainly of large and medium sized structures.
2. Oxy-acetylene burning, welding and brazing, as above.
3. Cleaning of parts in proprietary unit (using paraffin based solvent).
4. Use of cutting oils on the lathe and milling machine.
5. Application of solvent-based primers by brush (not spray). (Some primers are designated as 'harmful').
6. Small scale use of a variety of cleaning solvents, lubricants, adhesives and paints using aerosol sprays or brush application. (Several of these are labelled as harmful, irritant or corrosive).

### Control measures

1. & 2. Limited work carried out – never more than five minutes in duration or a total of 20 minutes per day. Workshop door normally open. Portable extraction unit available but currently broken.

3. Unit includes brush applicator. Suitable gauntlets provided and used. Solvent changed regularly by suppliers.
4. Splash guards in place. Suitable gloves provided and used for handling oils and swarf. General ventilation adequate to remove any fume or mist. Employees exposed report no breathing or skin problems.
5. Never more than fifteen minutes work per day. Priming done near open workshop door if possible but sometimes there is a strong smell. Suitable gloves are provided and worn.
6. Substances only used for extremely short periods of time. Gloves and eye protection (safety spectacles) provided.

### Recommendations

1. & 2.
   a) Arrange for portable extraction unit to be repaired.
   b) Carry out weekly visual check on extraction unit.
   c) Arrange for Insurance Company engineer to conduct examination and test every 14 months.

3. None.
4. Check annually with staff that they are not experiencing problems (make diary note).
5. Investigate the feasibility of using water-based primer.
6. 
   a) Prepare a table showing which substances require the use of gloves and/or safety spectacles;
   b) Display the table on the notice-board and draw it to the attention of all employees.

Signed: *A. F. Rogerson* Date: 4.08.2000

Follow up of recommendations: *October 2000 (make diary note)*

Review assessment: *August 2002*

## *RAINBOW PRODUCTS*

## COSHH ASSESSMENT

| | |
|---|---|
| ASSESSMENT UNIT | Mixing Hall |
| ACTIVITIES | Manufacture of solvent-based paints and other surface treatments.<br><br>Solvents are pumped into the mixing vessels from an external tank farm.<br><br>Solid constituents and some liquid components are charged into the mixing vessels from platforms above.<br><br>After mixing, the products are pumped directly to filling stations in a neighbouring building. |
| SUBSTANCES USED<br>(Data sheet file references) | 4, 7, 14, 23, 49, 50, 51, 60, 73, 80, 92, 106, 117.<br>Detailed formulations for each product are available from the Quality Control Department. |
| MAIN RISKS | Dust – from solid constituents during charging<br>Solvent vapours • escaping from the charging hatches<br>• from minor leaks at valves and pipe connections<br>• from liquid components during charging<br>Entry into mixing vessels for cleaning or maintenance purposes. |
| THOSE AT RISK | Mixing Hall production employees.<br>Maintenance staff when working in the area.<br>Contractors involved in vessel cleaning or maintenance work |
| CONTROLS AND OTHER PRECAUTIONS IN PLACE | Good general ventilation (specification 20 air changes per hour).<br><br>Annual surveys of solvent vapours show levels well below all OESs.<br><br>Hoods with LEV over each vessel charging position.<br><br>These are examined and tested annually by the Maintenance Dept.<br><br>Exposure Monitoring Surveys (Aug 1996, May 1999) show production employees as well within OESs for all dusts and solvents.<br><br>Disposable dust masks are available for vessel charging, although their use is not compulsory.<br><br>A portable vacuum cleaning unit with suitable filter is available when required.<br>Maintenance carry out an annual physical inspection of all mixer vessels and pipelines.<br><br>A weigh station is provided in a fume cupboard for weighing out smaller quantities of solid constituents (this also is examined and tested annually).<br><br>Entry into vessels is controlled by the permit to work system.<br><br>All employees are subject to the company's annual health screening programme. |

| | |
|---|---|
| OBSERVATIONS | Discarded empty paper sacks were strewn on several loading platforms.<br><br>Liquid component transfer containers had been left open on platforms 1 and 4 (still containing residual materials).<br><br>The ventilation at charging stations 2 and 4 appeared inadequate.<br><br>There were dust accumulations on all loading platforms.<br><br>A brush appears to have been used to sweep up dust on some platforms.<br>A pipe flange below mixer 3 had developed a small leak. |
| RECOMMENDATIONS | 1 Improve the sack disposal containers on all loading platforms.<br>2 Remind staff of the importance of disposing of sacks correctly.<br>3 Remind staff that liquid transfer containers should have their lids replaced after use.<br>4 Rectify the ventilation at charging stations 2 and 4.<br>5 Introduce simply weekly checks on the ventilation at all charging stations.<br>6 Introduce weekly cleaning for all loading platforms.<br>7 Remind staff of the importance of using vacuum methods for cleaning.<br>8 Investigate obtaining vacuum units which can be lifted onto the platforms more easily.<br>9 Repair the leaking flange below mixer 3.<br>10 Increase the frequency of pipeline inspections to six monthly.<br>11 Develop a standard procedure for entering vessels for cleaning or maintenance purposes (linked to the permit to work system).<br>12 Investigate alternative cleaning methods avoiding the need for entry eg immersion in solvent over weekend periods. |

Signatures: *A Storm, P Gold* Date: *2 July 2000*
Recommendation follow up: *October 2000*
Assessment Review: *July 2002*

# After the assessment

## Review and implementation of recommendations

**9.24** The guidance provided in CHAPTER 4: CARRYING OUT RISK ASSESSMENTS on the review of recommendations resulting from risk assessments and the implementation of an action plan is equally applicable to assessments made under the *COSHH Regulations*. Some recommendations could relate to the ongoing maintenance of effective control measures and many of these aspects are covered by further specific requirements of the COSHH Regulations.

## Use of control measures

**9.25** *Regulation 8* places duties on both employers and employees in respect of the proper use of control measures, including PPE:

> '(1) Every employer who provides any control measure, personal protective equipment or other thing or facility pursuant to these Regulations shall take all steps to ensure that it is properly used or applied as the case may be.
>
> (2) Every employee shall make full and proper use of any control measure, personal protective equipment or other thing or facility provided pursuant to these Regulations and shall take all reasonable steps to ensure it is returned after use to any accommodation provided for it and, if he discovers any defect therein, shall report it forthwith to his employer.'

As far as the employer is concerned, this should form part of the monitoring stage in the management cycle described in CHAPTER 8: IMPLEMENTATION OF PRECAUTIONS. Aspects where monitoring is likely to be particularly relevant are:

- correct use of LEV equipment;
- compliance with specified systems of work;
- compliance with PPE requirements;
- storage and maintenance of PPE;
- compliance with requirements relating to eating, drinking or smoking;
- condition of washing and showering facilities and personal hygiene standards.

Where employees are unwilling to use control measures properly, employers should consider the use of disciplinary action, particularly in relation to persistent offenders.

## Maintenance, examinations and test of control measures

**9.26** *Regulation 9* contains both general and specific requirements for the maintenance of control measures:

> '(1) Every employer who provides any control measure to meet the requirements of *Regulation* 7 shall ensure that it is maintained in an efficient state, in efficient working order and in good repair and, in the case of personal protective equipment, in a clean condition.
>
> (2) Where engineering controls are provided to meet the requirements of *Regulation* 7, the employer shall ensure that thorough examinations and tests of those engineering controls are carried out–
>
> (a) in the case of local exhaust ventilation plant, at least once every 14 months, or for local exhaust ventilation plant used in conjunction with a process specified in *Column 1* of *Schedule 4*, at not more that the interval specified in the corresponding entry in *Column 2* of that Schedule;
>
> (b) in any other case, at suitable intervals.
>
> (3) Where respiratory protective equipment (other than disposable respiratory protective equipment) is provided to meet the requirements of *Regulation* 7, the employer shall ensure that at suitable intervals thorough examinations and, where appropriate, tests of that equipment are carried out.
>
> (4) Every employer shall keep a suitable record of the examinations and tests carried out in pursuance of paragraphs (2) and (3) and of any repairs carried out as a result of those examinations and tests, and that record or a suitable summary thereof shall be kept available for at least 5 years from the date on which it was made.'

### *General maintenance of controls*

**9.27** The COSHH ACOP states that, where possible, all engineering control measures should receive a visual check at least once every week. Such checks may simply confirm that there are no apparent leaks from vessels or pipes and that local exhaust ventilation ('LEV') or cleaning equipment appear to be in working order. No records of such checks need to be kept, although it is good practice (and prudent ) to do so.

Paragraph (2) requires thorough examinations and tests of engineering controls. Requirements relating to LEV are reviewed below but for other engineering controls such examinations and test must be 'at suitable intervals', and suitable records must be kept for at least five years. The nature of examinations and tests will depend upon the engineering control involved and the potential consequences of its deterioration or failure. Examples might involve:

- detailed visual inspections of tanks and pipelines;
- inspections and non-destructive testing of critical process vessels;
- testing of detectors and alarm systems;
- planned maintenance of general ventilation equipment;
- checks on filters in vacuum cleaning equipment.

### LEV Plant

**9.28** Most LEV systems must be thoroughly examined and tested at least once every 14 months, although *Schedule 4* to the *COSHH Regulations* requires increased frequencies for LEV used in conjunction with a handful of specified processes. Dependent upon the design and purpose of the LEV concerned, the examination and test might involve one or more of the following:

- visual inspection of the LEV equipment;
- air flow measurements using an air velocity meter (involving comparisons with recommended capture and duct velocities);
- static pressure measurements (and comparison with design or commissioning pressures);
- visual checks of efficiency using smoke generators or dust lamps;
- air sampling to confirm efficiency levels (applying the sampling methods described later in this chapter);
- filter integrity tests to confirm filter efficiency.

Further guidance is available in an HSE booklet (REF. 28).

Details of the records which should be kept in relation to those examinations and tests is contained in paragraph 66 of the COSHH ACOP (REF. 1).

### *Personal protective equipment*

**9.29** All types of PPE are subject to the general maintenance requirements contained in *paragraph (1)* of *Regulation 9* whilst *paragraph (3)* contains specific requirements relating to non-disposable respiratory protective equipment (RPE). Some types of PPE can easily be seen to be defective by the user whilst in other cases (eg for gloves or clothing providing protection against strongly corrosive chemicals) it may be appropriate to introduce more formalised inspection systems.

For non-disposable RPE the COSHH ACOP states that thorough examinations and, where appropriate, tests should be made at least once every month, although it suggests that for half mask respirators, used more occasionally in relatively low risk situations, periods up to three months are acceptable.

For simple respirators a visual examination of the condition of the facepiece, straps, filters and valves is sufficient. However, for airline-fed RPE the quality and flow of the air supply should also be tested. For RPE supplied from compressed gas cylinders more detailed examinations and testing will be required, including a check on the pressure in the cylinders. Details of the records which should be kept are contained in paragraph 68 of the COSHH ACOP (REF. 1). Further guidance is available in an HSE booklet (REF. 26).

## Monitoring exposure at the workplace

**9.30** Reference was made earlier in the chapter to the possible need to carry out air testing in the workplace as part of the COSHH assessment process in order to determine the adequacy of control measures. Such testing may also be necessary in order to ensure that adequate control is maintained and this is a requirement of *Regulation 10*:

> '(1) In any case in which–
>
> (a) it is requisite for ensuring the maintenance of adequate control of the exposure of employees to substances hazardous to health; or
>
> (b) it is otherwise requisite for protecting the health of employees,
>
> the employer shall ensure that the exposure of employees to

substances hazardous to health is monitored in accordance with a suitable procedure.

(2) Where a substance or process is specified in Column 1 of Schedule 5, monitoring shall be carried out at least at the frequency specified in the corresponding entry in Column 2 of that Schedule.

(3) The employer shall keep a suitable record of any monitoring carried out for the purpose of this Regulation and that record or a suitable summary thereof shall be kept available–

(a) where the record is representative of the personal exposures of identifiable employee, for at least 40 years;

(b) in any other case, for at least 5 years.'

*Schedule 5* to the Regulations automatically requires monitoring to be carried out in processes using vinyl chloride monomer and electrolytic chromium plating.

The range of equipment available for monitoring air quality in the workplace is constantly expanding but there are three main types

- Chemical indicator tubes.
- Direct reading instruments.
- Sampling pumps and filter heads.

### *Chemical indicator tubes*

**9.31** Tubes are available to measure a wide range of air-borne substances. A measure volume of air is drawn through the tube, usually using a hand bellows or a mechanical pump. The contaminant (usually a gas, vapour or aerosol) reacts with the chemicals contained in the tube to produce a colour change. The concentration is measured by calibrated markings showing how far the colour change has penetrated into the tube or by comparing the intensity of the colour change with a calibrated chart. Different types of tubes can measure concentrations both in the short term and long term.

### *Direct reading instruments*

**9.32** Instruments can provide direct measurements of the concentrations of gases, vapours or dust present in the atmosphere. Some instruments are portable (particularly useful for measuring contaminants in confined spaces) whereas others are fixed, sometimes as part of detection networks. As well as providing instant measurement of concentrations, instruments can be set to trigger off alarms when specified concentrations are reached eg 50% of the MEL or 80% of the OES.

### *Sampling pumps and filter heads*

**9.33** Small battery operated pumps can be used to draw air through filter heads or some other absorbent medium. The samples collected can then be weighed, chemically analysed or counted under microscopes (eg in the case of asbestos fibres). The concentration can be determined from the weight of the sample (or the number of fibres counted) and the volume of air drawn through by the pump. Different filtration and absorbent materials are available to sample a wide range of contaminants.

Most types of monitoring equipment can be used either to monitor the concentration of a substance in a given part of a workplace or to measure the concentration in the breathing zone of an individual employee, to provide an indication of their exposure. Care should be taken in interpreting all survey results – the conditions measured may not be representative of those normally encountered and allowances should be made for the accuracy of the sampling method. Some occupational hygienists deliberately sample what they believe to be the worst conditions first. If these circumstances produce concentrations which are comfortably within the relevant MEL or OES then the need for further monitoring may be greatly reduced or eliminated. Note should be taken of the requirement to retain all exposure monitoring records for five years and those relating to the personal exposure of identifiable individuals for at least 40 years. The HSE provide considerable technical guidance on monitoring methods (REF. 29).

## Health surveillance

**9.34** *Paragraphs (1)* and *(2)* of *Regulation 11* contain the main requirements relating to the need for health surveillance.

> '(1) Where it is appropriate for the protection of the health of his employees who are, or are liable to be, exposed to a substance hazardous to health, the employer shall ensure that such employees are under suitable health surveillance.
>
> (2) Health surveillance shall be treated as being appropriate where–
>
> (a) the employee is exposed to one of the substances specified

in *Column 1* of *Schedule 6* and is engaged in a process specified in *Column 2* of that Schedule, unless that exposure is not significant; or

(b) the exposure of the employee to a substance hazardous to health is such that an identifiable disease or adverse health effect may be related to the exposure, there is a reasonable likelihood that the disease or effect may occur under the particular conditions of his work and there are valid techniques for detecting indications of the disease or the effect.'

The remaining parts of the Regulation (*Paragraphs (3)* to *(12)*) relate to the manner in which health surveillance is conducted and used, together with the maintenance of and access to surveillance records.

The decision as to whether health surveillance is appropriate to protect the health of employees is one that would normally be taken at the time of a COSHH assessment or during its subsequent review. However, for those processes and substances specified in *Schedule 6* surveillance must be carried out – in the main continuing requirements which were in place prior to the *COSHH Regulations.*

Normally health surveillance programmes would be initiated and carried out under the overall supervision of a registered medical practitioner, and preferably one with relevant occupational health experience. However, the surveillance itself (as described below) may be carried out by an occupational health nurse, a technician or a responsible member of staff, providing that individual was competent for the purpose.

There are many different procedures available for health surveillance including:

### Biological monitoring

Measurement of the concentrations of hazardous substances or their metabolites within the body through testing of:

- blood eg for lead or solvents,
- urine eg for fluoride or solvents,
- exhaled air eg for carbon monoxide, other gases or solvent vapours.

### *Biological effect monitoring*

The measurement of the effects of hazardous substances on exposed workers:

- eg possible deterioration in the lungs through lung function and/or peak flow testing.

### *Medical surveillance*

Physical examinations or measurements to identify possible alterations in body functions.

### *Interviews and/or examinations*

Enquiries about possible symptoms by a competent person

- eg the appearance of warts or lumps, possibly indicating skin cancer amongst pitch workers; inspections for possible ulceration amongst chrome workers.

For health surveillance to be 'appropriate' there must firstly be a significant enough risk to justify it and there must also be a valid technique (such as those above) for detecting indications of related occupational diseases or ill-health effects. The HSE provide specialist guidance on the subject (REF. 30).

Records of health surveillance must contain information specified in an Appendix to the COSHH ACOP and must be retained for at least 40 years.

## Information, instruction and training

**9.35** *Regulation 12* contains requirements relating to information, instruction and training:

> '(1) An employer who undertakes work which may expose any of his employees to substances hazardous to health shall provide that employee with such information, instruction and training as is suitable and sufficient for him to know–
>
> (a) the risks to health created by such exposure; and
>
> (b) the precautions which should be taken.

(2) Without prejudice to the generality of Paragraph (1), the information provided under that paragraph shall include–

(a) information on the results of any monitoring of exposure at the workplace in accordance with *Regulation 10* and, in particular, in the case of any substance hazardous to health for which a maximum exposure limit has been approved, the employee or his representatives shall be informed forthwith, if the results of such monitoring show that the maximum exposure limit is exceeded; and

(b) information on the collective results of any health surveillance undertaken in accordance with *Regulation 11* in a form calculated to prevent it from being identified as relating to any particular person.

(3) Every employer shall ensure that any person (whether or not his employee) who carries out any work in connection with the employer's duties under these Regulations has the necessary information, instruction and training.'

The requirements of Paragraph (1) mirror those found in various other codes of Regulations. It is important that workers are aware of the risks that their work exposes them to – if they understand the risks they are much more likely to take the necessary precautions. Instruction and training will be particularly relevant in relation to:

- awareness of safe systems of work;
- correct use of LEV equipment;
- use, adjustment and maintenance of PPE (especially RPE);
- the importance of good personal hygiene standards;
- requirements relating to eating, drinking and smoking;
- emergency procedures;
- arrangements for cleaning and disposal of waste.

Paragraph (2) requires employers to inform employees or their representatives of the results of workplace exposure monitoring – immediately if the MEL is shown to have been exceeded. Employees must also be informed of the *collective* results of health surveillance eg the average urinary fluoride concentration within a department or on a particular shift, or the numbers of employees referred for further investigation following a skin inspection.

Any person carrying out work on the employer's behalf (whether or not an employee) is required by Paragraph (3) to have the necessary information, instruction and training. Thus a consultant making a COSHH assessment or an occupational hygienist conducting exposure monitoring must be verified by the employer as being competent for the purpose and be furnished with the information necessary to carry out their work effectively.

## Review of assessments

**9.36** *Paragraph (2)* of *Regulation 6* requires COSHH assessments to

> 'be reviewed regularly and forthwith if:
>
> - there is reason to suspect the assessment is no longer valid; or
> - there has been a significant change in the work to which the assessment relates'.

### *Assessments no longer valid*

**9.37** Assessments might be shown to be no longer valid because of:

- new information on health risks eg information from suppliers, changes in the MEL or OES;
- results from inspections or thorough examinations or tests (*Regulation 9*) eg indicating fundamental flaws in engineering controls;
- results from workplace exposure monitoring (*Regulation 10*) eg showing the OES or MEL is regularly being exceeded (or approached);
- results from health surveillance (*Regulation 11*) eg demonstrating an unsatisfactory or deteriorating position;
- a confirmed case of an occupational disease.

### *Significant changes*

**9.38** Changes necessitating a review of an assessment might involve:

- the substances used, their form or their source;
- equipment used for the process or activity (including control measures);

- methods of work or operational procedures;
- volume, rate or type of production.

### *Regular review*

**9.39** The periods elapsing between reviews should relate to the degree of risk involved and the nature of the work itself. The COSHH ACOP states that assessments should be reviewed at least every five years.

A review would not necessarily require a revision of the assessment – it may conclude that existing controls are still adequate despite changed circumstances. However, where changes are shown to be required, *paragraph (2)* of *Regulation 6* requires that these be implemented.

## *Some pitfalls*

**9.40** The author has encountered many situations where employers have not met the objectives of the *COSHH Regulations*, sometimes despite the expenditure of considerable time and effort. Amongst the more common pitfalls are:

### The data sheet library

**9.41** Employers have collected a vast library of manufacturers and suppliers data sheets (many of which relate to substances they do not use) in the belief that this constitutes a COSHH assessment. Whilst acquiring relevant data sheets is an important preparatory step and their availability can assist in respect of emergency medical treatment, simply acquiring data sheets is a long way short of what is required.

### Armchair assessments

**9.42** Some employers have been known to simply arrange for information from data sheets to be transcribed onto their own COSHH assessment form without anyone actually visit the workplace to review the circumstances of use. Observations and discussions in the workplace are an essential part of assessing what control measures are necessary for individual processes or activities.

### Overkill

**9.43** Manufacturers and suppliers often identify precautions which *may* be appropriate for the use of their products. The unquestioning adoption of these precautions can often result in precautions (particularly PPE requirements) which are unnecessary, impractical for employees and extremely expensive. Whilst advice in data sheets is undoubtedly relevant, it is ultimately for the assessor(s) to determine what is appropriate in their workplace for their working methods and quantity of use.

### Not seeing the wood for the trees

**9.44** Particularly in larger organisations where large numbers of hazardous substances are in use, assessors often try to assess each and every substance individually. Assessing processes or activities is much more productive – looking at the layout and density of the forest rather than individual trees. Where a variety of substances are used in a process or activity, adopting a 'worst first' approach can often pay off. If control measures are adequate for the most hazardous substances they are likely to be adequate for other substances used in the same way.

### Slaves to record systems

**9.45** There is no single correct method for recording COSHH assessments – providing the appropriate information is included many different formats can be used (as the examples in this chapter demonstrate). The imposition of standard forms (particularly over-complicated ones) can be a recipe for much grief and unnecessary work.

## *References*

### (All HSE publications)

**9.46**


| | | |
|---|---|---|
| 1 | L 5: | General COSHH ACOP, Carcinogens ACOP and Biological Agents ACOP (1999) |
| 2 | L 9: | Control of vinyl chloride at work ACOP (1995) |
| 3 | L 86: | Control of substances hazardous to health in fumigation operations ACOP (1996) |
| 4 | INDG 198: | Working with sewage: the health hazards. A guide for employers (1995) |
| 5 | INDG 230: | Storing and handling ammonium nitrate (1996) |

| | | |
|---|---|---|
| 6 | INDG 257: | Pesticides: Use them safely (1997) |
| 7 | INDG 300: | Skin cancer by oil (1999) |
| 8 | ⋆MSA 1: | Lead and you (1998) |
| 9 | MSA 7: | Cadmium and you (1995) |
| 10 | MSA 8: | Arsenic and you (1996) |
| 11 | MSA 13: | Benzene and you (1997) |
| 12 | MSA 14: | Nickel and you (1997) |
| 13 | MSA 15: | Silica dust and you (1997) |
| 14 | MSA 16: | Chromium and you (1991) |
| 15 | MSA 17: | Cobalt and you (1995) |
| 16 | MSA 18: | Beryllium and you (1995) |
| 17 | MSA 19: | PCBs and you (1995) |
| 18 | MSA 21: | MbOCA and you (1996) |
| 19 | MSB 4: | Skin cancer caused by pitch and tar (1996) |
| 20 | ⋆ COP 2: | Control of lead at work ACOP (1998) |
| 21 | ⋆ L 27: | Work with asbestos insulation, asbestos coating and asbestos insulating board ACOP (1999) |
| 22 | L 8: | The prevention or control of legionellosis including legionnaires disease (2000) |
| 23 | EH 40: | Occupational exposure limits (published annually) |
| 24 | HSG 37: | An introduction to local exhaust ventilation (1993) |
| 25 | HSG 53: | The selection, use and maintenance of respiratory protective equipment (1998) |
| 26 | L 25: | Personal protective equipment at work (1992) |
| 27 | HSG 54: | The maintenance, examination and testing of local exhaust ventilation (1998) |
| 28 | HSG 173: | Monitoring strategies for toxic substances (1997) |
| 29 | HSG 61: | Health surveillance at work (1999) |

⋆ Whilst strictly speaking outside the scope of the *COSHH Regulations*, these references are included for the benefit of those conducting assessments under the regulations applying to lead and asbestos.

# 10 Noise assessment

**In this chapter:**

## *Introduction*

**10.1** The risks associated with exposure to noise have been understood for many years. HM Factory Inspectorate (a forerunner of the HSE) published its booklet 'Noise and the Worker' in 1963 and the courts have deemed that employers should have been aware of the risks since that date and been taking action to control them. However, employers were slow to move and as a result there have been many successful compensation claims for occupational deafness and many workers are also in receipt of disablement benefit from the DSS in respect of noise – induced hearing loss.

Occupational deafness has occurred in many industries – mining, shipbuilding, engineering, textiles, construction and the wood trades being some of the more common. However, there was no specific legislation dealing with noise until 1990 when the *Noise at Work Regulations 1989* came into operation. At the heart of these Regulations is a requirement for employers to make an assessment of the risks from noise.

## *How noise damages hearing*

### Damage to the hearing cells

**10.2** Hearing takes place through the action of sound waves on the eardrum. The eardrum vibrates, activating the bones of the inner ear which in turn exert pressure on the cochlea, a snail-shaped organ containing a liquid. Motion of liquid within the cochlea is detected by tiny hair cells which transmit sound to the brain. It is these hair cells which are damaged by excessive exposure to noise.

An analogy is to consider the hair cells as similar to grass on a lawn. One person's path across the lawn may be visible for a short while but the grass will soon return to its previous position. The path of several people walking across the lawn will be visible for rather longer but will have disappeared by the following day. However, a large number of people walking to and fro on a daily basis will eventually damage the grass beyond its ability to recover.

Similarly the hair cells in the ear may suffer a short term threshold shift from which they can recover but longer exposure to higher levels of noise will cause permanent damage to the hearing. Usually the frequencies at the higher end of the scale are affected first. This means that the victim can still hear sounds but loses the ability to differentiate between them, particularly the consonants. This may result in accusations that others are not speaking clearly rather than an acceptance that hearing damage has taken place. Many individuals also become quite adept at lip reading to overcome their hearing loss. A certain amount of hearing loss also occurs naturally as part of the ageing process.

### Other damage

**10.3** Very loud noises (such as explosions and gunfire) can cause perforated ear drums although this is relatively rare and the eardrum usually heals up. Severe cases of occupational deafness are often accompanied by tinnitus – a continuous ringing, buzzing or whistling in the ear – although this may have other causes. Noise may also create other work-related problems not associated with hearing damage – it may hinder communication, cause stress and sudden loud noises may startle workers. Whilst outside the scope of the *Noise at Work Regulations 1989*, significant risks of these types should still be assessed as part of the employer's general risk assessment.

## *Noise measurement*

### The decibel scale

**10.4** The ear can hear sounds at frequencies between 20 and 20,000 cycles per second or Hertz (Hz). It is most sensitive to frequencies between 3000 and 6000 Hz, those used in human speech. Sound levels are measured in decibels (dB) with the range going from zero decibels (the threshold of hearing) up to around 140 decibels (a very painful and dangerous level of exposure). A correction is made to allow for the human ear's varying ability to hear sounds at different frequencies. This is called the 'A weighting' and noise levels corrected in this way are shown in dB(A).

The decibel scale is logarithmic. Consequently a rise of 10 dB(A) (eg from 90 dB(A) to 100 dB(A)) actually represents a tenfold increase in noise. An increase of 3 dB(A) results approximately in a doubling of the noise. This feature of the decibel scale is particularly important in assessing the risks from noise – an apparently small increase in dB(A) can in fact significantly increase the risks.

Most noises in the workplace are a mixture of a wide range of frequencies – pure tone noises (ie noise of a single frequency) are usually only generated by test instruments or tuning forks. Instruments normally measure a combination of all of the noise frequencies they are exposed to. However, more sophisticated instruments (see later) can select noise from particular frequencies. This is known as octave band analysis.

An approximate guide to typical sound levels is provided by the table below:

| DB(A) | |
|---|---|
| 0 | Faintest audible sounds |
| 10 | Leaf rustling, quiet whisper |
| 20 | Very quiet room |
| 30 | Subdued speech |
| 40 | Quiet office |
| 50 | Normal conversation |
| 60 | Busy office |
| 70 | Loud radio or TV |
| 80 | Busy street |
| 90 | Heavy vehicle close by |
| 100 | Bandsaw cutting metal |
| 110 | Woodworking machine shop |
| 120 | Chainsaws |
| 130 | Riveting |
| 140 | Jet aircraft taking off close by |

## Daily personal noise exposure

**10.5** The degree of damage to hearing caused by excessive noise depends on both the noise level and the duration of exposure. The *Noise at Work Regulations 1989* are based on the 'daily personal noise exposure' (usually denoted as $L_{EP,d}$) related to an eight hour working day. The Regulations contain two action levels referring to the daily personal noise exposure:

- First action level – $L_{EP,d}$ of 85 dB(A).
- Second action level – $L_{EP,d}$ of 90 dB(A).

(There is also a 'peak action level' which is defined as a peak sound pressure of 200 pascals. This is relevant in relation to infrequent but loud noises, usually from explosions or major impacts).

In calculating the daily personal noise exposure it is important to appreciate the logarithmic nature of the decibel scale. Each of the following exposures will produce a daily personal noise exposure of 85 dB(A) – assuming that the remainder of the working day is relatively quiet.

| dB(A) | |
|---|---|
| 85 | 8 hours |
| 88 | 4 hours |
| 91 | 2 hours |
| 94 | 1 hour |
| 104 | 6 minutes |
| 114 | 36 seconds |

Similarly 4 hours exposure to a sound level of 94 dB(A) will produce a $L_{EP,d}$ of 91 dB(A).

## Measurement instruments

**10.6** There is a wide range of noise measuring instruments available, with varying levels of accuracy and different facilities. They can be categorised into three main types:

### *Sound level meters*

These provide a simple read out of sound levels (usually in dB(A)). Better instruments have both a fast and slow response time – the latter can be useful in providing an average level where the sound is fluctuating. Sound level meters are useful in measuring fairly uniform noise levels or for situations where the time of exposure to different levels of noise is fairly well known. The HSE's guidance booklet on the Regulations (REF 1) shows how the $L_{EP,d}$ for employee exposure can be calculated from this information using a 'fractional exposure' value f.

### *Integrating sound levels meters*

These meters integrate the sound levels in a particular location over a sample period or a whole day's exposure, allowing easy calculation of the $L_{EP,d}$. Better instruments will also provide a noise profile over the sample period which can help to highlight noisy occurrences or activities.

Static meters of this type are very useful in helping to identify whether areas need to be designated as hearing protection zones. However, they are only of limited value in determining the exposures of individual workers, especially if those workers move around significantly in the course of their activities.

### *Personal noise dosemeters*

Dosemeters are designed to be worn by workers as they carry out their work. A small microphone is placed in the worker's hearing zone (but at least 4cm from the head to avoid sound reflection from the body). Essentially dose meters are a portable version of integrating sound level meters.

They are of most value where workers have to move regularly between noisy and quiet areas or carry out a wide range of tasks. However, the results relate to the range of tasks carried out by an individual worker over a specific sampling period – caution should be exercised in applying the results to other employees, carrying out slightly different activities on other days.

Personal dosemeters and integrating sound level meters are both prone to being sabotaged through deliberate exposure to excessive noise. Instruments capable of providing noise profiles over the sample period are useful here as they can show the times that particularly high sound levels occurred. These can then be related to the working activities which were (or should have been) taking place. A check should usually be made on the calibration of instruments before they are used and most also require laboratory calibration periodically. Further information on measurement instruments is provided in the HSE guidance booklet (REF. 1).

## *The Noise at Work Regulations 1989 summarised*

**10.7** The *Noise at Work Regulations 1989* are contained in full in the HSE guidance booklet '*Reducing noise at work*' (REF. 1) together with detailed guidance on their interpretation.

### Action levels

**10.8** The 'daily personal action levels' ($L_{EP,d}$) which are referred to throughout the Regulations are defined in full within *Regulation 2* and *Part 1* of the *Schedule* to the Regulations. These are:

- First action level $L_{EP,d}$ of 85 dB(A).
- Second action level $L_{EP,d}$ of 90 dB(A).
- Peak action level a peak sound pressure of 200 pascals.

Where employers have duties under the Regulations in respect of their employees they are also given like duties (so far as is reasonably practicable) in respect of others at work who may be affected. Employees with noisy premises have a duty to contractors and others working in noisy locations. Also employers whose employees carry out noisy activities elsewhere have duties to those working there eg contractors have duties to clients' employees.

## Assessment of exposure

**10.9** *Regulation 4(1)* requires an employer to '*ensure that a competent person makes a noise exposure which is adequate . . .* ' *when any of his employees is likely to be exposed to the first action level or above or to the peak action level or above.*

Not all employers will need to make assessments. As a rough guide, if people need to shout or have difficulty being heard clearly by someone two metres away then exposure may be above the first action level and an assessment is necessary. More detailed guidance on conducting and reviewing assessments and the keeping of assessment records (referred to in *Regulation 5*) is provided later in the chapter.

## Reduction of risk of hearing damage

**10.10** *Regulation 6* contains an overriding duty that 'Every employer shall reduce the risk of damage to the hearing of his employees from exposure to noise to the lowest level reasonably practicable.'

This applies even where a noise assessment is not required. A small risk still exists below 85 dB(A) and employers may need to consider whether it is reasonably practicable to reduce exposure further.

## Reduction of noise exposure

**10.11** *Regulation 7* states that where exposure is likely to be at or above the second action level (90 dB(A)) or the peak action level, employers must reduce the exposure of employees, so far as is reasonably practicable, *other than by the provision of personal ear protectors*. As in other Regulations the use of PPE (in this case hearing protection) should be the last resort. Guidance on how noise exposure might be reduced is provided later in the chapter.

## Ear protection

**10.12** *Regulation 8* requires that where employees are exposed to noise at or above the first action level (85 dB(A)), their employer must provide them with hearing protection if they request it. If exposure is at or above the second action level (90 dB(A)) or the peak action level then the employer must provide hearing protection. Guidance on the types of hearing protection available is provided later.

## Ear protection zones

**10.13** *Regulation 9* requires that zones where hearing protection must be worn must be demarcated and identified using standard blue and white signs (as required under the *Health and Safety (Safety Signs and Signals) Regulations 1996*). Once a compulsory hearing protection zone has been designated employers must enforce it as such, even in respect of people (including contractors and visitors) who may only be in the zone for a short time. (Many employers also choose to identify zones where the first action level is exceeded using signs indicating that hearing protection is recommended or advised, as opposed to compulsory forms of wording).

## Maintenance and use of equipment

**10.14** Employers are required by *Regulation 10* to ensure (so far as is reasonably practicable) that anything they provide under the Regulation '*is fully and properly used*'. This applies both to noise reduction equipment and ear protection, although not to ear protection provided on request to employees exposed to between the first and second action levels. Compulsory ear protection zones must be enforced by the employer. All equipment (ear protection and noise reduction measures) must be '*maintained in an efficient state, in efficient working order and in good repair.*'

Employees must fully and properly use ear protection if they are likely to be exposed to the second or peak action levels or above (ie in compulsory ear protection zones) and also any other protective measures provided under the Regulations (eg by closing doors on acoustic enclosures). They must also report any defects in equipment to their employer.

## Provision of information to employees

**10.15** Employers have a duty under *Regulation 11* to provide employees likely to be exposed at or above the first or peak action levels with '*adequate information, instruction and training*'.

This must include:

- the risk of damage to hearing that such exposure may cause;
- what steps the employees can take to minimise the risk;
- how to obtain ear protection;
- employees' own duties under the Regulations.

The methods used will depend upon the type of workplace and the degree of risk involved but might include:

- oral briefing or explanation;
- individual counselling and training;
- use of leaflets or posters (see REF. 2);
- use of videos, films etc;
- formal training sessions.

### Duties of manufacturers etc

**10.16** *Regulation 12* extends the duties of manufacturers, suppliers etc under *section 6* of *HASAWA 1974* to require them to provide information on noise likely to be generated by articles for use at work, where this is likely to reach the first or peak action level. Much more detail on this topic is provided in the HSE guidance booklet and elsewhere (REFS. 1 AND 3).

## *Reducing noise exposure*

**10.17** Before carrying out a noise assessment it is important to have an awareness of the different measures which can be adopted to reduce the exposure of employees to noise, including the different types of hearing protection available. Whilst noise control engineering is a specialist subject in its own right, an appreciation of the techniques available can be very useful in identifying measures which may be effective in given situations and for evaluating the recommendations being made by so-called specialists. The HSE have published an excellent booklet called 'Sound Solutions' which contains 60 case studies of noise control techniques which have been used successfully in a wide variety of industrial situations. (REF. 4).

## Equipment specification

**10.18** Reference was made earlier to the requirements of *Regulation 12* in relation to the supply of information on noise likely to be generated by work equipment. In some cases there may be a choice between different products stated to generate different levels of noise. In other situations the client may stipulate that the equipment must not generate more than a specified level.

In all cases it is important to consider the specification carefully – where exactly is the noise to be measured and at what stage of the equipment's operating cycle (eg idling or operating at maximum capacity). Obviously the equipment must also be checked before being formally accepted in order to ensure that it meets the appropriate noise specification. This topic is covered extensively in the HSE guidance booklet in the Regulations (REF. 1).

There may also be scope to introduce less noisy work methods or equipment eg:

- use of hydraulic pile driving instead of impact methods;
- high pressure water jetting rather than abrasive cleaning methods.

## Reducing noise generation

**10.19** Noise is generated by vibrating sources – either a vibrating surface or vibration in a fluid. If the vibration can be eliminated or reduced then so will the noise. It may be important to consider other parts which vibrate in sympathy (secondary vibration) as well as the primary source of the vibration. Noise reduction measures might include:

### *Vibrating surfaces*

- cushioning impacts (eg with plastic or nylon surfaces),
- replacing metal gears by nylon/polyurethane gears or by belts,
- using isolating or anti-vibration mountings,
- separating large vibrating surfaces from moving parts,
- stiffening structural parts or panels,
- placing machines on vibration absorbing pads,
- using damping materials on metal surfaces,

- using mesh in place of sheet metal,
- placing absorbent gaskets around doors and lids,
- replacing rigid pipework and flexible materials.

### *Vibration in gases*

- choosing centrifugal rather than propeller fans,
- using large diameter, low speed fans,
- using large diameter, low pressure ductwork,
- streamlining ductwork to avoid turbulence (this will also improve its efficiency),
- using effective silencers to reduce turbulence at exhausts,
- using low-noise air nozzles or pneumatic ejectors (at the minimum pressure necessary).

### *Efficient maintenance*

Good maintenance standards are also important in reducing noise generation eg by:

- replacing worn or badly fitting parts,
- securing loose parts,
- balancing rotating and other moving parts correctly,
- providing good lubrication.

## Reducing noise transmission

**10.20** Many of the measures described to reduce noise generation will also reduce noise transmission within work equipment. However, it is also important to reduce the transmission of noise through the air.

### *Acoustic enclosures*

Noisy equipment can be placed in acoustic enclosures. Alternatively where the noise source is large or there are several noise sources, it may be better to place the workers inside an acoustic enclosure. This may be an acoustically protected control booth, in which case it should contain all the relevant controls and provide adequate visibility of the equipment or process being controlled. (These are commonly used in large printing plants eg in the newspaper industry). In some cases the enclosure may simply be a noise refuge to which workers can go when their duties do not require them to be out on the noisy plant (such refuges are often used in power generation plants).

Important considerations in designing acoustic enclosures are:

- covering the surfaces of the enclosure in sound absorbent material;
- minimising the openings in the enclosure;
- installing absorbent gaskets around doors, windows, service inlets etc;
- avoiding the enclosure being in contact with vibrating parts.

### *Applying sound absorbent materials*

Transmission of noise can be reduced by the application of sound absorbent materials to prevent noise reflection from the walls and ceilings of rooms. Such materials will generally be most efficient if they are installed close to the source of the noise but benefits can also be obtained from installing them close to positions where people work. Hanging panels of sound absorbent material close to noise sources may also be effective. Portable sound absorbent screens can also be useful, especially for protecting maintenance employees working for limited periods in close proximity to noisy equipment.

### *Separation measures*

The transmission of noise to workers can be reduced by situating them further away from noise sources or, if possible, by putting them in different rooms. Care should always be taken in the positioning of noisy exhaust or extraction systems to ensure that noise (together with any gas, dust or fumes) is directed away from working positions.

## Ear protection

**10.21** There are three main types of hearing protection:

## *Ear muffs*

Ear muffs (also known as ear defenders) consist of plastic cups which fit over the ears. They are sealed against the head by cushions containing foam or a viscous liquid or gel. The inside part of the cups is filled with soft plastic foam or similar sound-absorbent material. The cups are pressed against the head by pressure bands which normally pass over the top of the head although they may be positioned behind the head or under the chin. Some types of ear muffs are designed to be attached to safety helmets.

The use of ear muffs over spectacles will decrease their efficiency as also may the presence of long hair or jewellery. Both the pressure exerted by the head band and the condition of the muffs seals are likely to deteriorate with age or misuse.

## *Ear plugs*

Ear plugs are intended to be fitted directly into the ear canal. Some types are reusable whilst others are disposable. Re-usable plugs are usually of plastic or rubber materials whilst disposable plugs are made of foam plastic or a down material coated in a plastic membrane. Some re-usable plugs are attached to cords to prevent their loss (an important consideration in food handling).

Hygiene is very important in relation to ear plugs as contamination or infections can easily be introduced into the ear. Re-usable plugs should always be washed prior to further use. Plugs should not be used by anyone suffering from an ear infection or irritation. Some employees are unable to tolerate anything within their ear at all.

Most re-usable plugs come in different sizes – some workers need different sizes for each ear. Simple instruction is usually necessary to show employees how to insert the plugs into their ears safely and efficiently.

## *Semi-inserts*

This type consists of plastic or rubber cups which are held against the entrance to the ear canal by a headband, often made of plastic. They can easily be slipped off and carried round the neck on the headband. The cups must be kept clean and the effectiveness of the headband may deteriorate with time.

The choice of hearing protection will depend upon a number of factors including those described below.

### *Level of protection required*

All suppliers of ear protection should supply information on the level of protection their products provide. This will not be identical for all noise frequencies – most types are more effective against the frequencies in the audible range. The protection overall can be calculated by a fairly complicated process which requires octave band analysis of the noise exposure. The methodology for such calculations is described in the HSE guidance booklet (REF. 1).

Complicating the situation further, research has shown that the attenuation figures provided by suppliers are not always achieved in practice. This may be due to poor fitting, deterioration of the ear protection, use with spectacles, long hair or jewellery. As a very rough rule of thumb, most types of hearing protection will provide attenuation of at least 15 dB(A) if they are fitted reasonably well.

### *Work limitations/personal preference*

Many people find ear muffs more comfortable for wearing in situations where they are exposed to noise for long periods. Semi-inserts are convenient for work which involves regularly going into and out of hearing protection areas. Plugs can be kept in the pocket for use in situations of occasional or unexpected exposure to noise. Some individuals find the presence of anything in their ear canal to be irritating.

Assuming that the degree of protection provided by the different types is similar (and this is often the case) it is generally best to provide employees with the type of protection that they prefer. If hearing protection is only worn by an employee for 90% of the time they are exposed to noise then the maximum exposure reduction which will be achieved overall can be shown mathematically to be only 10 dBA. If hearing protection is only worn for half of the exposure period then noise exposure will only be reduced by 3 dBA.

### *Cost*

If hearing protection is not worn then any cost saving in opting for cheaper types is a false economy. Although disposable plugs may seem to be a relatively cheap option, they will be used in large numbers in workplaces where there is regular or continuous exposure to noise. Reusable types of hearing protection will usually prove more economical in the long run in these environments. However, disposable plugs (kept readily available in pockets) may be the better option for occasional exposure situations.

## Planning and preparation

**10.22** The principles to be followed in noise assessments are similar to those for general risk assessments (covered in CHAPTER 4: CARRYING OUT RISK ASSESSMENTS) and for most of the other more specific type of assessments. Some specific factors relating to noise assessments are referred to below.

### Who will carry out the assessments?

**10.23** The assessment must be carried out by a competent person and noise assessments probably require a greater degree of technical expertise than other types of risk assessment. HSE guidance (REF. 1) refers to skills and knowledge needed as including:

- the purpose of the assessments;
- an appreciation of one's own limitations (knowledge, experience or equipment);
- how to record results and explain them to others;
- the reasons for using different kinds of instruments and their limitations;
- how to interpret information provided by others eg in order to calculate probable exposures.

That is not to say that noise assessment is solely the preserve of specialists. Straightforward situations, particularly those involving steady noise, can be assessed by anyone with an understanding of the decibel scale who is capable of using simple instruments and relating readings to the requirements of the Regulations. However, more complex noise exposure will require a greater degree of knowledge and experience in its assessment. The HSE guidance booklet (REF. 1) provides advice on the extent of training which may be necessary. Creation of an in-house assessment team may be appropriate in larger workplaces.

### How will the assessments be organised?

**10.24** As with other types of assessment, some workplaces may need to be divided into manageable assessment units. These may be based on:

- Departments or sections.
- Buildings or rooms.
- Process lines.
- Use of types of equipment.
- Specific activities.

Some areas or activities may be ruled out of the assessment process because it is known that noise exposure is below the first action level. In other cases it may be determined that the noise exposure is sufficiently complex to require competent outside assistance in order to make an adequate assessment.

However, employers should be cautious in contracting out noise assessments. There have been many instances where outside consultancies have carried out extensive measurement of noise levels in workplaces using some very sophisticated instrumentation and at considerable expense, but without getting round to answering the basic questions that the assessment process should be addressing.

It will also be necessary at this stage to check that the noise measuring instruments likely to be required during the assessment are not only available but are also in full working order with up to date calibration certificates.

### Gathering information

**10.25** Prior to starting the assessment relevant information should be gathered such as:

- What equipment, processes, activities, areas are thought to be noisy.
- Previous noise surveys or previous noise assessments.
- Noise specifications for relevant equipment.
- HSE guidance material – (REFS. 5 to 14 relate to specific occupational sectors).

## *Making the assessment*

### The purpose of the assessment

**10.26** In making a noise assessment it is important to keep in mind the basic purpose of the assessment required by *Regulation 4*. In essence answers must be provided to the following questions:

- Is there a noise problem in this situation?
- Who is exposed and to what extent? (in particular in relation to the action levels).
- What must be done to comply with the Regulations?
  - reduction of noise exposure (equipment specification, noise generation, noise transmission),
  - provision of ear protection,
  - creation of ear protection zones,
  - provision of information to employees.

Whilst noise survey work will need to be carried out, this should only be to the extent required to answer the above questions. Extremely detailed noise surveys are not a requirement of the Regulations in their own right.

## Information required

**10.27** A combination of noise survey work, observations and discussions with employees will be required in order to determine:

- What equipment, processes, activities, areas are noisy?
- What are the actual noise levels?
- Do the noise levels vary?–
  - at different stages of activities,
  - for different materials, products, equipment.
- How long is noise emitted at each level?
- How long are employees exposed to each level of noise?
- What is their position in relation to the noise source?
- Are different employees exposed to different levels of noise?

Each of these questions need not be answered precisely but enough information must be obtained in order to decide whether the exposure reaches the first action level (85 dbA), the second action level (90 dBA) or, in some cases, the peak action level.

During the assessment the availability and effectiveness of any existing noise exposure reduction measures should also be evaluated eg:

- acoustic enclosures;

- types of hearing protection provided;
- designated hearing protection zones;
- compliance with hearing protection requirements;
- quality of equipment maintenance.

Consideration should also be given to the feasibility of introducing additional noise exposure reduction measures such as:

- changes to processes or equipment;
- reduction in noise generation;
- reduction in noise transmission;
- additional hearing protection requirements.

## Drawing conclusions

**10.28** At the end of the assessment the assessors must make conclusions in respect of:

### *Where the problems are–*

- which equipment, processes, activities, areas involve exposure above the action levels.

### *Noise reduction measures–*

- existing measures which are proving effective,
- additional measures which should be introduced,
- alternative possibilities requiring evaluation.

### *Hearing protection–*

- existing hearing protection zones,
- the need for additional zones,
- types of hearing protection provided,
- enforcement of hearing protection requirements,
- the quality, wording and positioning of signs,
- the supply and maintenance of hearing protection.

*Information to employees–*

- whether employees need further education on noise risks,
- are there any specific noise-related training needs.

## Assessment records

**10.29** *Regulation 5* of the *Noise at Work Regulations 1989* requires that an adequate record of each assessment is kept until a new one is made. (The demands of possible civil litigation usually dictate that records are kept much longer, although the Regulations do not require this).

Records should include details of the workplaces, areas or tasks assessed, the date of the assessment, who carried out the assessment and what the results of the assessment were.

There is no standard format for assessment records but they might contain:

- noise exposure tables (identified by equipment, area, activity or person);
- plans showing noise exposures at various locations;
- details of exposure times;
- details of activities carried out by peripatetic workers (including noise exposure levels and times);
- recommendations on actions required;
- reference to more detailed assessments which may be required.

An example of an assessment record is provided later in this chapter. Several examples are also included in the HSE guidance booklet (REF. 1).

# SPHINX ENGINEERING
# NOISE ASSESSMENT REPORT

*Dates of assessment:* 7–9 June 1999 *Assessment by:* D Barr
*Instruments used:* Acme Sound Level Meter Model D2
Reliant Personal Dosemeters Type R2

## RESULTS OF NOISE SURVEY

| Location | Sound Level Average or range | Average Daily Exposure | Assessed Action Level | | | Comments |
|---|---|---|---|---|---|---|
| | (dBA) | (hours) | 0 | 1 | 2 | |
| MACHINE SHOP | | | | | | |
| Bandsaw | 98 | 2 | | | ✓ | Operators do not generally move between machines |
| Power press A | 95-97 | 4 | | | ✓ | |
| Power press B | 94-96 | 4 | | | ✓ | Machines are well separated. |
| Milling Machine | 87 | 6 | | ✓ | | Some operators wearing hearing protection. |
| Drilling Machines | 80 | 6 | ✓ | | | |
| Background | 74-78 | 8 | ✓ | | | No signs in position. |
| PLASTIC SHOP | | | | | | Dosemeter readings: |
| Cross cut saw | 98 | 2 | | | ✓ | 91.7 dBA and 90.9 dB(A) (employee 1); |
| Portable saw | 100 | 2 | | | ✓ | 90.6 dB(A) (employee 2). |
| Assembly bench | | | | | | |
| – saw operating | 93-95 | 4 | | | ✓ | Employee 2 wears hearing protection, Employee 1 does not. No signs. |
| – assembly only | 74-77 | | ✓ | | | |

### *Recommendations*

1 Noise reduction

1.1 Investigate means of reducing noise at–

- the bandsaw and power presses in the Machine Shop,
- the saws in the Plastic Shop (see separate proposals).

2 Ear protection

2.1 Continue to make hearing protection available to all employees;

2.2 Make the following compulsory hearing protection activities–

- work at the bandsaw and power presses in the Machine Shop,
- work in the Plastic Shop whenever a saw is operating.

3 Ear protection zones

3.1 Provide suitable signs to indicate compulsory hearing protection activities (as in 10.35: EAR PROTECTION) on the bandsaw and power presses (Machine Shop) and at the entrance to the Plastic Shop.

4 Information to employees

4.1 At the next staff meeting–

- show the video about risks from noise,
- explain the results of the noise survey,
- emphasise the compulsory hearing protection activities,
- show the hearing protection available and how to use it.

# *After the assessment*

## Review and implementation of recommendations

**10.30** CHAPTER 4: CARRYING OUT RISK ASSESSMENTS provides general guidance on the review of recommendations and the implementation of an action plan resulting from risk assessments. The nature of noise problems is such that specialist external resources may be required to provide guidance on the feasibility or practicalities of noise reduction measures or to conduct detailed noise surveys or assessments. This may result in the timescale for implementation of some actions being rather longer than for other types of risk assessment.

Recommendations should also be followed up in order to ensure that they have actually been implemented and, where relevant, to measure the new levels of noise exposure. Either the previous assessment records should be annotated with the findings of the follow-up or a revised assessment record should be prepared.

## Assessment review

**10.31** *Regulation 4(2)* requires the assessment to be reviewed when there is reason to suspect it is no longer valid or significant changes have taken place. Circumstances justifying a review might include:

- evidence of hearing loss (eg from audiometric tests on employees);
- changes in work equipment or equipment layout;
- changes in workload, work pattern or machine speeds;
- changes in materials used or products manufactured;
- significant alterations in employees' duties or hours of work.

As for other assessments, periodic reviews should also take place. These may detect the cumulative effects of minor changes or of wear and tear in equipment. Such reviews may involve simple spot checks rather than detailed reviews or re-assessments.

## *References*

### (All HSE publications.)


| | | |
|---|---|---|
| 1 | L 108: | Reducing Noise at work. Guidance on the *Noise at Work Regulations 1989* (1998) |
| 2 | INDG 99: | Noise at work: Advice to employees (1995) – priced sets of leaflets |
| 3 | INDG 263: | Keep the noise down: Advice for purchasers of workplace machinery (1997) – free leaflet. |
| 4 | HSG 138: | Sound solutions. Techniques to reduce noise at work (1995) |
| 5 | INDG 127: | Noise in construction: Further guidance on the *Noise at Work Regulations 1989* (1995) |
| 6 | HSG 109: | Control of noise in quarries (1993) |
| 7 | PM 56: | Noise from pneumatic systems (1985) |
| 8 | PBIS 1: | Noise assessments in paper mills (2000) – free leaflet |
| 9 | AS 8: | Noise (in agriculture) (1999) – free leaflet |
| 10 | WIS 4: | Noise reduction at band re-saws (1990) – free leaflet |
| 11 | WIS 5: | Noise enclosure at band re-saws (1990) – free leaflet |
| 12 | WIS 8: | Noise reduction at multi-spindle planning and moulding machines (1990) – free leaflet |
| 13 | WIS 13: | Noise at woodworking machines (1997) – free leaflet |
| 14 | | Noise control in the rubber industry (1990) |

# 11 Assessment of manual handling

## In this chapter:

**Introduction**

**What the Regulations require**

**Risk of injury from manual handling**

Assessment guidelines
Task related factors
Load related factors
Factors relating to the working environment
Capability of the individual
Other factors

**Avoiding or reducing risks**

Elimination of handling
Automation or mechanisation
Reduction of the load
Task-related measures
Load-related measures
Improving the work environment
Individual capability

**Planning and preparation**

Who will carry out the assessments?
How will the assessments be arranged?
Gathering information

**Making the assessment**

**Manual handling assessment checklist**

Observations
Discussions
Notes

**After the Assessment**
Assessment records
Review and implementation of recommendations
Assessment review
Training

**References**

## Introduction

**11.1** The *Manual Handling Operations Regulations 1992* came into operation on 1 January 1993 as part of the so-called 'six pack' of new Regulations. Although the Regulations implemented *European Directive 90/269/EEC*, the HSE had previously attempted to introduce Regulations on manual handling in an attempt to reduce the huge toll of accidents from this source. At the time of the introduction of the Regulations more than a quarter of the accidents reported each year to the enforcing authorities (the HSE and local authorities) were associated with manual handling. In 1990/91 65% of handling accidents resulted in sprains and strains, whilst 5% were fractures. Many manual handling injuries have cumulative effects eventually resulting in physical impairment or even permanent disability.

There is already evidence of the beneficial effects of the Regulations, particularly in respect of the increasing use of mechanical handling aids and improved manual handling training. By 1996/97 the proportion of handling accidents causing fractures had been reduced to 3.3%. However, the battle was far from over with 54% of RIDDOR reportable accidents in the health and social work sector still attributable to handling. Several other sectors had over 30% of accidents involving handling, including food and drink, textiles, construction, wholesale and retail, transport/storage and education.

## What the Regulations require

**11.2** Various terms used in the Regulations are defined in *Regulation 2* which states:

'manual handling operations' means any transporting or supporting of a load (including the lifting, putting down, pushing, pulling, carrying or moving thereof) by hand or by bodily force.

'Injury' does not include injury caused by any toxic or corrosive substance which:

(a) has leaked or spilled from a load;

(b) is present on the surface of a load but has not leaked or spilled from it; or(c)
is a constituent part of a load;

and 'injured' shall be construed accordingly;'

(This in effect establishes a demarcation with the *COSHH Regulations* – where there is oil on the surface of a load making it difficult to handle that is a matter for the *Manual Handling Operations Regulations*, whereas any risk of dermatitis is covered by the *COSHH Regulations*).

'Load includes any person and any animal'

(This is of great importance to a number of work sectors including health and social care, agriculture and veterinary work).

HSE guidance accompanying the Regulations states that an implement, tool or machinery being used for its intended purpose is not considered to constitute a load – presumably establishing a demarcation with the requirements of PUWER 98. However, when such equipment is being moved before or after use it will undoubtedly be a load for the purpose of these Regulations.

*Regulation 2(2)* imposes the duties of an employer to his employees under the Regulations on a self-employed person in respect of himself. *Regulation 3* excludes the normal ship-board activities of a ship's crew under the direction of the master from the application of the Regulations (these are subject to separate Merchant Shipping legislation).

The duties of employers under the Regulations are all contained in *Regulation 4* which (as in the COSHH Regulations) establishes a hierarchy of measures that employers must take. *Regulation 4* states:

'(1) Each employer shall –

(a) so far as is reasonably practicable, avoid the need for his employees to undertake any manual handling operations at work which involve a risk of their being injured; or

(b) where it is not reasonably practicable to avoid the need for his employees to undertake any manual handling operations at work which involve a risk of their being injured–

(i) make a suitable and sufficient assessment of all such manual handling operations to be undertaken by them, having regard to the factors which are specified in column 1 of Schedule 1 to these Regulations and considering the questions which are specified in the corresponding entry in column 2 of that Schedule,

(ii) take appropriate steps to reduce the risk of injury to those employees arising out of their undertaking any such manual handling operations to the lowest level reasonably practicable, and

(iii) take appropriate steps to provide any of those employees who are undertaking any such manual handling operations with general indications and, where it is reasonably practicable to do so, precise information on –

(aa) the weight of each load, and

(bb) the heaviest side of any load whose centre of gravity is not positioned centrally.

(2) Any assessment such as is referred to in paragraph (1)(b)(i) of this Regulation shall be reviewed by the employer who made it if –

(a) there is no reason to suspect that it is no longer valid; or

(b) there has been a significant change in the manual handling operations to which it relates,and where as a result of any such review changes to an assessment are required, the relevant employer shall make them.'

The hierarchy of measures which must be taken by employers where there is a risk of injury can be summarised as:

- Avoid the operation (if reasonably practicable);
- Assess the remaining operations;
- Reduce the risk (to the lowest level reasonably practicable);
- Inform employees about weights.

Reference will be made later in the chapter to a variety of measures which can be taken to avoid or reduce risks. The factors to which regard must be given during the assessment (as specified in *Schedule 1* to the Regulations) are the *tasks, loads, working environment* and *individual capability* together with other factors eg hindrance from PPE or clothing. These factors and the questions specified by *Schedule 1* are also covered later in the chapter.

*Regulation 5* places a duty on employees. It states:

> 'Each employee while at work shall make full and proper use of any system of work provided for his use by his employer in compliance with *Regulation 4(1)(b)(ii)* of the *Regulations*.'

*Regulation 6* provides for the Secretary of State for Defence to make exemptions from the requirements of the Regulations in respect of home forces and visiting forces and their headquarters.

*Regulation 7* extends the Regulations to apply to offshore activities such as oil and gas installations, including diving and other support vessels. Previous provisions relating to manual handling were replaced or revoked by *Regulation 8*. The Regulations themselves are extremely brief but they are accompanied by considerable HSE guidance, much of which will be referred to during this chapter.

## *Risk of injury from manual handling*

### Assessment guidelines

**11.3** Appendix 1 of the guidance accompanying the Regulation (REF. 1) provides assessment guidelines which can be used to filter out manual handling operations involving little or no risk and help to identify where a detailed risk assessment is necessary. However, it must be stressed that *these are not weight limits* – they must not be regarded as safe weights nor must they be treated as thresholds which not be exceeded. The HSE guidance states that application of the guidelines will provide a reasonable level of protection to around 95% of working men and women. Some workpeople will require additional protection (eg pregnant women, frail or elderly workers) and this should be considered in relation to the assessment of individual capability.

#### *Lifting and lowering*

The guidelines for lifting and lowering operations are shown in the accompanying diagram. They assume that the load can be easily grasped with both hands and that the operation takes place in reasonable working conditions, using a stable body position. Where the hands enter more than one box, the lowest weights apply. A detailed assessment should be made if the weight guidelines are exceeded or if the hands move beyond the box zones.

These guideline weights apply up to approximately 30 operations per hour. They should be reduced for more frequent operations

- by 30% for 1 or 2 operations per minute;
- by 50% for 5 to 8 operations per minute;
- by 80% for more than about 12 operations per minute.

Other factors likely to require a more detailed assessment are where:

- workers do not control the pace of work eg on assembly lines;
- pauses for rest are inadequate;
- there is no change of activity allowing different muscles to be used;
- the load must be supported for any length of time.

### *Carrying*

Similar guidelines figures can be applied for carrying where the load is held against the body and carried up to 10 metres without resting. For longer distances or loads held below knuckle height a more detailed assessment should be made. The guideline figures can be applied for carrying loads on the shoulder for distances in excess of 10 metres but an assessment may be required for the lifting of the load onto and off the shoulder.

### *Pushing and pulling*

Where loads are slid, rolled or supported on wheels the guideline figures assume that force is applied with the hands between knuckle and shoulder height. The guideline figure for starting or stopping the load is a force of about 25kg (about 250 Newtons) for men and 10kg (about 100 Newtons) for keeping the load in motion (these figures reduce to 16kg and 7kg respectively for women).

In practice it is extremely difficult to make a judgement as to whether forces of these magnitude are being applied. Many employers are likely to make assessments of significant pushing or pulling activities anyway. There

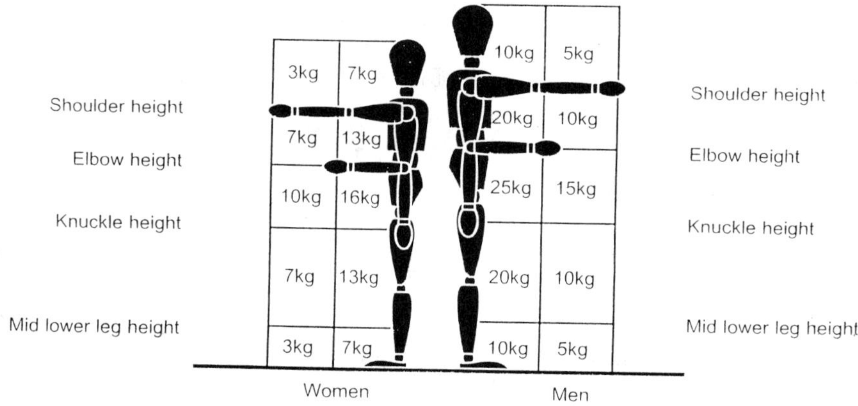


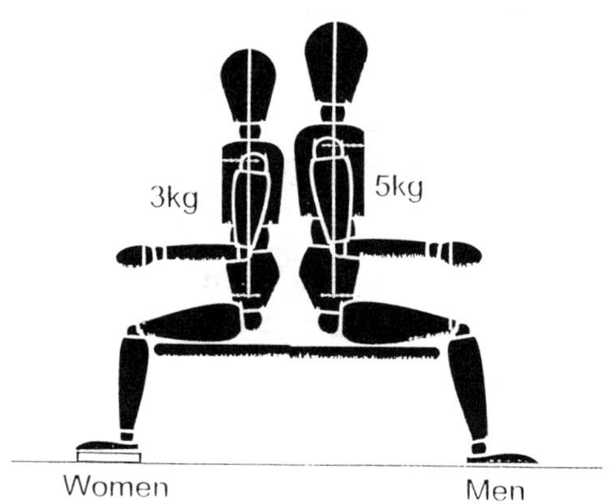


are no guideline limits on distances over which loads may be pushed or pulled, providing there is sufficient opportunity for rest.

### *Handling when seated*

The accompanying diagram illustrates the guideline figures for handling whilst seated. Any handling activities outside the specified box zones should be assessed in any case.

*Schedule 1* to the Regulations contains a list of questions which must be considered during assessments of manual handling operations. All of these indicate factors which may increase the risk of injury. (Most of these factors have been included in the checklist for assessments provided later in the chapter).

## Task related factors

### *Holding or manipulating loads at a distance from the trunk*

**11.4** Stress on the lower back increases as the load is moved away from the trunk. Holding a load at arms length imposes five times the stress as the same load very close to the trunk.

### *Unsatisfactory body movement or posture*

The risk of injury increases with poor feet or hand placings eg feet too close together, body weight forward on the toes, heels off the ground.

*Twisting the trunk* whilst supporting a load increases stress on the lower back – the principle should be to move the feet, not twist the body.

*Stooping* also increases the stress on the lower back whilst reaching upwards places more stress on the arms and back and lessens control on the load.

### *Excessive movement of loads*

Risks increase the further loads must be *lifted or lowered*, especially when lifting from floor level. Movements involving a *change of grip* are particularly risky. Excessive *carrying* of loads increases fatigue – hence the guidance figure of about 10 metres carrying distance before a more detailed assessment is made.

### *Excessive pushing or pulling*

Here the risks relate to the forces which must be exerted, particularly when starting to move the load, and the quality of the grip of the handler's feet on the floor. Risks also increase when pushing or pulling below knuckle height or above shoulder height.

### *Risk of sudden movement*

Freeing a box jammed on a shelf or a jammed machine component can impose unpredictable stresses on the body, especially if the handler's posture is unstable. Unexpected movement from a client in the health care sector or an animal in agricultural work can produce similar effects.

### *Frequent or prolonged physical effort*

Risk of injury increases when the body is allowed to become tired, particularly where the work involves constant repetition or a relatively fixed posture. The periodic inter-changing of tasks within a work group can do much to reduce such risks.

### *Insufficient rest and recovery*

The opportunity for rest and recovery will also help to reduce risks, especially in relation to tasks which are physically demanding.

### *Rate of work imposed by a process*

In such situations workers are often not able to take even short breaks, or to stretch or exercise different muscle groups. More detailed assessments should be made of assembly line or production line activities. Again periodic role changes within a work team may provide a solution.

## Load related factors

### *Is the load too heavy?*

**11.5** The guideline figures provided earlier are relevant here but only form part of the picture. Task-related factors (eg twisting or repetition) may also come into play or the load may be handled by two or more people. Size, shape or rigidity of the load may also be important.

### *Is the load bulky or unwieldy?*

Large loads will hinder close approach for lifting, be more difficult to get a good grip of or restrict vision whilst moving. The HSE guidance suggests that any dimension exceeding 75cm will increase risks and the risks will be even greater if it is exceeded in more than one dimension. The positioning of suitable handholds on the load may somewhat reduce the risks.

Other factors to consider are the effects of wind on a large load, the possibility of the load hitting obstructions or loads with offset centres of gravity (not immediately apparent if they are in sealed packages).

### *Is the load difficult to grasp?*

Where loads are large, rounded, smooth, wet or greasy, inefficient grip positions are likely to be necessary, requiring additional strength of grip. Apart from the possibility of the grip slipping there are likely to be inadvertent changes of grip posture, both of which could result in loss of control of the load.

### *Is the load unstable?*

The handling of people or animals was referred to earlier. Not only do such loads lack rigidity, but they may also be unpredictable and protection of the load as well as the handler is of course an important consideration. Other potentially unstable loads are those where the load itself or its packaging may disintegrate under its own weight or where the contents may shift suddenly eg a stack of books inside a partially full box.

### *Is the load sharp, hot etc?*

Loads may have sharp edges or rough surfaces or be extremely hot or cold. Direct injury may be prevented by the use of protective gloves or clothing but the possibility of indirect risks (eg where sharp edges encourage an unsuitable grip position or cold objects are held away from the body) must not be overlooked.

## Factors relating to the working environment

### *Space constraints*

**11.6** Areas of restricted headroom (often the case in maintenance work) or low work surfaces will force stooping during manual handling and obstructions (eg in front of shelves) will result in other unsatisfactory postures. Restricted working areas or the lack of clear gangways will increase risks in moving loads, especially heavier or bulkier items.

### *Uneven, slippery or unstable floors*

All of the above can increase the risks of slips, trips and falls. The availability of a firm footing is a major factor in good handling technique – such a footing will be a rarity on a muddy construction site. Moving workplaces (eg trains, boats, elevating work platforms) will also introduce unpredictability in footing. (The guideline weights should be reduced in such situations).

### *Variation in levels of floors or work surfaces*

Risks will increase where loads have to be handled on slopes, steps or ladders, particularly if these are steep. Any slipperiness of their surface eg due to ice, rain, mud will create further risks. The need to maintain a firm handhold on ladders or steep stairways is another factor to consider. Movement of loads between surfaces or shelving may also need to be considered, especially if there is considerable height change eg floor level to above shoulder height.

### *Extremes of temperature or humidity*

High temperatures or humidity will increase the risk of fatigue, with perspiration possibly affecting the grip. Work at low temperatures (eg in cold stores or cold weather) is likely to result in reduced flexibility and dexterity. The need for gloves and bad weather clothing is another factor to consider.

### *Ventilation problems or gusts of wind*

Inadequate ventilation may increase fatigue whilst strong gusts of wind may cause considerable danger with larger loads eg panels being moved on building sites.

### *Poor lighting*

Lack of adequate lighting may cause poor posture or an increased risk of tripping. It can also prevent workers identifying risks associated with individual loads eg sharp edges or corners, offset centres of gravity.

## Capability of the individual

**11.7** Manual handling capabilities will vary significantly between individual workers. Reference was made earlier in the chapter to the assessment guideline weights providing a reasonable level of protection to around 95% of workers and those guideline figures differed for men and women. Factors to be taken into account in relation to individual workers are:

### *Gender*

Whilst there is overlap between the capabilities of men and women, generally the lifting strength of women is less than men.

### *Age*

The bodies of younger workers will not have matured to full strength (see CHAPTER 3: SPECIAL CASES) whilst with older workers there will be a gradual decline in their strength and stamina, particularly from the mid 40's onwards.

### *Experience*

More mature workers may be better able to recognise their own capabilities and pace themselves accordingly, whilst also having acquired better handling techniques.

### *Pregnancy*

The need to protect new or expectant mothers was emphasised in CHAPTER 3: SPECIAL CASES.

### *Previous injury*

Workers with long term musculoskeletal problems, a history of such injuries or short term injuries (including those from non-work related causes) will all justify additional protection.

### *Physique and stature*

These factors will vary considerably within any workforce. Whilst bigger will often mean stronger, it must not be overlooked that some tasks or work locations may force taller workers to stoop or adopt other unsuitable handling postures.

Generally the objective should be to ensure that all manual handling operations can be performed satisfactorily by most reasonably fit and healthy employees, although a minority of workers may justify restrictions on their handling activities (see later in the chapter).

During the assessment process it is important that special note is taken of any manual handling operations which:

- Require unusual strength, height etc, eg reels of wrapping paper can only be safely positioned in a machine by persons above a certain height.
- Create additional risk to workers who are pregnant, disabled or have health problems.

Such tasks may need to be reassessed to reduce risks or it may be necessary to restrict some individuals from carrying them out.

- Require special information or training.

The health care sector provides many examples of situations where both the worker and the client (the load) may be at risk if correct technique is not used. Many other tasks are likely to require specific techniques to be adopted – whether in manual handling itself or the use of handling aids.

## Other factors

**11.8** The use of PPE or clothing eg gloves, protective suits, breathing apparatus may significantly affect the user's mobility or dexterity in respect of manual handling. Similarly uniforms or costumes (eg in the entertainment industry) may also be a factor to be taken into account.

# *Avoiding or reducing risks*

**11.9** The Regulations require employers to avoid the need for employees to undertake manual handling operations involving a risk of injury, so far as is reasonably practicable. Measures for avoiding such risks can be categorised as:

- Elimination of handling.
- Automation or mechanisation.
- Reduction of the load.

## Elimination of handling

**11.10** It may be possible for employers to eliminate manual handling altogether (or to eliminate handling by their own employees) by means such as:

### *Redesigning processes or activities*

Eg so that activities such as machining or wrapping are carried out in situ, rather than a product being manually handled to a position where the activity take place; a treatment is taken to a patient rather than vice versa (this may have other benefits to the patient).

### *Using transport better*

Eg allowing maintenance staff to drive vehicles carrying tools or equipment up to where they are working, rather than manually handling them into place.

### *Requiring direct deliveries*

Eg requiring suppliers to make deliveries directly into a store rather than leaving items in a reception area (such suppliers may be better equipped in terms of handling aids and their staff may be better trained in respect of manual handling).

## Automation or mechanisation

**11.11** The automation or mechanisation of a work activity is best considered at the design stage although there is no reason in principle why such changes cannot be made later eg as the result of a risk assessment. In making changes it is important to avoid creating additional risks eg the use of fork lift trucks for a task in an already cramped workplace may not be the best solution. However, as employers have become more aware of manual handling risks (many prompted by the advent of the Regulations) a much greater range of mechanical handling solutions to manual handling problems have become available.

These include:

### *Mechanical lifting devices*

Fork lift trucks, mobile cranes, lorry mounted cranes, vacuum devices and other powered handling equipment are commonly used to eliminate or greatly reduce the manual handling of loads.

### *Manually-operated lifting devices*

Pallet and stacker trucks, manually operated chain blocks or lever hoists can all be used to move heavy loads using very limited physical force.

### *Powered conveyors*

As well as fixed conveyors (both belt and driven roller types), mobile conveyors are being used increasingly, particularly for the loading and unloading of vehicles eg stacking of bundles of newspapers in delivery vans.

### *Non-powered conveyors, chutes etc*

Free-running roller conveyors, chutes or floor-mounted trolleys allow loads to move under the effects of gravity or to be moved manually with little effort. Such devices may operate between different levels or be set into the workplace floor.

### *Trolleys and trucks*

Trolleys and trucks can be used to greatly reduce the manual handling effort required in transporting loads. Some types also incorporate manual or mechanically-powered lifting mechanisms. Specialist trolleys are designed for carrying drums or other containers whilst an ingenious triple wheel system can be lifted to some trucks to aid them in climbing or descending stairs.

### *Lifting tools*

Special lifting tools are available to reduce the manual handling effort required for lifting or lowering certain loads eg paving slabs, manhole covers, drums or logs.

All of these and many other types of devices are illustrated in an HSE booklet 'Manual handling: solutions you can handle' (REF. 2).

## Reduction of the load

**11.12** There is considerable scope to avoid the risk of injury by reducing the sizes of the loads which have to be handled. In some cases the initiative for this has come from suppliers of a particular product whereas in others the impetus has come from customers or from users of equipment, often as a result of their manual handling assessments. Examples include:

- Packaged building materials (eg cement) reduced to 25kg.
- Photocopying paper now supplied in 5 ream boxes (approximately 12kg) – 10 ream boxes were previously commonplace.
- Newspaper bundle sizes reduced below 20kg (printers reduce the number of copies in a bundle as the number of pages in the paper increases).
- Customers specifying maximum container weights they will accept from suppliers eg weights of brochures from commercial printers.
- Equipment being separated into component parts and assembled where it is to be used eg emergency equipment used by fire services.

Where it is not reasonably practicable to avoid a risk of injury from an manual handling operation, the employer must carry out an assessment of such operations with the aim of reducing the risks to the lowest level reasonably practicable . The four main factors to be taken into account during the assessment are *the task, the load, the working environment* and *individual capability*. Possible risk reduction measures related to each of these factors are described below.

(Later in the chapter these are summarised in an assessment checklist).

## Task-related measures

### *Mechanical assistance*

**11.13** The types of mechanical assistance described earlier can be used to reduce the risk of injury, even if such risks cannot be avoided entirely. The use of roller conveyors, trolleys, trucks or levers can reduce considerably the amount of force required in manual handling tasks.

### *Task layout and design*

The layout of tasks, storage areas etc should be designed so that the body can be used in its more efficient modes eg:

- heavier items stored and moved between shoulder and mid lower leg height;
- allowing loads to be held close to the body;
- avoiding reaching movements eg over obstacles or into deep bins;
- avoiding twisting movements or handling in stooped positions eg by repositioning work surfaces, storage areas or machinery;
- providing resting places to aid grip changes whilst handling;
- reducing lifting and carrying of loads eg by pushing, pulling, sliding or rolling techniques;
- utilising the powerful leg muscles rather than arms or shoulders;
- avoiding the need for sustaining fixed postures eg in holding or supporting a load;
- avoiding the need for handling in seated positions.

### *Work routines*

Work routines may need to be altered to reduce the risk of injury using such measures as:

- limiting the frequency of handling loads (especially those that are heavier or bulkier);
- ensuring that workers are able to take rest breaks (either formal breaks or informal rest periods as and when needed);
- introducing job rotation within work teams (allowing muscle groups to recover whilst other muscles are used or lighter tasks undertaken).

### *Team handling*

Tasks which might be unsafe for one person might be successfully carried out by two or more. HSE guidance indicates that the capability of a two person team is approximately two thirds of the total of their individual capabilities; and of a three person team approximately one half of their total. Other factors to take into account in team handling are:

- the availability of suitable handholds for all the team;
- whether steps or slopes have to be negotiated;
- possibilities of the team impeding each other's vision or movement;
- availability of sufficient space for all to operate effectively;
- the relative sizes and capabilities of team members.

## Load-related measures

### *Weight or size reduction*

**11.14** The types of measures described earlier in the chapter might be adopted to reduce the risk of injury even if it is not possible to avoid the risk entirely. However, reducing the individual load size will increase the number of movements necessary to handle a large total load. This could result in a different type of fatigue and also the possibility of corners being cut to save time. Sizes of loads may also be reduced to make them easier to hold or bring them closer to the handler's body.

### *Making the load easier to grasp*

Handles, grips or indents can all make loads easier to handle (as demonstrated by the handholds provided in office record storage boxes). It will often be easier handling a load placed in a container with good handholds than handling it alone without any secure grip points. The positioning of handles or handholds on a load can also influence the handling technique used eg help avoid stooping. Handholds should be wide enough to accommodate the palm and deep enough to accommodate the knuckles (including gloves where these are worn).

The use of slings, carrying harnesses or bags can all assist in gaining a secure grip on loads and carrying them in a more comfortable and efficient position.

### *Making the load more stable*

Loads which lack rigidity themselves or are in insecure packaging materials may need to be stabilised for handling purposes. Use of carrying slings, supporting boards or trays may be appropriate. Partially full containers may need to have their contents wedged into position to prevent them moving during handling.

### *Reducing other risks*

Loads may need to be cleaned of dirt, oil, water or corrosive materials for safe handling to take place. Sharp corners or edges or rough surfaces may have to be removed or covered over. There may also be risks from very hot or very cold loads. In all cases the use of containers (possibly insulated) other handling aids or suitable gloves or other PPE may need to be considered.

## Improving the work environment

### *Providing clear handling space*

**11.15** The provision of adequate gangways and sufficient space for handling activities to take place will be linked with general workplace safety issues. Low headroom, narrow doorways and congestion caused by equipment and stored materials are all to be avoided. Good housekeeping standards are essential to safe manual handling.

### *Floor condition and design*

Even in temporary workplaces such as construction sites, every effort should be made to ensure that firm, even floors are provided where manual handling is to take place. Special measures may be necessary to allow water to drain away or to clear promptly any potentially slippery materials (eg food scraps in kitchens). Where risks are greater special slip-resistant surfaces may need to be considered. In outdoor workplaces the routine application of salt or sand to surfaces made slippery by ice or snow may need to be introduced.

### *Differing work levels*

Measures may be necessary to reduce the risks caused by different work levels. Slopes may need to be made more gradual, steps may need to be provided or existing steps or stairways made wider to accommodate handling activities. Work benches may need to be modified to provide a uniform and convenient height.

### *Thermal environment and ventilation*

Unsatisfactory temperatures, high humidity or poor ventilation may need to be overcome by improved environmental control measures or transferring work to a more suitable area. For work close to hot processes or equipment, in very cold conditions (eg refrigerated storage areas) or carried on out of doors the use of suitable PPE may be necessary.

### *Gusts of wind*

Where gusts of wind (or powerful ventilation systems) could affect larger loads extra precautions, in addition to those normally taken, may be necessary eg:

- using handling aids (eg trolleys);
- utilising team handling techniques;
- adopting a different work position;
- following an alternative transportation route.

### *Lighting*

Suitable lighting must be provided to permit handlers to see the load and the layout of the workplace and to make accurate judgements about distance, position and the condition of the load.

## Individual capability

**11.16** In ensuring that individuals are capable of carrying out manual handling activities in the course of their work, account must be taken both of factors relating to the individual and those relating to the activities they are to perform. Steps which may be appropriate include:

### *Medical screening*

Workers may be screened both prior to being offered employment and periodically thereafter to check whether they are physically capable of carrying out the full range of manual handling tasks in the workplace. In some extreme situations (eg the emergency services) an individual may be deemed unsuitable for employment if they are not sufficiently fit. However, legislation prevents employers discriminating against those with disabilities *without good reason*. In most workplaces the results of such screening may simply result in restrictions on the range of tasks individuals are allowed to perform.

### *Long term restrictions*

Long term restrictions may be appropriate where workers are identified through screening programmes as not being capable of carrying out certain manual handling activities without undue risk, or they become incapable due to some long term injury or the effects of the ageing process. It may be necessary to place long term restrictions on young workers until they attain an appropriate age at which their capabilities can be re-assessed.

### *Short term restrictions*

Relatively short term restrictions on manual handling activities may be necessary because of:

- pregnancy (or a particular stage of pregnancy) – see CHAPTER 3: SPECIAL CASES;
- recently having given birth (also referred to in CHAPTER 3: SPECIAL CASES);
- injury or illness of short duration.

### *Fitness programmes*

An increasing number of employers actively encourage employers to be physically fit, thus reducing their risk of injury during manual handling activities. A number of Fire Services have particularly pro-active programmes.

### *General manual handling training*

Many employers offer general training in manual handling, either to all employees or to all those employees expected to engage in significant manual handling work. Aspects to cover in such training include:

- recognition of potentially hazardous operations;
- avoiding manual handling hazards;
- dealing with unfamiliar handling operations;
- correct use of handling aids;
- proper use of PPE;

- working environment factors;
- importance of good housekeeping;
- factors affecting individual capability (knowing one's limitations);
- good handling technique (summarised in REF. 3).

### *Task specific training and instruction*

Training and instruction will often need to relate to the safety of specific manual handling tasks:

- how to use specific handling aids;
- specific PPE requirements;
- specific handling techniques.

The health care sector contains many such specific training needs (REF. 4) but there are also likely to be many specific needs in other occupational areas.

## *Planning and preparation*

**11.17** The principles of planning and preparation for manual handling assessments are no different from those for general risk assessments. Reference should be made to the relevant section of CHAPTER 4: CARRYING OUT RISK ASSESSMENTS if further guidance is required in addition to that provided below.

### Who will carry out the assessments?

**11.18** HSE guidance contained in booklet L 23 (REF. 1) states that while one individual may be able to carry out an assessment in relatively straightforward cases, in others it may be more appropriate to establish an assessment team. It also refers to employers and managers with a practical understanding of the manual handling tasks to be performed, the loads to be handled, and the working environment being better able to conduct assessments than someone outside the organisation, (Although it is not stated in the guidance, in-house personnel will also usually be more aware of the capabilities of employees carrying out manual handling tasks.)

The guidance refers to the individual or team performing the assessments needing to possess the following knowledge and expertise:

- the requirements of the Regulations;
- the nature of the handling operations;
- a basic understanding of human capabilities;
- awareness of high risk activities;
- practical means of reducing risk.

The HSE also acknowledge that there will be situations where external assistance may be required. These might include:

- training of in-house assessors;
- assessing risks which are unusual or difficult to assess;
- re-designing equipment or layouts to reduce risks;
- training of staff in handling techniques.

## How will the assessments be arranged?

**11.19** As for general risk assessments, the workplace or work activities will often need to be divided into manageable assessment units. Depending on how work is organised, these might be based on:

- Departments or sections.
- Buildings or rooms.
- Parts of processes.
- Product lines.
- Work stations.
- Services provided.
- Job titles.

Members of the assessment team can then be allocated to the assessment units where they are best able to make a contribution.

## Gathering information

**11.20** It is important to gather information prior to the assessment in order to identify potentially high risk manual handling activities and the precautions which ought to be in place to reduce the risks. Relevant sources might include:

### *Accident investigation reports*

Dependent upon the requirements of the organisation's accident investigation procedure, these may only include the more serious accidents resulting from manual handling operations.

### *Ill health records*

These may reveal short absences or other incidents due to manual handling which may have escaped the accident reporting system.

### *Accident treatment records*

Accident books or other treatment records may identify regularly recurring minor accidents which do not necessarily result in any absences from work eg cuts or abrasions from sharp or rough loads.

### *Operating procedures etc*

Reference to manual handling activities and precautions which should be adopted may be contained in operating procedures, safety handbooks etc.

### *Work sector information*

Trade associations and similar bodies publish information on manual handling risks and how to overcome them.

### *HSE Guidance*

Much guidance is available from the HSE – some of the more important publications are identified in the reference section of this chapter (References 1 to 3 will be relevant to most work activities). Additional guidance is also available on individual work sectors (see References 4 to 13).

## *Making the assessment*

**11.21** As with other types of assessments, visits to the workplace are an essential part of manual handling assessment. Manual handling operations need to be observed (sometimes in some detail) and discussions with those carrying out manual handling work, their safety representatives and their supervisors or managers need to take place.

The assessment checklist provided on the following pages provides guidance on the factors which may need to be taken into account during the observations and discussions and also on possible measures to reduce the risk. The checklist utilises the four main factors specified in the Regulations – task, load, working environment and individual capability. In practice each of these will have greater or lesser importance, depending upon the manual handling activity.

## MANUAL HANDLING ASSESSMENT CHECKLIST

### THE TASK

| ***ASSESSMENT FACTORS*** | ***REDUCING THE RISK*** |
|---|---|
| DISTANCE OF THE LOAD FROM THE TRUNK | TASK LAYOUT |
| BODY MOVEMENT/POSTURE<br>• Twisting<br>• Reaching<br>• Stooping | USE THE BODY MORE EFFECTIVELY<br>eg SLIDING OR ROLLING THE LOAD |
| • Sitting | SPECIAL SEATS |
| DISTANCE OF MOVEMENT<br>• Height (? Grip Change)<br>• Carrying (? Over 10m)<br>• Pushing or Pulling | RESTING PLACE/TECHNIQUE<br>USE OF TROLLEYS etc<br>TECHNIQUE/FLOOR SURFACE |
| RISK OF SUDDEN MOVEMENT | AWARENESS/TRAINING |
| FREQUENT/PROLONGED EFFORT | IMPROVED WORK ROUTINE<br>eg Job rotation |
| RATE OF WORK IMPOSED BY A PROCESS | ADEQUATE REST OR RECOVERY PERIODS |

### THE LOAD

| ***ASSESSMENT FACTORS*** | ***REDUCING THE RISK*** |
|---|---|
| HEAVY | MAKE THE LOAD LIGHTER<br>TEAM LIFTING<br>MECHANICAL AIDS |
| BULKY<br>(Any Dimension above 75cm) | MAKE THE LOAD SMALLER |
| UNWIELDY<br>(Offset Centre Of Gravity) | INFORMATION/MARKING |
| DIFFICULT TO GRASP<br>(Large, Rounded, Smooth, Wet, Greasy) | MAKE IT EASIER TO GRASP<br>• Handles<br>• Handgrips<br>• Indents<br>• Slings<br>• Carrying Devices<br>• Clean the Load |
| UNSTABLE<br>• Contents Liable to Shift<br>• Lacking Rigidity | WELL-FILLED CONTAINERS<br>USE OF PACKING MATERIALS<br>SLINGS/CARRYING AIDS |
| SHARP EDGES/ROUGH SURFACES | AVOID OR REDUCE THEM<br>GLOVES OR OTHER PPE |
| HOT OR COLD | CONTAINERS (? Insulated) |

## WORKING ENVIRONMENT

| ***ASSESSMENT FACTORS*** | ***REDUCING THE RISK*** |
|---|---|
| SPACE CONSTRAINTS<br>AFFECTING POSTURE | ADEQUATE GANGWAYS,<br>FLOORSPACE, HEADROOM |
| UNEVEN, SLIPPERY OR<br>UNSTABLE FLOORS | WELL MAINTAINED SURFACES<br>PROVISION OF DRAINAGE<br>SLIP-RESISTANT SURFACING<br>GOOD HOUSEKEEPING<br>PROMPT SPILLAGE CLEARANCE |
| VARIATION IN WORK SURFACE<br>LEVEL<br>eg steps, slopes, benches | STEPS NOT TOO STEEP<br>GENTLE SLOPES<br>UNIFORM BENCH HEIGHT |
| HIGH OR LOW TEMPERATURES<br>HIGH HUMIDITY<br>POOR VENTILATION<br>STRONG WINDS OR<br>OTHER AIR MOVEMENT | BETTER ENVIRONMENTAL<br>CONTROL<br>RELOCATING THE WORK<br>SUITABLE CLOTHING<br>RELOCATING THE WORK<br>ALTERNATIVE ROUTE<br>HANDLING AIDS |
| LIGHTING<br>MOVING WORKPLACE<br>• Boat<br>• Train<br>• Vehicle | TEAM HANDLING<br>SUFFICIENT WELL-DIRECTED<br>LIGHT |

## INDIVIDUAL CAPABILITY

| ***ASSESSMENT FACTORS*** | ***REDUCING THE RISK*** |
|---|---|
| *INDIVIDUAL FACTORS* | |
| STRENGTH<br>HEIGHT<br>FLEXIBILITY<br>STAMINA | BALANCED WORK TEAMS<br>'SELF SELECTION'<br>MAKE ASSISTANCE AVAILABLE<br>ENCOURAGE FITNESS |
| PREGNANCY<br>HEALTH PROBLEM<br>• Back Trouble<br>• Hernia<br>• Temporary Injury | SPECIAL ASSESSMENTS<br>FORMAL RESTRICTIONS<br>CLEAR INSTRUCTIONS |

| *TASK FACTORS*<br>OPERATIONS OR SITUATIONS<br>REQUIRING PARTICULAR | FORMALISED WORK<br>PROCEDURES<br>CLEAR INSTRUCTIONS<br>ADEQUATE TRAINING |
|---|---|
| • Awareness of risks<br>• Knowledge<br>• Method of approach<br>• Technique | • Recognising potentially hazardous operations<br>• Dealing with unfamiliar operations<br>• Correct use of handling aids Proper use of PPE<br>• Environmental factors<br>• Importance of housekeeping<br>• Knowing one's own limitations<br>• Good technique |

## Observations

**11.22** Sufficient time should be spent in the workplace to observe a sufficient range of the manual handling activities taking place and to take account of possible variations in the loads handled (raw materials, finished product, equipment etc). Aspects to particularly be considered include:

- comparison of actual methods used with those specified in operating procedures, industry standards etc;
- the level and manner of use of handling aids and their effectiveness;
- handling techniques adopted;
- physical conditions eg access, housekeeping, floor surfaces, lighting;
- variations between employees eg size, strength, technique adopted.

## Discussions

**11.23** In discussing manual handling issues with workpeople a similar approach should be taken to that described in CHAPTER 4: CARRYING OUT RISK ASSESSMENTS ie utilising open-ended questions wherever possible. Aspects which might be discussed include:

- whether normal conditions are being observed;
- their awareness of procedures, rules etc;
- their training in the use of handling aids or handling techniques;
- possible variations in work activities eg product changes, seasonal variations, differences between day and night shift;

- what happens if handling equipment or handling aids break down or are unavailable;
- whether assistance is available if required;
- what manual handling problems have been experienced?;
- have there been any injuries with manual handling?;
- reasons precautions are not being taken.

### Notes

**11.24** Notes should be taken during the assessment of anything considered to be of relevance. Further guidance is provided in the equivalent section of CHAPTER 4: CARRYING OUT RISK ASSESSMENTS on what may be of relevance and on note taking techniques.

## *After the assessment*

### Assessment records

**11.25** HSE guidance states that the significant findings of the assessment must be recorded unless:

- the assessment could very easily be repeated and explained at any time because it is so simple and obvious; or
- the manual handling operations are quite straightforward, of low risk, are going to last only a very short time, and the time taken to record them would be disproportionate.

As has been recommended in relation to other types of assessment, it is better to make a simple record if there is any doubt.

There is no standard format for recording an assessment. The HSE Guidance booklet L 23 (REF. 1) includes a sample record format together with a useful worked example. This record format includes a checklist of assessment factors under the four main headings (task, load, working environment, capability) in a similar listing the assessment checklist we have provided. Alongside each checklist item the assessor has space to

- identify whether the risk from this factor is low, medium or high;
- provide a more detailed description of the problems;
- identify possible remedial action.

Some will no doubt find this checklist format meets their needs. However, the author has found that many assessment factors often have little or no relevance to a specific manual handling operation. As a result, the eventual record contains a lot of blank paper, with only occasional comments. Consequently he has preferred to keep the checklist separate and only include within the record a reference to the risks, precautions and recommended improvements which are relevant to the operation being assessed. Two worked examples of this type of record are included in the chapter.

## Review and implementation of recommendations

**11.26** The guidance provided in CHAPTER 4: CARRYING OUT RISK ASSESSMENTS in relation to the review of recommendations and implementation of action plans is equally applicable to manual handling assessments. Similarly recommendations will need to be followed up in order to ensure that they have actually been implemented and also to assess any new risks which may have been introduced. This latter point is particularly relevant to manual handling as changes in working practice may have resulted in different techniques being adopted (with their own attendant risks) or the introduction of handling aids may have created additional training needs.

## Assessment review

**11.27** *Paragraph 4(2)* of the Regulations requires a manual handling assessment to be reviewed if:

'(a) there is reason to suspect that it is no longer valid; or

(b) there has been a significant change in the manual handling operations to which it relates;'

As is the case for other assessments, a review would not necessarily result in the assessment being revised, although a revision may be deemed to be necessary. A significant manual handling related injury should automatically result in a review of the relevant assessment. It is recommended that assessments are reviewed periodically in any case in order to take account of small changes in work practices which will eventually have a cumulative effect. The periods for such reviews might vary between two and five years – depending upon the degree of risk involved and the potential for gradual changes to take place.

| MANUAL HANDLING ASSESSMENT | | AREA: *Stores* | DATE: *24/3/00* | ASSESSOR: *B Strong* |
|---|---|---|---|---|
| No. | OPERATION | RISKS | EXISTING PRECAUTIONS | RECOMMENDATIONS |
| 1 | HANDLING OF INCOMING PARTS AND MATERIALS | Some items are both large and heavy eg drums and some boxed materials.<br><br>Palletised items must be transferred onto trolley by hand.<br>(no fork-lift access into stores) | Vehicles are unloaded as close as possible to stores entrance.<br>Trolley and sack barrow available and used.<br>Heavy items are lifted by two people.<br>(Stores staff have been trained in handling techniques). | Provide a suitable drum handling trolley.<br>Investigate which items can be delivered in smaller containers.<br><br>Provide a hand-operated pallet truck. |
| 2 | MOVEMENT OF PARTS AND MATERIALS WITHIN STORES | Transfer of items between stores sections (step between old and new sections causes problems).<br><br>Movement of items onto and off shelves etc. | Trolley and sack barrow and two-person lifts as above.<br>Stores lighting is good.<br><br>Heaviest items are mainly stored on shelves between knee and shoulder height. Clear access to shelves is maintained.<br>Some items are rolled or pushed into fixtures. | Provide a gradual ramp alongside the step (or alternatively a 'climbing barrow').<br><br>Ensure assistance is available when required for moving heavier items.<br><br>Some parts of the floor in the old store require repair. |
| 3 | DESPATCH OF ITEMS TO OPERATING DEPARTMENTS | A few heavy items are despatched, sometimes over long distances.<br><br>Rough ground must be negotiated en route to annex building.<br>Some transfers take place during hours of darkness | Stores trolley and barrow are loaned, where necessary.<br>Sometimes stores staff assist in moving loads. | Ensure all operating dept. staff collecting heavy items receive suitable training in handling techniques.<br>Provide a suitable footpath to the annex.<br>Check lighting levels of external areas. |

| MANUAL HANDLING ASSESSMENT | | AREA: *Newspaper Despatch* † | DATE: *11/5/00* | ASSESSOR: *A. Loader* |
|---|---|---|---|---|
| No. | OPERATION | RISKS | EXISTING PRECAUTIONS | RECOMMENDATIONS |
| | GENERAL COMMENTS | Weight of bundles controlled at 16–17 kg each.<br><br>Waste paper and strapping can create tripping risks. | Lighting and floor surface in despatch area and loading bay good.<br><br>Bins readily available for disposal of waste paper and strapping. | <br><br>Enforce safe disposal of strapping more rigorously. |
| 1 | PREPARATION OF BUNDLES FOR DESPATCH | Manual removal and refeeding of mis-stacked and unstrapped bundles.<br>Some bundles are stored temporarily on the floor. | Automated line with conveyors between stacking, strapping and loading positions.<br>Staff trained in handling techniques. | Provide a table close to the conveyor line for temporary storage. |
| 2 | DELIVERY OF BUNDLES INTO VANS | Vans at bay C are loaded manually by company and contract delivery staff. | Adjustable mobile conveyors feed into vans at bays A and B.<br><br>Company staff trained in handling techniques. | Provide a similar mobile conveyor at bay C (See below also). |
| 3 | STACKING BUNDLES INSIDE VANS | Stacking may involve:<br>stooping (due to low headroom)<br>moving bundles at floor level<br>moving bundles above shoulder height | Company staff trained (see above).<br>Newer company vans now have adequate headroom.<br>Bundles should be slid across the floor (rakes available).<br>This should normally be avoided by fully utilising the floor area. | Make company manual handling training available to contract staff ⋆.<br>Complete conversion of fleet by 2002.<br>Recommend contractors use similar vans ⋆. |

Notes: † A separate assessment of delivery activities would be necessary.
⋆ The company has no legal obligation to do this.

## Training

**11.28** The need for specific manual handling technique training may frequently be one of the recommendations made as a result of a manual handling assessment. With manual handling activities featuring in a wide range of work sectors many employers have chosen to provide all or a significant proportion of their workforce with general training in good handling technique. Such training is often provided as part of a more comprehensive health and safety induction programme. Guidance on the content of such general training is contained in paragraphs 173 and 174 of the HSE Guidance booklet (REF. 1) and also in other HSE publications (see references below).

## *References*

### (All HSE publications.)

**11.29**


| | | |
|---|---|---|
| 1 | L 23: | Manual Handling Operations 1992. Guidance on the Regulations (1998) |
| 2 | HSG 115: | Manual Handling: Solutions you can handle (1994) |
| 3 | INDG 143: | Getting to grips with manual handling: A short guide for employers (1993) – free leaflet |
| 4 | | Manual handling in the health service (1998) |
| 5 | | Getting to grips with handling problems: Worked examples of assessment and reduction of risk in the health service (1993) |
| 6 | HSG 119: | Manual handling in drinks deliveries (1994) |
| 7 | HSG 171: | Well handled: Offshore manual handling solutions (1997) |
| 8 | | Safe handling of bales (textile and clothing sector) (1994) |
| 9 | | Manual handling in paper mills (1998) |
| 10 | | Picking up the pieces: Prevention of musculoskeletal disorders in the ceramics industry (1996) |
| 11 | AS 23: | Handling loads in agriculture (1996) |
| 12 | INDG 125: | Handling and stacking bales in agriculture (1998) – free leaflet |
| 13 | IACL 106: | Handling the news: Advice for newsagents and employees on safe handling of bundles (1999) – free leaflet |

# 12 Assessment of DSE workstations

**In this chapter:**

## *Introduction*

**12.1** The *Health and Safety (Display Screen Equipment) Regulations 1992*, together with the other 'six pack' *Regulations*, came into operation on 1 January 1993. Their aim was to combat upper limb pains and discomfort, eye and eyesight effects, together with general fatigue and stress associated with work at display screen equipment ('DSE'). The Health and Safety Executive state in the guidance booklet to the Regulations (REF. 1) hat they do not consider there are any radiation risks from DSE or special problems for pregnant women. The Regulations require Assessments to be carried out to identify any health and safety risks at workstations used by 'users' or 'operators' (as defined). 'Users' have the right to an eye and eyesight test and any spectacles (or contact lenses) found to be necessary for their DSE work must be provided by their employer.

## *The Regulations summarised*

### Definitions

**12.2** *Regulation 1* contains a number of important definitions:

- Display screen equipment
  Any alphanumeric or graphic display screen, regardless of the display process involved.

- Workstation
  An assembly comprising display screen equipment, any optional accessories, any disk drive, telephone, modem, printer, document holder, work chair, work desk, work surface or other peripheral item and the immediate environment around.

- User
  An employee who habitually uses DSE as a significant part of his normal work.

- Operator
  A self-employed person who habitually uses DSE as a significant part of his normal work.

Factors to consider in determining whether a person is a 'user' or 'operator' are:

  - dependence on DSE to do the job;
  - no discretion on whether to use the DSE;

- significant training or DSE skills required;
- use normally for continuous spells of an hour or more;
- use more or less daily;
- fast transfer of information is an important requirement;
- high attention and concentration required, where the consequences of an error may be critical.

Detailed examples are given in the HSE Guidance to the Regulations (REF. 1).

## Exclusions

**12.3** The Regulations do not apply to:

- drivers' cabs or control cabs for vehicles or machinery;
- DSE on board a means of transport;
- DSE mainly intended for public use;
- portable systems not in prolonged use;
- calculators, cash registers or other equipment with small displays;
- window typewriters.

## Assessment of workstations and reduction of risk

**12.4** *Regulation 2* requires employers to perform a 'suitable and sufficient' analysis of all workstations which are:

- used for their purposes by 'users';
- provided by them and used for their purpose by 'operators';

to assess the health and safety risks in consequence of that use. They must then reduce the risks identified to the lowest level reasonably practicable. As for other types of assessments, an assessment must be reviewed if there is reason to suspect it is no longer valid or there have been significant changes. Further guidance on assessment, including an assessment checklist, is provided later in the chapter.

## Requirements for workstations

**12.5** *Regulation 3* states that all workstations which may be used by 'users' or 'operators' must meet the requirements laid down in the

Schedule to the Regulations. (Workstations first put into service prior to 1 January 1993 were given until 31 December 1996 to meet the requirements). The requirement must be relevant in relation to the health, safety and welfare of workers – for example there is no need to provide a document holder (referred to in the Schedule) if there is little or no inputting from documents.

## Daily work routine of users

**12.6** Employers are required by *Regulation 4* to plan the activities of 'users' so that their DSE work is periodically interrupted by breaks or changes of activity. Breaks should be taken before the onset of fatigue and preferably away from the screen. It is best if users are given some discretion in planning their work and are able to arrange breaks informally rather than having formal breaks at regular intervals.

## Eyes and eyesight

**12.7** *Regulation 5* gives 'users' the right (at their employer's expense) to an appropriate eye and eyesight test by a competent person before becoming a 'user' and at regular intervals thereafter. (Some employers are re-testing at two yearly to five yearly intervals – in some cases varying the period depending on the age of the employee. Professional advice should be sought in cases of doubt). They are also entitled to tests on experiencing visual difficulties which may reasonably be considered to be caused by DSE work. Such tests are an entitlement for 'users' and are not compulsory.

Tests are normally carried out by opticians and involve a test of vision and an examination of the eye. Where companies have vision screening facilities, 'users' may opt for a screening test to see if a full eye test is needed. If the eye test shows a need for spectacles (other than the 'user's' normal spectacles) the basic cost of these must be met by the employer, but employees must pay for extras eg designer frames or tinted lenses.

## Provision of training

**12.8** 'Users' are required by *Regulation 6* to be provided with adequate health and safety training in the use of any workstation upon which they may be required to work. Training may also be required where workstations are substantially modified. The training should include:

- the causes of DSE-related problems eg poor posture, screen reflections;
- the user's role in recognising risks;

- the importance of comfortable posture and postural change;
- equipment adjustment mechanisms eg chairs, contrast, brightness;
- use and arrangement of workstation components;
- the need for regular screen cleaning;
- the need to take breaks and changes of activity;
- arrangements for reporting problems;
- information about the Regulations (especially sight tests and breaks);
- the user's role in assessments.

The HSE have published a leaflet (REF. 2) which provides a useful reference for training purposes.

### Provision of information

**12.9** *Regulation 7* requires employers to ensure that operators and users at work within their undertaking are provided with adequate information. The table below shows the responsibility of the 'host' employer in this respect (and also gives a good guide to his responsibilities generally under the Regulations).

| The 'host' employer must inform on: | Regulation: | Own users: | Other users (Agency Staff): | Operators (Self-employed): |
|---|---|---|---|---|
| Dse/Workstation Risks | | YES | YES | YES |
| Risk Assessment and Reduction | 2 and 3 | YES | YES | YES |
| Breaks and Activity Changes | 4 | YES | YES | NO |
| Eye and Eyesight Tests | 5 | YES | NO | NO |
| Initial Training | 6(1) | YES | NO | NO |
| Training when Workstation Substantially Modified | 6(2) | YES | YES | NO |

## *Planning and preparation*

### Who will carry out the assessments?

**12.10** As with other types of assessments, DSE workstation assessments within an organisation may be carried out by an individual or by members of an assessment team. Those responsible for making assessments should have received appropriate training so that they are familiar with the requirements of the Regulations and they should have the ability to:

- assess risks from the workstation and the kind of work;
- use additional sources of information or expertise as appropriate (recognising their own limitations);

- draw valid and reliable conclusions;
- make a clear record and communicate the findings to those who need to take action.

They may be health and safety specialists, IT managers or line managers, and there will often be benefits in involving employees' safety representatives in the assessment process.

## How will the assessments be organised?

### *Identify the 'users'*

**12.11** An important first step is to identify the users' (together with any 'operators') of display screen equipment within the organisation. The definitions in *Regulation 1* refer to habitual use of DSE. The HSE guidance booklet (REF. 1) provides considerable advice on the factors which must be taken into account, of which time spent using DSE is the most significant. Some organisations have adopted a rule of thumb that anyone spending more than 50% of their time in DSE work is a DSE 'user'. However, the HSE guidance indicates that a less simplistic approach should be taken.

The checklists provided later in the chapter include reference to the other factors which the HSE state should be taken into account in deciding whether an individual is a 'user' or an 'operator'. It should be noted that employers have duties to assess workstations used for the purposes of their undertaking by *all* 'users' or 'operators'. This includes 'users' employed by others (eg agency-employed staff), 'operators' (eg self-employed draughtsmen or journalists), peripatetic staff (eg journalists, sales staff, careers advisors) and homeworkers.

In practice, most employers have not found it too difficult to decide who their 'users' and 'operators' are. Many have taken the approach of assessing the workstations of those individuals where doubt exists and, if necessary, making a final decision then. More time and expense can often be wasted debating a few borderline cases than would be involved in including them in the definition.

### *Decide on the assessment approach*

Most of the author's practical experience of assessment work has involved his personal assessment of each individual 'user's' or 'operator's' workstation, using a simple checklist (a completed example of this checklist is provided later in the chapter). Many others have taken a similar approach to assessments.

However, in some organisations the number of DSE workstations may be so large that this approach would either be impracticable or would require an unnecessarily large input of resources. In such cases the issuing of a self-assessment checklist to identified 'users' will often be more appropriate. (A sample checklist, together with guidance to 'users' on its completion, is provided later in the chapter). In the author's view the issue of such checklists would not in its own right fully satisfy the requirements of the Regulations. It should be supported by other actions such as:

- an inspection of areas where DSE workstations are situated (evaluating general issues such as lighting, blinds, housekeeping, desk space and the standards of chairs and DSE hardware);
- providing employees with the option of an assessment of their individual workstation by a specialist;
- responding promptly to problems identified in the completed checklists.

## *Making the assessments*

### Observations

**12.12** Where workstations are to be assessed on an individual basis the assessment checklist questions are intended to identify the principal factors that the assessor(s) need to look out for (as illustrated in the completed example).

Some of the more common problems identified are related to:

- Posture:
  - height of screen;
  - height of seat or position of backrest;
  - position of keyboard or keyboard technique;
  - need for footrest or document holder.
- Vision:
  - angle of screen;
  - position of lights or need for diffusers;

- need for blinds to control sunlight;
- adjustment of brightness or contrast controls.

## Discussions

**12.13** One of the dangers of self-assessments is that a minority of employees will blame their DSE work for a variety of problems from flat feet to halitosis. An individual assessment provides an opportunity for a two-way dialogue between the assessor(s) and the 'user' and allows the assessor to evaluate whether stated problems are related to deficiencies in the workstation.

Common causes of problems are:

- Back, shoulders, neck;
  - height or position of screen;
  - positioning of seat;
  - need for footrest or document holder.
- Hands, wrists, arms;
  - position of keyboard;
  - keyboard technique.
- Tired eyes or headaches;
  - failure to take breaks or change activities;
  - reflected light (artificial or sunlight).
- Discussions with 'users' can also reveal other important pieces of information, eg;
  - there are problems with sunlight at certain times of day or periods of the year;
  - the 'user' does not know how to adjust their chair or brightness/contrast controls;
  - the 'user's' chair is broken and incapable of being adjusted;
  - the 'user' has never been offered an eye test.

## Assessment records

**12.14** As for other types of assessment, there is no standard format for DSE workstation assessment records. The completed sample assessment checklist and the self-assessment checklist (both below), together with the guidance on its completion are offered as examples of record formats that have been found successful in practice.

The HSE guidance booklet (REF. 1) states that records may be stored in electronic as well as paper form. Self-assessment checklists would particularly lend themselves to being completed and submitted electronically. No guidance is provided on how long records should be kept. Prudent employers may prefer to retain them indefinitely, bearing in mind that civil claims for alleged DSE-related conditions may be submitted many years after it is claimed the condition was first initiated.

## Display screen equipment workstation assessment

USER'S NAME: *Caroline Smith* LOCATION: *Accounts*

| FACTOR | | COMMENT |
|---|---|---|
| 1 | WORK PATTERNS | |
| 1.1 | Most time spent per day at DSE | *6 Hours* |
| 1.2 | Average time per day at DSE | *4–5 Hours* |
| 1.3 | Number of days per week at DSE | *5* |
| 1.4 | Longest spell without break | *1–2 Hours* |
| 1.5 | Can breaks be taken? | *YES – at Caroline's discretion* |
| 1.6 | Concentration important? | *Fairly Important – Accuracy* |
| 1.7 | Speed of operation important? | *NO* |
| 'USER' STATUS CONFIRMED | | *Yes/No* |
| 2 | PROBLEMS EXPERIENCED<br>Has the user significant experience of problems with: | |
| 2.1 | Back, shoulders or neck | *Pains in shoulder and neck* |
| 2.2 | Hands wrists or arms | *None* |
| 2.3 | Tired eyes or headaches | *Occasionally* |
| 2.4 | Suitability of software | *No problems* |
| 2.5 | Other problems | *None* |
| 3 | LIGHTING/ENVIRONMENT | |
| 3.1 | Artificial Lighting: Adequate to see documents | *YES* |
| | Any reflection or glare problems | *Some reflection from striplight (diffuser fitted)* |
| 3.2 | Sunlight: Any reflection or glare problems | *In mornings from window behind.* |
| | Suitable blinds available (if necessary) | *Good vertical blinds provided* |
| 3.3 | Noise: Hindering to communication | |
| | Distracting or stressful | *No problems* |
| 3.4 | Temperature & ventilation: Satisfactory in summer and winter | *Office hot and stuffy in summer* |
| 4 | SCREEN | |
| 4.1 | Set at suitable height | *Screen too low* |
| 4.2 | Stable Image with clear characters | *Good. Able to vary colours* |
| 4.3 | Brightness and contrast adjustable | *Both have adjustable controls* |
| 4.4 | Swivels and tilts easily | *YES* |
| 4.5 | Cleaning materials available | *In stationery store* |
| 5 | KEYBOARD | |
| 5.1 | Separate and tiltable | *YES* |
| 5.2 | Sufficient space in front | *Too near edge of desk* |
| 5.3 | Keys clearly visible | *YES* |

| 6 | DESK AND CHAIR | |
|---|---|---|
| 6.1 | Desk size adequate | *Satisfactory* |
| 6.2 | Sufficient leg room | *Materials being stored in desk well* |
| 6.3 | Desk surface low reflectance | *YES – wooden surface* |
| 6.4 | Suitable document holder (if required) | *Not available* |
| 6.5 | Chair comfortable and stable | *YES* |
| 6.6 | Chair height adjustable | *YES* |
| 6.7 | Back adjustable (height and tilt) | *Adjustment not working* |
| 6.8 | Footrest available (if required) | *Not required* |

OTHER COMMENTS
*Caroline was advised to take short breaks more frequently.*
*Some lengthy jobs seem to be the cause of her tired eyes and headaches.*
*Repositioning of the screen and provision of a document holder should overcome the shoulder and neck problems.*

| No. | Actions required | Responsibility |
|---|---|---|
| 3.1 | Modify screen position to avoid light reflection. | *C Smith* |
| 3.2 | Close blinds when sunlight bright. | *C Smith* |
| 3.4 | Free up seized office windows. | *Office Manager* |
| 4.1 | Provide screen stand and keep top of screen at eye level. | *Office Manager/C Smith* |
| 5.2 | Keep wrist resting space in front of keyboard. | *C Smith* |
| 6.2 | Remove items from desk well. | *C Smith* |
| 6.4 | Provide document holder. | *Office Manager* |
| 6.7 | Repair chair back adjustment. | *Office Manager* |

Assessor's name: *C Moore* Signature: *C Moore* Date: *14/5/99*

PROGRESS WITH ACTIONS
All recommendations acted upon although Caroline needs to remember to close the blinds on sunny days. No more problems with shoulders/neck or tired eyes/headaches.
*C Moore 15/7/99*

Planned date for assessment review: July 2001

| DISPLAY SCREEN EQUIPMENT WORKSTATION<br>SELF ASSESSMENT CHECKLIST<br>USER'S NAME: LOCATION: | | |
|---|---|---|
| 1 | LIGHTING AND WORK ENVIRONMENT | COMMENTS |
| 1.1<br>1.2<br><br>1.3<br><br>1.4<br>1.5 | Is artificial lighting adequate?<br>Does it cause any reflection or glare problems?<br>Any reflection or glare problems from sunlight?<br>Are suitable blinds available (if necessary)?<br>Are temperature and ventilation satisfactory in summer and winter? | |
| 2 | SCREEN AND KEYBOARD | |
| 2.1<br>2.2<br>2.3<br>2.4<br>2.5<br>2.6<br>2.7 | Is your screen set at a suitable height?<br>Stable image with clear characters?<br>Brightness and contrast adjustable?<br>Screen swivels and tilts easily?<br>Cleaning materials available?<br>Is your keyboard tiltable?<br>Have you sufficient space in front of it? | |
| 3 | DESK AND CHAIR | |
| 3.1<br>3.2<br>3.3<br><br>3.4<br>3.5<br>3.6<br><br>3.7 | Is your desk size adequate?<br>Is there sufficient leg room under it?<br>Do you have a suitable document holder (if required)?<br>Is your chair comfortable and stable?<br>Can you adjust your seat height?<br>Can you adjust the height and tilt of your chair back?<br>Do you have a footrest (if required)? | |
| 4 | HAVE YOU HAD SIGNIFICANT EXPERIENCE OF PROBLEMS WITH: | |
| 4.1<br>4.2<br>4.3<br>4.4<br>4.5 | Your back, shoulders or neck?<br>Your hands, wrists or arms?<br>Tired eyes or headaches?<br>The suitability of the software you use?<br>Other problems? | |

| ANY OTHER PROBLEMS OR COMMENTS? |
|---|
| WOULD YOU LIKE YOUR WORKSTATION TO BE ASSESSED BY A SPECIALIST ? Yes/No |
| Signature: Date: |

# GUIDANCE ON COMPLETING THE DSE WORKSTATION SELF-ASSESSMENT

## Lighting and work environment

1.1 Artificial lighting should be adequate to see all the documents you work with.

1.2 Recessed lights with diffusers shouldn't cause problems. Lights suspended from ceilings might.

1.3 There may be problems in the early morning or afternoon, especially in winter when the sun is low.

1.4 Blinds provided should be effective in eliminating glare from the sun.

1.5 Strong sunlight may create significant thermal gain at times.

## Screen and keyboard

2.1 The top of your screen should normally be level with your eyes when you are sitting in a comfortable position.

2.2 There should be little or no flicker on your screen.

2.3 You should know where the brightness and contrast controls are.

2.4 The screen should swivel and tilt so that you can avoid reflections.

2.5 You should know where to get cleaning items for your screen (and keyboard, if necessary).

2.6 Small legs at the back of your keyboard should allow you to adjust its angle.

2.7 Space in front the keyboard allows you to rest your hands and wrists when not keying in.

## Desk and chair

3.1 Your desk should have sufficient space to allow you to have your screen and keyboard in a comfortable position and accommodate documents, document holder, phone etc.

3.2 There should be enough space under the desk to allow you to move your legs freely.

3.3 If you are inputting from documents, using a document holder helps avoid frequent neck movements.

3.4 Chairs with castors must have at least five (four is very unstable).

3.5 You should be able to adjust your seat height to work in a comfortable position (arms approx. horizontal and eyes level with the top of the screen).

3.6 The angle and height of your back support should be adjustable so that it provides a comfortable working position.

3.7 DSE users who are shorter may need a footrest to help them keep comfortable when sitting at the right height for their keyboard and screen (see 3.5).

## Possible problems

4.1 Problems with back, shoulders or neck might indicate your screen is at the wrong height, an incorrectly adjusted chair or need for a document holder.

4.2 Problems with hands, wrists or arms might indicate incorrect positioning of the keyboard or a poor keying technique. Hands should not be bent up at the wrist and a soft touch should be used on the keyboard, not overstretching the fingers.

4.3 Tired eyes or headaches could indicate problems with lighting, glare or reflections.

They may also indicate the need to take regular breaks away from the screen. Persistent problems might need an eye test – contact Human Resources to request one.

4.4 The software should be suitable for the work you have to do.

IF YOU HAVE A PROBLEM OR WOULD LIKE A SECOND OPINION, WE CAN ARRANGE FOR A SPECIALIST TO COME TO ASSESS YOUR WORKSTATION

## *After the assessment*

### Review and implementation of recommendations

**12.15** The general guidance provided in CHAPTER 4: CARRYING OUT RISK ASSESSMENTS is equally applicable to recommendations made as a result of DSE workstation assessments. It should be noted that the sample assessment checklist includes a space which can be used at a follow-up of an assessment to describe 'Progress with actions'.

### Assessment review/re-assessments

**12.16** Changes to the layout of office accommodation often take place with bewildering rapidity. Some of these changes have significant implications for DSE workstations, others do not. To carry out a re-assessment every time the office layout is changed would be an inefficient use of resources.

A better approach is to make both management and DSE 'users' aware that a review or reassessment should be requested from the assessor or assessment team whenever significant changes take place. This can be supported by observations by the assessor(s) of changes which have occurred or are in progress.

Because of the frequency of changes a periodic review of DSE workstation assessments would be beneficial. The HSE do not provide any guidance on this aspect. Reviews at two yearly intervals may be appropriate for larger workplaces where changes are regularly taking place whilst five yearly intervals would probably be suitable for smaller workplaces where the layout of workstations is more static.

## *References*

### HSE publications

**12.17**



| | | |
|---|---|---|
| 1 | L26: | Display screen equipment work. *Health and Safety (Display Screen Equipment) Regulations* 1992. Guidance on Regulations (1992). |
| 2 | INDG 36: | Working with VDUs (1998) – priced pack of leaflets. |
| 3 | | VDUs: An easy guide to the Regulations |

# 13 Assessment of Personal Protective Equipment ('PPE') requirements



## *Introduction*

**13.1** The *Personal Protective Equipment at Work Regulations 1992* ('the *PPE Regulations*') replaced much outdated law on PPE. Unlike many of the previous Regulations (which often only applied to limited processes or activities), these Regulations require an assessment of the PPE needs, whatever the work activity. If the assessment shows PPE is necessary then the employer must provide it, maintain it, instruct and train employees in its use, and take reasonable steps to ensure that they do use it. The self-employed are also covered by the Regulations.

However, several other sets of Regulations also contain important PPE requirements. They include:

- the *Control of Lead at Work Regulations 1998*;

- the *Ionising Radiations Regulations 1999*;
- the *Control of Asbestos at Work Regulations 1987*;
- the *Construction (Head Protection) Regulations 1989*;
- the *Noise at Work Regulations 1989*;
- the *Control of Substances Hazardous to Health Regulations 1999.*

## The Regulations summarised

### PPE defined

**13.2** PPE is defined in *Regulation 2* of the *PPE Regulations* as,

> 'all equipment (including clothing affording protection against the weather) which is intended to be worn or held by a person at work and which protects him against one or more risks to his health or safety'.

This might include safety helmets, eye protection, safety footwear, gloves, high visibility clothing etc. Waterproof, weatherproof or insulated clothing is subject to the Regulations if it is needed to protect employees against health and safety risks, but not otherwise.

Under *Regulation 3* certain types of equipment are excluded from the application of the Regulations, including ordinary working clothes and uniforms (not specifically giving protection), self defence or deterrent equipment (eg panic alarms) and portable devices for detecting and signalling risks and nuisances (eg gas monitors).

### Assessment of PPE Requirements

**13.3** Under *Regulation 3* of the *Management of Health and Safety at Work Regulations 1999* ('the *Management Regulations*'), employers must have made an assessment of the risks to their employees' health and safety whilst at work, in order to identify the most appropriate way of reducing those risks to an acceptable level. *Regulation 4* of the *PPE Regulations* requires that PPE is only chosen as the last resort ie after such measures as elimination at source, engineering controls or safe systems of work. If the risk cannot be adequately controlled by such other means then the employer must provide employees with suitable PPE free of charge. This PPE must be readily available. Whilst much PPE is provided on a personal basis, in some circumstances PPE may be shared.

The Regulations refer to many factors which should be considered when selecting suitable PPE.

The PPE must:

- be appropriate for the risks and the conditions;
- take account of ergonomic requirements and the wearer's state of health;
- be capable of adjustment to fit correctly;
- prevent or adequately control the risk, without increasing overall risk;
- comply with appropriate standards (normally bearing the CE mark);
- be compatible with other types of PPE being used (*Regulation 5* refers).

*Regulation 6* requires the employer to ensure that an assessment is made in respect of PPE needs. This must include:

- identifying risks not avoided by other means;
- defining the characteristics required of the PPE;
- comparing these with the characteristics of PPE available.

In simple and obvious cases the assessment need not be recorded. In more complex cases it must be recorded and kept readily available. It may be incorporated within the general risk assessment required by the *Management Regulations* (Some of the sample assessment records in CHAPTER 5: ASSESSMENT RECORDS refer to PPE requirements). Examples of specific PPE assessment records are also provided later in this chapter. Assessments must be reviewed if it is suspected they are no longer valid or in the event of significant changes taking place.

## Maintenance, replacement and accommodation

**13.4** *Regulation 7* states that employers must ensure that PPE is maintained in an efficient state, efficient working order and in good repair. Depending upon the type of PPE and its circumstances of use, this might require specific arrangements to be made for its cleaning, disinfecting, inspection, examination, testing or repair. Responsibility for this maintenance should be clearly identified.

Some tasks could be given to the user but more complex work may require specially trained personnel. Records should be kept, where appropriate. In most cases it will be sufficient to follow manufacturers' instructions. Some types of PPE may need to be replaced periodically eg many manufacturers recommend replacing safety helmets at least every five years.

*Regulation 8* requires appropriate accommodation to be provided for PPE when it is not being used. This will vary according to the type of PPE – pegs (for helmets or weatherproof clothing), carrying cases (for safety spectacles), lockers, containers etc. Storage accommodation may need to protect the PPE from contamination, damage or loss. Where PPE may become contaminated in use, it must be kept separate from other clothing and equipment.

## Ensuring that PPE is used properly

**13.5** *Regulation 9* states that employees must be given adequate and appropriate information, instruction and training on PPE they are required to use, including:

- why and when it must be used (this might include providing relevant signs);
- how to use it, and its limitations;
- arrangements for its maintenance and/or replacement.

For some PPE, correct fitting or adjustment may be necessary. Practical training as well as theoretical instruction will be required in some cases.

### *Employers*

Employers have a clear duty under *Regulation 10* to take all reasonable steps to ensure that PPE is properly used by employees. This will normally involve taking a pro-active approach to policing standards of compliance.

### *Employees*

Employees also have duties under *Regulation 11*:

- to use PPE in accordance with their training and instruction;
- to return PPE after use to the accommodation provided;
- to immediately report loss of or obvious defect in their PPE.

## PPE assessment in practice

### What PPE may be required

**13.6** The HSE Guidance accompanying the Regulations (REF. 1) gives much detailed advice on what types of PPE are likely to be necessary to protect against many common types of risk. Further guidance is included in other HSE publications, some of which have been listed in the reference section of this chapter.

The main types to be considered are:

#### *Head protection*

Safety helmets are necessary whenever there is significant risk from falling objects or impact with fixed objects. Other types of head protection which may be appropriate are bump caps (providing limited impact protection), caps or hairnets (protecting against scalping or entanglement) and crash helmets (for use on certain types of transport eg all-terrain vehicles).

#### *Eye protection*

Activities and processes involving risks to the face and eyes include:

- contact with acids, alkalis and corrosive or irritant substances;
- work with power-driven tools creating chippings etc;
- work with molten metal and other molten substances;
- welding or burning operations and other activities producing intense light or other significant optical radiation;
- use of liquid, gas or vapour under pressure.

The type of eye protection chosen will depend on the nature of the risk and the circumstances of use. Types available include safety spectacles, goggles, eyeshields and visors.

#### *Foot protection*

Safety boots or shoes are necessary for any situation where there is risk from items falling onto the feet or from penetration through the soles or heels of footwear. They are likely to be required for construction, maintenance and warehouse work and heavier industrial processes. Work with hot metal is likely to require the use of foundry boots with quick release fastenings and without external features such as laces which could trap molten metal. Wellington boots may also be necessary for some activities or external locations.

### *Hand and arm protection*

Gloves or gauntlets are necessary for protection against:

- cuts and abrasions;
- extremes of temperature;
- skin irritation and dermatitis;
- contact with toxic or corrosive liquids;
- molten metal.

The choice of glove material is important as it must be capable of protecting against the risk (or a combination of risks) but should also be comfortable for the wearer and compatible with the work being done.

### *Body protection*

Types of body protection which may be necessary include:

- Overall and aprons – to protect against hazardous substances, welding spatter etc;
- Outdoor clothing – providing protection against cold, rain etc;
- High visibility clothing – for work on or close to roadways or mobile plant;
- Specialist clothing – eg for work with chain-saws;
- Life jackets or buoyancy aids – for work close to water;
- Harnesses or fall arrestors – for some types of work at height;
- Molten metal clothing – for work at furnaces etc (this may also need to protect against radiant heat).

### *Respiratory protection*

See CHAPTER 9: COSHH ASSESSMENTS dealing with COSHH assessments.

### *Hearing protection*

See CHAPTER 10: NOISE ASSESSMENTS dealing with noise assessments.

(These last two types of PPE are not subject to the *PPE at Work Regulations* but are included for completeness).

Once the risk has been identified through the assessment process there is a wide range of British Standards and European Standards which can be consulted to select the most appropriate type of PPE. Many suppliers will provide well-illustrated catalogues to aid in the selection process and their technical staff can provide more detailed guidance if required.

## Carrying out assessments

**13.7** Personal protective equipment needs should really be identified during other types of risk assessment – as described elsewhere in this book.

- General risk assessments – The need for head, eye, foot, hand/arm or body protection;
- Manual handling assessments – The need for hand/arm protection and also possibly for foot and body protection;
- COSHH assessments – The need for respiratory, hand/arm, eye and body protection and occasionally also foot protection;
- Noise assessments – The need for hearing protection.

However, some employers may prefer to carry out a separate review of their PPE requirements and arrangements in order to ensure that:

- no PPE needs have been overlooked;
- suitable PPE is available to meet those needs;
- employees are fully aware of PPE requirements and know how to obtain it and use it;
- suitable arrangements for maintaining and storing PPE are in place;
- signs are in place indicating PPE requirements, where appropriate;
- PPE requirements are actually being complied with.

It may also be the case that an employer becomes aware that other risk assessments are either inadequate or out of date. Such an employer may wish to carry out a review of PPE needs in the short term, prior to carrying out a more comprehensive and lengthier risk assessment programme.

Individuals or team members carrying out assessments of PPE needs are likely to be similar to those carrying out general risk assessments (as described in CHAPTER 4: CARRYING OUT RISK ASSESSMENTS). As well as having the qualities referred to in that chapter, they should also have a practical working knowledge of the requirements of the *PPE at Work Regulations*. Where PPE assessments are carried out separately the methodology will be similar to that described for other types of assessments ie:

- planning and preparation (including reference to HSE material and other relevant sources of information);
- assessment in the workplace (including observations and discussions with workpeople);
- the review and implementation of recommendations;
- subsequent review of the assessments (if suspected to be no longer valid or in the event of significant change).

## Assessment records

**13.8** As stated earlier and demonstrated in CHAPTER 5: ASSESSMENT RECORDS and elsewhere, PPE requirements can be incorporated within general risk assessment records or the records kept in relation to more specific risk assessment requirements (eg manual handling , COSHH, noise). The last sample record included in CHAPTER 5: ASSESSMENT RECORDS shows how PPE requirements can be included in comprehensive operating procedures, which also detail other health and safety precautions that are required.

However, many employers also choose to list PPE requirements separately for a variety of reasons which include:

- As an aid in communicating PPE requirements to employees (particularly during induction training);
- As a clear reference point to assist in the enforcement of PPE rules;
- As a demonstration to others (HSE Inspectors, clients, main contractors) that the employer has carried out a thorough PPE assessment.

Some examples of this type of PPE assessment record follow. These relate to:

- The manufacture of pre-stressed concrete beams (the same process referred to in the final example in CHAPTER 5: ASSESSMENT RECORDS);
- Maintenance activities in a newspaper printing plant;
- The erection of timber framed structures on building sites.

In each of these examples no differentiation has been made between PPE required under the *PPE at Work Regulations* and that required to comply with Manual Handling Operations, COSHH or *Noise at Work Regulations*.

# *Manufacture of pre-stressed concrete beams*

## Personal Protective Equipment Requirements

**13.9**

| TYPE OF PPE | MUST BE USED IN THESE LOCATIONS OR FOR THESE ACTIVITIES |
|---|---|
| Safety footwear: | |
| Safety boots, shoes or wellington boots | By all operatives at all times.<br>By anyone else directly involved in the manufacturing process or the stacking of beams. |
| Eye protection: | |
| Face visor or goggles | Using a Stihl saw or electric saw.<br>Cutting wires under tension.<br>Using an airline to clean the moulds. |
| Hearing protection: | |
| Ear muffs or ear plugs | Using a Stihl saw or electric saw to cut wires or concrete.<br>(and by anyone working in the immediate vicinity)<br>Using an airline to clean the moulds.<br>(Use of hearing protection is recommended when the vibrating beam is operating nearby.) |
| Dust masks: | |
| Disposable masks for nuisance dusts | Using a Stihl saw or electric saw to cut out spacers or to cut beams. |
| Gloves: | |
| | Using a Stihl saw or electric saw.<br>Placing wooden spacers under or on top of beams.<br>Turning beams.<br>Repositioning beams on the fork lift truck.<br>Spraying moulds with releasing oil.<br>Pulling the locator bar.<br>Raking, cleaning and smoothing concrete. |

# *Newspaper Printing*

## Personal Protective Equipment Requirements

**13.10**

| **Section: Maintenance** | | |
|---|---|---|
| **PPE normally required (to be worn at all times when working in operational areas):** | | |
| • | Safety footwear | |
| • | Two piece suit | |
| **PPE required for specific activities or locations:** | | |
| • | When using most power tools or workshop machinery ( inc. grinding, drilling, milling, turning): | Eye protection (goggles or safety spectacles) |
| • | When blowing down with compressed air: | Eye protection (goggles or safety spectacles)<br>Dust mask (if significant dust likely) |
| • | When burning or welding: | Visor or goggles (with appropriate shade of filter)<br>Leather gauntlets or gloves |
| • | When working on the press solvent system: | Solvent resistant gloves (at all times)<br>*Eye protection (goggles or safety spectacles)<br>*Protective suits (unless exposure to solvent is minimal)<br>*Respirators suitable for solvent vapours<br>(*unless exposure to solvent is minimal) |
| • | When working on the press fount spray system | Chemical resistant gloves are recommended |
| • | When handling rough materials or equipment | General purpose gloves |
| • | When working in designated hearing protection zones | Hearing protection (muffs, plugs on bands, disposable plugs) |
| • | EMPLOYEES MUST:<br>❍ use PPE as designated above;<br>❍ take care of PPE which is in their care;<br>❍ obtain replacements of PPE which has been damaged or lost;<br>❍ report to management any difficulties in obtaining suitable PPE. | |

## *Erection of timber-framed structures on building sites*

### Personal protective equipment (PPE) standards

All staff carrying out erecting work on site must conform to the PPE Standards set out in the table below. Specific activities or specific sites may require additional PPE to be provided and used as necessary.

| TYPE OF PPE | REQUIREMENTS |
|---|---|
| Safety footwear | At all times when working on sites. |
| Safety helmet | At all times when working on sites. |
| Eye protection (safety glasses or goggles) | When using nail guns or powered woodworking machines.<br>When using timber treatment chemicals. |
| Hearing protection | When using nail guns or powered woodworking machines. |
| Gloves (a suitable type) | When handling rough materials.<br>When using timber treatment chemicals. |
| Waterproof clothing | If work is carried out in rain, hail or snow. |
| High visibility clothing | Work in the vicinity of lifting operations.<br>If required by the Principal Contractor or Client. |

Staff supervising site activities must ensure that all staff comply with these standards. (Individual employees and subcontractors also have legal duties to comply with PPE requirements).

## *References*

### (HSE publications)

**13.12**


| | | |
|---|---|---|
| 1 | L 25: | Personal Protective Equipment at Work. *Personal Protective Equipment at Work Regulations 1992. Guidance on Regulations (1992).* |
| 2 | INDG 174: | *A Short Guide to the Personal Protective Equipment at Work Regulations 1992* (1995)(Free leaflet). |
| 3 | APIS 1: | *PPE, High visibility clothing for airport workers* (1994) (Free leaflet). |
| 4 | HSG 150: | *Health and Safety in Construction (1996)* – pages 80–82. |

# 14 Fire risk assessment

**In this chapter:**

## Introduction

**14.1** The *Fire Precautions (Workplace) Regulations 1997* came into force on 1 December 1997, rather belatedly implementing fire safety provisions contained in the European Framework and Workplace Directives. Whilst in the long term the Regulations should undoubtedly have beneficial effects, they have added further complexity to what was already a confusing picture on workplace fire safety. There are many who believe that a wholesale revision of legislation in this area is long overdue.

The Regulations introduced an amendment to the *Management Regulations 1992*, making it explicit that a risk assessment of fire provisions must be carried out by all employers. This amendment with other fire-related amendments were incorporated into the *Management Regulations 1999.*

## An outline of workplace fire safety legislation

### Fire Precautions (Workplace) Regulations 1997

**14.2** These Regulations (which for brevity will be referred to as the Fire Regulations) as well as containing the requirement for fire risk assessments also introduced some specific requirements in respect of workplaces which were not already subject to the *Fire Precautions Act 1997* or other fire safety legislation. These related to:

- Fire-fighting and fire detection (*Regulation 4*).
- Emergency routes and exits (*Regulation 5*).
- Maintenance of fire equipment and devices (*Regulation 6*).

Each of these topics will be examined in greater detail later in the chapter under the heading 'Fire Risk Assessment Factors'. (It is perhaps illustrative of the complex nature of fire safety legislation that only 3 out of 22 Regulations in the *Fire Regulations 1997* relate to specific fire topics – the remainder refer to amendments, enforcement, application and other administrational matters!)

### Fire Precautions Act 1971

**14.3** Employers must apply for a Fire Certificate under this Act if:

- more than 20 people work on the premises at any one time;
- more than 10 work on other than the ground floor at any one time;

- explosive or highly flammable materials are stored or used on the premises.

For buildings in multiple occupancy the total number of people at work is the operative figure. Certificates are also required under the Act for larger hotels and boarding houses.

The *Fire Certificates (Special Premises) Regulations 1976* also define premises requiring a Fire Certificate, based on the storage and use of specified quantities of hazardous substances or the existence of certain hazardous activities.

## Other licensing, registration and approval requirements

### *The Explosives Act 1875*

**14.4** Explosive manufacturing facilities and large explosives stores must be licensed by the HSE. Smaller stores are licensed by or registered with local authorities. Licensing conditions usually include fire safety requirements.

### *Local authority licensing*

Various work related activities require licences from the local authority or licensing magistrates whose licensing conditions can include fire safety requirements. Typical activities requiring such licences are:

- the sale of alcohol;
- music and dancing;
- theatrical performances, showing of films and other types of public entertainment;
- gambling;
- certain sporting activities.

### *Registration schemes*

Some uses of premises must be registered with local authorities or other official bodies who may require fire safety precautions as a condition of registration. These registration schemes may include:

- nursing and residential care homes;

- childrens' homes;
- independent schools;
- child care activities.

### *Building Regulations*

The Building Regulations apply to new buildings, extensions or material alterations to existing buildings or to material changes of use of buildings. The Regulations include fire safety requirements which are enforced by local building control authorities or similar bodies.

## Related legal duties

**14.5** Various other legal duties interrelate to fire safety requirements–

- *Highly Flammable Liquids and Liquefied Petroleum Gas Regulations 1972* – These Regulations apply to the storage and use of highly flammable substances.
- *Control of Major Accident Hazardous Regulations 1999* (COMAH) – The *COMAH Regulations* apply where specified quantities of dangerous substances are present. They require the preparation of a Major Accident Prevention Policy, dealing with risks both inside and outside the premises.
- *Confined Spaces Regulations 1997* – The Regulations require entry into confined spaces (which may involve fire or explosion risks) to be in accordance with a safe system of work. Arrangements must also be in place to deal with possible emergencies, including fires either inside or outside the confined space.
- *Health and Safety at Work etc Act 1974 ('HASAWA 1974')* – The general requirements of *HASAWA 1974* will apply to fire issues associated with work processes and activities, as opposed to work premises.
- *Management of Health and Safety at Work Regulations 1999* – Various requirements of the *Management Regulations* are of particular relevance to fire safety precautions, including those relating to–
    - establishing procedures for serious and imminent danger (*Regulation 8*)
    - ensuring contacts with external services (*Regulation 9*)
    - providing information for employees (*Regulation 10*)

- co-operating and co-ordinating with other employers (*Regulation 11*)
- providing information to other employers and their employees working in your undertaking (*Regulation 12*)

### Enforcement

**14.6** In general the local fire authority enforces the *Fire Regulations 1997*, the *Fire Precautions Act 1971* and the parts of the *Management Regulations* relating to general fire safety precautions.

The Health and Safety Executive (or the local authority if they enforce health and safety law generally in the workplace) enforce *HASAWA 1974*, the *Management Regulations* in respect of processes and work activities, and specific Regulations such as the *Highly Flammable liquids and liquefied Petroleum Gases Regulations 1972*, *COMAH 1999* and the *Confined Spaces Regulations 1997*. Where local authorities and others administer registration, licensing or approval systems they are likely to rely heavily on support from the fire authority or, to a lesser extent, the HSE.

The fire authorities are allowed to exempt premises from the certification requirements of the *Fire Precautions Act 1971* if they consider them to be of low risk. There is already evidence that some fire authorities are using this exemption power more readily and generally putting less emphasis on their fire certification role. This places much greater reliance on the fire risk assessments which must be carried out by employers – it will be interesting to see if this trend continues.

## *Planning and preparation*

### Who will carry out the assessment?

**14.7** Previous chapters of this book (particularly CHAPTER 4: CARRYING OUT RISK ASSESSMENTS) have reviewed whether assessments should be conducted by individuals or by assessment teams and also the possible composition of assessment teams. the qualities required by assessors will depend upon the size, complexity and fire risks of the workplace concerned. employers, managers or safety representatives without any specialist knowledge should be capable of dealing with small, low risk situations but more complex, higher risk premises will require a greater degree of knowledge and experience.

All those involved in the fire risk assessment (including experienced health and safety practitioners) can benefit from using the Home Office booklet *'Fire Safety: An employer's guide' Home Office/HMSO (1999)* (REF. 1). this booklet was published in conjunction with the hse and other government departments as a practical guide to compliance with fire legislation. it provides both an invaluable training resource for the inexperienced and a useful refresher and reference for those who already have some specialist knowledge.

## How will the assessment be organised?

**14.8** As for other types of assessment, it may be appropriate to divide the workplace into assessment units. However, the size of the units is likely to be larger than for general risk assessments. This is partly because only fire issues need to be considered as opposed to a multiplicity of types of risk. This is also likely as fire protection systems (fire detection, fire alarms, sprinklers, evacuation procedures) are usually integrated within large buildings.

However, there is no reason why fire issues cannot be dealt with during general risk assessments in each assessment unit (as described in CHAPTER 4: CARRYING OUT RISK ASSESSMENTS), with the fire protection systems then being assessed separately for the premises as a whole. if workplaces are divided into units purely for fire assessment, then the division may be on the basis of:

- separate buildings;
- major sections of buildings eg operational departments;
- separate floors.

It is also important that fire risks in all parts of the workplace are properly assessed. Areas which could be overlooked are:

- outbuildings such as boiler-houses or stores;
- basements or pits below equipment;
- overhead crane and similar control cabs;
- upper walkways and platforms;
- roof areas where provision is made for maintenance access;
- plant rooms;
- confined spaces to which access is made periodically.

(Fire safety in construction work is subject to separate requirements (see REF. 2)).

Where the workplace is in a shared building there will need to be liaison with other occupants and/or the landlord or managing agent. This liaison is particularly important where the landlord, the managing agent or a major occupier is responsible for fire protection systems eg fire detection or fire alarms.

## Gathering information

### *Fire certificate*

**14.9** The Fire Certificate, if one exists, will be a key document in the fire risk assessment, particularly if it is up to date. Assessors should be able to have some confidence that if a fully trained fire officer has considered the fire evacuation routes and fire protection systems to be good enough to issue the certificate, then they met relevant standards at the time of issue. However, the existence of the Fire Certificate only provides a valuable starting point. The assessor(s) will still need to:

- look for changes eg to premises, activities, materials used or stored;
- ensure that fire protection equipment is being inspected, maintained, tested (the Fire Certificate will usually specify standards for this); and
- evaluate the standards of fire prevention within the workplace.

In practice many Fire Certificates have been allowed to become considerably out of date due to the failure of employers to notify changes or failure of fire authorities to react to such notifications. The assessment may reveal the need for a new Fire Certificate – in which case the employer will need to liase closely with the fire authority, especially before making any major changes following recommendations resulting from the fire risk assessment.

### *Plans and drawings*

Where there is no Fire Certificate or the certificate is out of date, plans and drawings of the premises are extremely useful in carrying out the fire risk assessment. Even simple layout plans can be marked up to show the fire evacuation routes and the positions of detectors, alarm call points, alarm sounders, fire fighting equipment etc These marked up drawings can form an important part of the eventual assessment records. Detailed drawings which already show the positions of such equipment are a bonus (although the assessors(s) should always be alert for possible inaccuracies).

### Records

Records of maintenance, tests and inspections of fire protection systems will need to be examined as part of the assessment. These could be checked prior to or during the assessment. Such records might include those relating to:

- fire detection equipment (smoke and heat alarms);
- fire alarms;
- emergency lighting;
- fire fighting equipment (extinguishers, hose reels, sprinklers);
- fire evacuation drills.

### Reference material

Favourable comment was made earlier about the value of '*Fire Safety: An Employer's Guide*' (REF. 1) as a reference source for those carrying out fire risk assessments. there are many other sources of reference in respect of different types of premises, specialist fire risks or particular types of fire precautions. a range of these are listed in the reference section of this chapter but far more are available.

## Fire risk assessment factors

**14.10** '*Fire Safety: An Employer's Guide*' (REF. 1) provides detailed guidance on the various factors which should be taken into account when carrying out a fire risk assessment. it is not possible to provide the same level of detail in a book of this nature but this section includes reference to the principles to be followed and some of the key standards relating to:

- Fire detection.
- Fire warning.
- Fire escape routes.
- Evacuation procedures.
- Fire fighting.

- Fire prevention.
- Fire-related signs.

## Fire Detection

**14.11** *Regulation 4(1)(a)* of the *Fire Regulations 1997* requires workplaces to be equipped with fire detectors, where necessary, in order to safeguard the safety of employees in case of fire. However, this does not mean that every workplace must have automatic fire detection equipment. In many workplaces fires can be detected during working hours by observation and smell.

During the assessment consideration must be given to the possibility of fires starting in unoccupied areas and spreading. Even during working hours fires could develop undetected:

- in storage areas or storerooms;
- in plant rooms;
- in thinly populated work areas;
- during break times.

If such a fire could significantly endanger the safety of employees (eg by cutting off a single escape route) then some sort of fire detection equipment must be provided. Fire detectors may also be justified in order to prevent or reduce property damage – many insurers will insist upon its provision in certain areas.

The nature of any fire detection equipment will vary according to the extent and type of fire risk present.

### *Domestic smoke alarms*

Where the only escape route from a work area (eg an office or workshop) is through an unoccupied outer area (eg a storeroom) the provision of a single domestic smoke alarm may be appropriate. Such an alarm should conform with British Standard 5446: '*Components of automatic fire alarm systems for residential premises. Part 1: Specifications for self-contained smoke alarms and point-type smoke detectors*' (REF. 12).

### *Interlinked systems*

Similarly such domestic smoke alarms can be interlinked to provide protection in slightly more complex situations. However, higher risk workplaces will require more sophisticated and reliable detection systems conforming with British Standard 5839: '*Fire detection and alarm systems for buildings Part 1*' (REF. 13).

### *Types of detectors*

Basic domestic smoke detectors are usually more sensitive than those in more sophisticated systems, leading to a greater possibility of false alarms. In some workplaces it may be better to install heat detectors because smoke, fumes or dust from work activities would trigger off any type of smoke detector. Specialist advice should be sought before installing any automatic fire detection system or an interlinked system of smoke alarms. Most fire authorities are willing to provide such advice.

## Fire warning

**14.12** Workplaces must also be equipped with fire alarms, where necessary, in order to safeguard the safety of employees in case of fire. (*Regulation 4(1)(a)* of the *Fire Regulations 1997*). As for fire detection, the degree of sophistication should match the size of the workplace and the extent of the fire risk. In many small buildings or larger, but open workrooms, a shout of 'Fire' can be heard by everyone, including those who may be in restrooms, toilets or storerooms.

Slightly larger workplaces may justify the use of a manually operated sounder (eg a rotary gong) or the installation of a single combined alarm point including a call point, bell and battery (plus charger). In both cases the unit should be positioned so that it can be reached quickly and operated without exposing the person using it to danger.

Workplaces of any significant size will require a conventional type of electrical fire alarm system incorporating a number of manually activated call points (usually situated at or close to principal exits from the building or sections of it). The system should have sufficient sounders for the alarm to be heard throughout the premises. In noisy workplaces sounders may need to be augmented by visual alarms eg distinctive flashing lights. (These may also be necessary where workers have hearing problems). Such systems are normally integrated with any automatic fire detection equipment which may have been installed – British Standard 5839: Part 1 provides a Code of Practice for design, installation and servicing (REF.13).

Some workplaces use a two-tier system of alarms. One type of sound indicates a fire problem which must be investigated whilst a different sound requires the premises to be evacuated. Some types of premises (eg large retail operations or places of entertainment) utilise public address systems as part of their fire alarm system. This can provide guidance on the action to be taken – important where many of those present will be unfamiliar with the building and evacuation procedures. BS 5839: Part 8 provides a Code of Practice for such systems (REF. 13).

## Fire escape routes

**14.13** *Regulation 5* of the *Fire Regulations 1997* establishes various principles which must be followed in relation to emergency routes and exits. Considerable guidance is provided in '*Fire Safety: An Employer's Guide*' (REF. 1) on how these principles must be followed in practice. essentially fire escape routes should be such that people can make their escape (once the alarm has been raised) before their means of escape are made unsafe by the fire. all escape routes should lead to a place of relative safety, defined in the guidance booklet as a 'storey exit'. this might be a final exit from the building, a protected lobby or stairway or an external stairway. whilst having more than one route to escape is always preferable, it is not possible in every case. there will be many parts of workplaces (individual offices, storerooms, kitchens, toilets) which only have one escape route.

The guidance booklet sets down the maximum lengths of escape routes from occupied parts of workplaces to storey exits. These distances are much greater where more than one escape route is provided than where there is only a single escape route. The distances also vary according to the level of fire risk present in the premises.

The maintenance of protected fire escape routes is extremely important – leaving self closing fire doors wedged open can result in fires and products of combustion (particularly smoke) spreading rapidly throughout buildings.

Other factors to be taken into account include:

- exit routes (corridors, stairways, doors) should be of adequate width for the numbers expected to use them;
- special arrangements may be necessary for people with disabilities;
- some doors may need to open in the direction of travel;
- doors should be easily opened from inside when the premises are occupied (this may need to be reconciled with any security issues);

- emergency lighting may be required in some cases;
- exit routes and doors not in regular use or otherwise obvious should be indicated with pictogram signs;
- exit routes must not be obstructed.

## Evacuation procedures

**14.14** A fire evacuation procedure should be established and communicated effectively to employees eg by notices in prominent positions around the workplace. It may also be passed on to employees in other ways eg contained in employee handbooks. The procedure should contain the following elements:

### *Action on finding a fire*

Usually setting off the alarm or shouting 'Fire'. Employees may be invited to tackle the fire, if they can do this without endangering themselves.

### *Reaction to the fire alarm*

Normally this would be to evacuate using the nearest safe exit route. Some employees may be designated to carry out specific tasks eg:

- telephoning the Fire Brigade (if the alarm does not do this automatically);
- collecting visitor books (or similar records);
- carrying out emergency shutdowns of equipment, if they can do this without risk.

### *A designated assembly point*

In large premises different groups may be allocated separate assembly points. At the assembly point a roll call should be carried out to establish whether everyone can be accounted for. Such roll calls would be carried out by fire wardens (each of whom would have a designated deputy). Administrative staff (who are aware of the movements of employees) are often more suitable for this post than more senior staff, who may not always be on the premises.

Fire wardens are expected to be the point of contact with the Fire Brigade and other emergency services, especially in respect of persons who cannot be accounted for and when it is safe for premises to be re-entered.

Regular fire evacuation drills are an essential part of ensuring that the evacuation procedure will be effective if it is really needed. Drill frequencies are usually specified in Fire Certificates, otherwise it is recommended that they are held at intervals of from 3 to 12 months, depending upon the level of fire risk. Records should be maintained of the dates of the drills, the time taken to account for the safe evacuation of the premises and any other relevant details.

Training of staff in the fire evacuation procedure should be a key element of induction. Arrangements should also be in place to inform contractors and others working on the premises.

## Fire fighting

**14.15** The assessment should also take account of the provision of means of fighting fire for use by people in the premises. Where there is a Fire Certificate in force the requirements for fire fighting equipment will usually be included in it. Insurers may also require certain types of equipment to be installed. Equipment may include:

- portable fire extinguishers (see below);
- fire blankets;
- hose reels;
- sprinkler systems;
- other fixed fire fighting systems (utilising carbon dioxide or other inert gas, foam, dry powder).

Extinguishers are usually best located in positions from which those using them can, if necessary, make a safe escape ie close to fire exit doors or on fire exit routes. Those hidden from view (eg in alcoves or containers) may need to be indicated by signs, but there is no automatic requirement for signs to be provided for all extinguishers.

Basic training should be provided for employees in the suitability of different extinguishers for different types of fires (see below) and also in practical fire fighting techniques – there is no substitute for 'hands-on' experience.

The Regulations on safety signs and signals now require fire extinguishers to be predominantly red, rather than each type being coloured differently, as was previously the case. However, extinguishers in the UK are still provided with additional coloured labels to denote the different types, in accordance with British Standard 7863: '*Recommendations for colour coding to indicate the extinguishing media contained in portable fire extinguishers*' (REF. 14). british standard 5423: '*portable fire extinguishers*' provides detailed guidance on portable fire extinguishers (REF. 15).

| EXTINGUISHER TYPE | Colour Code | Suitability |
|---|---|---|
| WATER | Red | Wood, paper, textiles<br>NOT electrical or flammable liquid fires |
| FOAM | Cream | Flammable liquids<br>Reasonable for wood, paper, textiles<br>NOT electrical fires |
| CARBON DIOXIDE | Black | Flammable liquids and best for electrical fires<br>NOT paper fires |
| DRY POWDER | Blue | Flammable liquids, electrical fires<br>Reasonable for wood, paper, textiles |
| VAPOURISING LIQUID | Green | Flammable liquids and electrical fires |
| FIRE BLANKET | – | Flammable liquids in containers eg deep fat friers, chip pans |

## Fire prevention

**14.16** The need to avoid fires occurring in the first place should not be overlooked in carrying out the fire risk assessment. Fire prevention measures which may require attention include:

- safe storage of all flammable materials, particularly flammable liquids and gases;
- minimising quantities of flammable liquids and gases in workrooms;
- safe methods of use of flammable materials;
- maintenance of plant and equipment (avoiding electrical short circuits, overheating);

- good standards of housekeeping;
- control of hot work (burning, welding etc);
- careful positioning of heating appliances;
- control of smoking;
- control and removal of flammable rubbish and waste;
- controlled burning of rubbish;
- checks before locking up and/or regular patrols by security staff;
- other measures to avoid arson.

## Fire-related signs

**14.17** The need for fire-related signs may be identified during the assessment although such signs are not an automatic requirement as some sales personnel may suggest. Any signs which are provided must comply with the requirements of the *Health and Safety (Safety Signs and Signals) Regulations 1996* (REF. 16).

Situations where signs may be required are:

### *Fire alarm call points*

Where call points may not be immediately obvious, particularly if they may need to be operated by people not familiar with the premises.

### *Fire escape routes*

Exit routes and doors not in regular use or not otherwise obvious (again taking into account persons not familiar with the building). All such signs must now include a pictogram symbol.

### *Evacuation procedures*

Fire Action Notices can be used to summarise evacuation procedures. Some types of sign allow the insertion of local details eg the fire assembly point. Such signs should be in addition to, not in place of, the provision of staff training.

### *Fire fighting equipment*

Signs may be used to indicate the positions of fire fighting equipment if this is not readily apparent.

### *Fire prevention*

Fire prevention requirements eg no smoking, no hot work, may be emphasised by signs.

Many types of fire sign are now available in luminous materials and fire exit route signs can be incorporated into emergency lighting installations.

## *Making the assessment*

### Observations

**14.18** Observations during a fire risk assessment should relate closely to the assessment factors described above. Aspects to particularly look out for will include:

- areas where fire might break out undetected;
- escape routes through unoccupied areas;
- positioning of fire alarm call points;
- single escape route situations;
- obstructed means of escape;
- wedged self-closing fire doors;
- easy opening of fire exit doors;
- signs indicating means of escape;
- display of information re evacuation procedures;
- positioning (and possible obstruction) of fire fighting equipment;
- condition and evidence of servicing of fire extinguishers;
- storage and use of flammable liquids and gases;
- housekeeping standards;
- other fire prevention measures.

## Discussions

**14.19** Questions to workpeople during the assessment will also relate to the assessment factors and might include:

- audibility of fire alarms;
- evidence of fire alarm tests;
- knowledge of evacuation routes and assembly point;
- awareness of roll-call arrangements etc;
- evidence of evacuation drills;
- fire-related training (at induction and other times);
- knowledge of safe systems of work relating to flammable materials or potential sources of ignition.

## Checks of records

**14.20** Records likely to be examined during the assessment (and where appropriate related to standards specified in the Fire Certificate) will include those of the testing and maintenance of:

- fire detection equipment;
- fire alarms;
- emergency lighting;
- fire fighting equipment.

Other records to be checked are those of:

- fire evacuation training;
- induction training;
- other fire-related training.

## Assessment records

**14.21** The fire risk assessment must comply with the requirements of the *Management Regulations 1992* and therefore all employers with five or more employees must record the significant findings of their risk assessment. As with other types of assessment, there is no standard format for recording fire risk assessments. The guidance booklet (*Fire Safety: An Employer's Guide* – REF. 1) provides only limited advice on the subject. The risk assessment forms demonstrated in CHAPTER 5: ASSESSMENT RECORDS can quite easily be used for recording this type of risk assessment.

The fire risk assessment factors described earlier in the chapter can be utilised as headings within the assessment record. Plans showing the layout of the workplace, including the location of any significant fire risks and the positioning of fire protection equipment, can be incorporated into the record. However, where an up to date Fire Certificate exists it will already contain much of this detail.

The headings below were included in a fire risk assessment for a large manufacturing plant and its associated offices. (The Fire Certificate for this building was significantly out of date).

1 Introduction.

2 Summary (inc. reference to the Fire Certificate).

3 Fire risks and their control.

4 Fire detection.

5 Fire alarm.

6 Means of escape (including provision of signs).

7 Fire evacuation arrangements.

8 Fire fighting equipment.

9 Recommendations–

- Appendices (drawings detailing)–
  - Escape routes and fire alarm call points,
  - Smoke detectors,
  - Fire fighting equipment.

## *After the assessment*

### Review and implementation of recommendations

**14.22** In some respects the process for reviewing and implementing recommendations will be similar to that for other types of assessment, as described in some detail in CHAPTER 4: CARRYING OUT RISK ASSESSMENTS. many simple recommendations should be capable of being implemented quite promptly such as those relating to:

- testing of fire alarms;
- wedging open of self-closing fire doors;
- holding of fire evacuation drills;
- positioning of fire extinguishers;
- housekeeping standards;
- working practices;
- fire-related signs.

However, other recommendations may require far more technical input – from the fire authority, from suppliers of specialist equipment or from both. Where a Fire Certificate is in force the fire authority will need to be consulted in any case. This technical input may be required in relation to:

- the need for fire detection and alarm equipment;
- the design of such equipment;
- the adequacy of means of escape in borderline situations(especially for single escape routes);
- other fire escape or fire separation issues;
- automatic sprinklers and other fixed fire fighting systems.

Where the assessment reveals issues involving the storage and use of highly flammable liquids or gases or relating to process activities, advice from the HSE may be required. (The reference section of this chapter includes some relevant publications).

## Maintaining fire precautions

**14.23** Where Fire Certificates have been issued they will normally include requirements relating to the inspection, testing and maintenance of fire precautions. As with other types of precautions they are subject to the 'management cycle' required by *Regulation 5* of the *Management Regulations 1992*, and in particular to the 'monitor' stage of that cycle. Fire precautions can be monitored through the use of general health and safety inspection and audit programmes (as described in CHAPTER 8: IMPLEMENTATION OF PRECAUTIONS) or, in the case of smaller workplaces, through informal inspections. testing and maintenance should also take place in workplaces not subject to a fire certificate.

Tests can usually be carried out by employees, providing they have received fairly basic training. Most employers prefer to contract out maintenance of fire equipment to specialist companies but there is no reason in law why this also cannot be done in house, providing the staff involved are competent for the purpose.

Frequencies of testing and maintenance where a Fire Certificate is not in force are suggested below, but these may need to be varied either because of the level of fire risk or the type of fire protection equipment in place.

### *Fire detection and alarm systems*

- weekly testing of the alarm, using different alarm call points each week in rotation (many employers prefer to test at the same time each week and also to inform staff and others that a test is taking place);
- annual inspection and test by a competent person, including testing and/or inspection of smoke and heat detectors.

### *Emergency lighting*

- testing at one to three monthly intervals;
- annual inspection and test by a competent person.

### *Fire evacuation procedures*

- evacuation drills at intervals of three to twelve months depending upon the fire risk (drills can be made more realistic by simulating the non-availability of exit routes).

### *Fire fighting equipment*

- annual checks by a competent person of extinguishers, sprinkler systems and other fixed fire fighting extinguishing systems.

## Assessment review

**14.24** Fire risk assessments, like other types of assessment, must be reviewed if they are thought to be no longer valid or if significant changes take place. It is recommended that periodic reviews should be carried out in any case. Such reviews should take place at intervals of from two to five years depending upon the level of fire risk and the potential for gradual change to take place.

## References

**14.25**


| | | |
|---|---|---|
| 1 | | Fire Safety: An employer's guide. Home Office/HMSO (1999). |
| 2 | HSG 168 | Fire safety in construction HSE (1997). |
| 3 | | Fire safety in the paper and board industry HSE (1995). |
| 4 | | Fire safety in the printing industry HSE (1992). |
| 5 | HSG 146: | Dispensing petrol: Assessing and controlling the risk of fire and explosion at sites where petrol is stored and dispensed as a fuel HSE (1996). |
| 6 | HSG 140: | Safe use and handling of flammable liquids HSE (1996). |
| 7 | IND G 227: | Safe working with flammable substances HSE(1996) – free leaflet. |
| 8 | HSG 178: | The spraying of flammable liquids HSE (1998). |
| 9 | HSG 51: | The storage of flammable liquids in containers HSE (1998). |
| 10 | HSG 176: | The storage of flammable liquids in tanks HSE (1998). |
| 11 | HSG 141: | Petrol filling stations: Construction and operation HSE (1990). |
| 12 | BS 5446: | Components of automatic fire alarm systems for residential premises. Part 1: Specifications for self-contained smoke alarms and point-type smoke detectors. |
| 13 | BS 5839: | Fire detection and alarm systems for buildings. |
| 14 | BS 7863: | Recommendations for colour coding to indicate the extinguishing media contained in portable fire extinguishers. |
| 15 | BS 5423: | Portable fire extinguishers. |
| 16 | L64: | Safety signs and signals. *Health and Safety (Safety Signs and Signals) Regulations 1996*. Guidance on Regulations HSE (1997). |

# 15 Risk assessment related concepts



## *Introduction*

**15.1** Risk assessment techniques are at the heart of the effective management of health and safety. This chapter examines several important concepts which involve risk assessment. These are:

- Safe systems of work.
- Dynamic risk assessments.

- Permits to work.
- CDM Health and Safety plans.
- Method statements.

## *Safe systems of work*

### What is a safe system of work?

**15.2** Under *section 2(2)(a)* of *HASAWA 1974* employers have a duty to ensure:

> 'the provision and maintenance of plant and systems of work that are, so far as is reasonably practicable, safe and without risks to health'.

Safe systems of work are also required directly or indirectly under several codes of Regulations including those applying to asbestos, carcinogens (COSHH), confined spaces, electricity and lifting operations. Employers also have duties under common law to establish safe systems of work.

A safe system of work can be defined as:

> 'the work method resulting from an assessment of the risks associated with a task and the identification of the precautions necessary to carry out the task in a safe and healthy way'.

The risk assessment may result in the elimination of risks or in the identification and application of controls at source eg guarding, enclosure, the use of local exhaust ventilation. However, a safe system of work will be necessary to ensure that those controls are properly applied and that any residual risks are adequately controlled.

The degree of formality necessary in identifying and defining a safe system of work will depend on factors such as:

- the level of risk involved;
- the frequency of the task;
- its complexity and variability;
- the capabilities of those performing the task;
- the complexity of the precautions required.

There are several ways in which a safe system of work may be defined including *task safety instructions* and *task procedures* (referred to below) together with *permits to work* and *method statements* (covered later in the chapter). The word 'task' is preferred to 'job' as the latter can be confused with 'occupation'.

In some situations only a relatively short time might be available to establish a safe system of work, requiring a *dynamic risk assessment* to be carried out in the workplace (see 15.8: DYNAMIC RISK ASSESSMENT). In others, a more formalised risk assessment will be appropriate, applying the types of approach already described elsewhere in the book.

## Task safety instructions

**15.3** A task safety instruction is a means of conveying essential safety information to those carrying out a task. It can use a variety of forms of communication:

- informal oral instructions, eg–
  - make sure someone is footing that ladder,
  - some of the castings are hot, you'll need to wear gloves.
- Safety signs or notices, eg–
  - wear eye protection when operating this machine,
  - fragile roof – crawling boards must be used.
- Written safety rules or key points–
  - summarising the risks involved and the precautions required.

## Task procedures

**15.4** A task procedure provides a step by step description of how a task should be performed. As well as including operational instructions and health and safety requirements, it can also contain efficiency and quality requirements relating to the task. Such formal procedures are more commonly prepared for routine production tasks but they may also be appropriate for some maintenance activities and emergency or breakdown situations. An extract from such a task procedure is provided in CHAPTER 5: ASSESSMENT RECORDS as the final example of a risk assessment record.

## Factors in establishing a safe system of work

**15.5** Whether a safe system of work is eventually defined by task safety instructions, a task procedure, a permit to work or a method statement, all relevant factors which might create risks must be taken into account. These will include:

- Equipment and materials used–
  - work equipment involved,
  - power sources and the effect of possible power failures,
  - materials used, including their movement or handling,
  - hazardous substances involved directly.
- The work environment–
  - access to and egress from the workplace,
  - hazardous substances present in the workplace,
  - neighbouring or passing equipment eg vehicles,
  - heat, light, dust, fumes and other environmental aspects,
  - weather conditions eg wind, ice, rain.
- The work methods–
  - frequency to which the task is carried out,
  - variability in the task,
  - complexity of the task,
  - skills required to carry out the task.
- Possible sources of error or problems–
  - lack of skill or concentration lapses,
  - fatigue,
  - short cuts likely to be taken,
  - pressure from deadlines or other factors,
  - breakdowns of equipment or emergency situations,
  - external factors eg major distractions.

## Development of task procedures

**15.6** Detailed task procedures are more likely to be appropriate for higher risk tasks and also for those lower risk tasks which are carried out more frequently. They contain full details of how the task should be performed, providing an important aid to training. They should incorporate all aspects of the task and not just the health and safety issues. These might include:

- The overall purpose of the task;
- Operational instructions–
  - in a logical sequence,
  - providing adequate detail.
- Health and safety points–
  - highlighting risks eg slippery floors,
  - specifying precautions eg wear safety spectacles.
- Equipment damage prevention–
  - detailing risks and precautions eg check oil levels.
- Quality considerations–
  - raw materials,
  - product specifications.
- Environment and waste issues.

The following documents may be useful in the preparation of task procedures:

- Engineering manuals or drawings.
- Quality control documents.
- Training material.
- General risk assessment records.
- COSHH assessments.
- Manual handling assessments.
- PPE requirements–
- Other assessments (noise, DSE),
- Safety rules,
- Accident records,
- Environmental guidelines,
- Waste requirements.

In preparing task procedures (or task safety instructions) it is important to observe and consult with those actually carrying out the task. It may be necessary to go through a couple of drafts before a procedure is produced that is both relevant and contains adequate information on health and safety and other issues. The procedure should be capable of easily being understood and followed by a newcomer to the task. Contentious issues (eg the suitability of certain types of PPE) may need to be resolved before the procedure can be finalised. Task procedures should be reviewed periodically to ensure that they are still relevant.

### Implementation of safe systems of work

**15.7** Employers must ensure that safe systems of work are communicated effectively to those who are expected to follow them and to supervise their use. Formal training is particularly likely to be necessary in relation to the communication of task procedures and also of more formal task safety instructions eg written safety rules. The safe systems of work must also be implemented in practice, requiring appropriate levels of supervision. The effectiveness of this implementation must be monitored – either formally through health and safety inspections and audits or informally by the employer during observations of work activities.

## *Dynamic risk assessments*

**15.8** The risk assessment techniques described elsewhere in the book and particularly in CHAPTER 4: CARRYING OUT RISK ASSESSMENTS result in what are now commonly described as generic risk assessments. They identify and evaluate the risks normally associated with work activities and the precautions necessary to control those risks to the standard required by legislation.

However, it is impossible for employers to take account in advance of all of the variables involved in work activities and the circumstances and environments in which those activities are carried out. A certain amount of reliance must be placed upon employees to make their own judgments in relation to health and safety. This process is called *dynamic risk assessment* and it is something we call carry out in our daily lives – for example, on every occasion we decide whether or not it is safe to cross the road. It involves:

- identification of risks 'in the field';
- evaluation of the precautions available;

- selection and implementation of the most suitable precautions (or a decision not to go ahead with the task).

Dynamic risk assessment should take place within the framework of a generic risk assessment ie where the risks likely to be associated with the task have been identified and the precautions likely to be necessary have been provided or made available. Those individuals who have received the appropriate level of information, instruction, training and supervision should then be able to carry out dynamic assessments.

Applying this approach to crossing the road, a generic risk assessment should ensure:

- provision of physical controls where appropriate eg light controlled crossings, zebra crossings, pedestrian central refuges, lighting, barriers etc;
- that those who are to cross have the physical capability to do so safely eg eyesight, hearing, walking ability;
- delivery of training in crossing technique eg Green Cross Code, benefits of using crossings;
- supervision of inexperienced people (children in this case) – until they demonstrate the capability to successfully carry out a dynamic risk assessment in practical situations.

Much installation or maintenance work involves work at heights using various types of temporary access equipment. A generic risk assessment should ensure that:

- suitable temporary access equipment is readily available eg stepladders, extension ladders, tower scaffolds etc;
- this equipment is maintained to a satisfactory standard;
- those who are to use it receive training–
    - in the safe use of the access equipment,
    - in which types are most appropriate for which circumstances.

Employees trained and equipped in this way should then be able to carry out a dynamic risk assessment of a range of work situations and select the most suitable type of access equipment. In some cases this may involve deciding that none of the equipment available is suitable and requesting alternatives eg full scaffolding or a mobile elevating work platform. It may sometimes be appropriate to decide not to go ahead with the task eg in strong winds or other adverse circumstances.

## The 'safe person'

**15.9** Some work activities require dynamic risk assessments to be made quite quickly in very dangerous and rapidly changing situations, in order to establish a safe system of work. The emergency services encounter many such situations and fire services in particular place reliance on the concept of the 'safe person'. This involves:

- selection of staff with the physical and mental attributes necessary for the work;
- development of procedures for carrying out key tasks;
- provision of equipment (including PPE) necessary to carry out anticipated activities safely;
- training of staff in procedures and the use of equipment;
- the ongoing provision of supervision and information.

The 'safe person' model is one which can be applied elsewhere. Those employees in whom investment has been made in terms of selection, training, procedures, equipment etc will be properly equipped to carry out dynamic risk assessments and to establish safe systems of work for themselves.

## *Permits to work*

**15.10** In essence a permit to work provides a formal mechanism for ensuring that a dynamic risk assessment of a work situation is carried out by a person competent for the purpose (a 'safe person') in order to ensure that a safe system of work is followed.

Organisations which use permit to work systems will normally require them where:

- The risks involved are high eg work involving high voltage electrical systems, highly flammable liquids or gases.
- Unusual risks are present eg sources of ionising radiation or lasers.
- Complex isolations are necessary to ensure safety eg of power sources, services, material feeds.
- Special precautions are required eg atmospheric testing, use of alarms or special access equipment.

- Personnel are unfamiliar with the environment or risks eg contractors or inexperienced staff.

Further examples of situations where permits to work may be appropriate are:

- work on overhead cranes or crane tracks;
- entry into confined spaces;
- work on potentially dangerous or complex machinery;
- work involving hazardous substances;
- pressure testing;
- high level access;
- excavation work.

## Designation of permit situations

**15.11** Those situations requiring permits to work should be clearly designated through written task procedures, listings in safety handbooks or rulebooks, the posting of relevant signs and notices or within method statements. It is important that all those likely to be involved (employees and contractors) are fully aware of when permits to work are required. However, it will never be possible to identify all permit situations in advance – staff should always be alert to new tasks which justify the use of a permit to work.

## The permit sequence

**15.12** For permit to work systems to be effective, isolations and the provision of other precautions prior to work starting (and their subsequent withdrawal) must take place in a strictly controlled sequence. This should be ensured by the manner in which the permit is issued and then cancelled, which would normally follow the sequence below:

- Request for permit issue–
    - from the person in charge of the work (or requiring it to be carried out).
- Clearance from person in charge of the area/equipment–
    - eg production agree that maintenance work can start.
- Isolations made/other precautions taken–

  - these must be done or directly supervised by the permit issuer.
- The permit issuer completes the PTW form–
  - detailing precautions taken or required, stating any restrictions eg on work activities or areas where work can take place.
- The permit holder signs the PTW form–
  - accepting any terms or restrictions.
- The permit is then issued–
  - the permit issuer signs the form to issue the permit if satisfied that the permit holder understands and is capable of meeting any requirements in it.

(Normally at least two copies are made – one issued to the permit holder (or put on display), the other retained by the permit issuer or in a central repository).

*When work is complete (or must cease)–*

- *All* permit copies must be brought together.
- The permit holder cancels *all* copies–
  - confirming work has terminated, people, equipment etc have been withdrawn and the area has been left safe.
- An authorised person cancels *all* copies–
  - the permit issuer (or another authorised person) permits the withdrawal of precautions, including isolation removal.
- Isolations are removed and other precautions withdrawn–
  - Checks may be made on the general safety of the area / equipment.
- Normal activity may resume.

## Permit to work forms

**15.13** The detailed design of the form should relate to the types of risks involved and precautions required. The form should include:

- a checklist of risks to be considered;
- some guidance on appropriate precautions;*

- logical places for signatures to issue and cancel the permit;
- clear statements of responsibilities at each stage in this process.

At least two copies of each permit should normally exist – one given to the permit holder or put on display, the other remaining with the permit issuer or at a central repository. Most forms use self-carbon paper, often with colour coding of the different copies. An example of a permit to work form is provided in this section of the chapter.

*In some workplaces standard lists of precautions have been developed for routine tasks controlled by permits to work. Nevertheless the permit issuer must still ensure that the necessary precautions are actually taken and also remain alert for any unexpected risks which may be present and the need for extra precautions.

## The permit issuer

**15.14** Those issuing and cancelling permits to work should have the following capabilities:

- an appreciation of the purpose of permits to work;
- a clear understanding of the issue and cancellation sequence;
- knowledge and experience of the activities and locations for which they are issuing permits (equipment, risks involved, isolation points, other precautions);
- the ability to carry out, supervise and prove isolations;
- knowledge of other relevant precautions eg gas testing;
- the ability to recognise and deal with problems;
- a positive attitude to health and safety.

Normally there should be a formal system for training, testing and authorising those who are to issue and cancel permits.

## Authorisation of permit issuers

**15.15** Authorisation should normally be by a well balanced panel or a very competent individual.

Candidates should be questioned on the theoretical aspects of PTW use–

- the reasons for using PTW systems;

- the issue and cancellation sequence;
- how they would deal with problem situations;

They should then demonstrate their practical knowledge and capabilities–

- the location and use of isolation points;
- the implementation of other precautions.

The panel should issue an authorisation certificate if it is satisfied that the candidate is competent.

The issuing of PTWs must not just 'come with the job'.

# PERMIT TO WORK

Serial No. 12345

<table>
<tr><td colspan="4">DETAILS OF PROPOSED WORK</td></tr>
<tr><td>Intended start date<br>Intended start time</td><td>Expected duration</td><td colspan="2">General clearance is given for this work to take place<br>Signature Position Date</td></tr>
<tr><td>SERVICE ISOLATION CHECKLIST</td><td>✓</td><td colspan="2">DETAILS OF ISOLATIONS MADE</td></tr>
<tr><td>ELECTRICITY</td><td></td><td colspan="2"></td></tr>
<tr><td>STEAM</td><td></td><td colspan="2"></td></tr>
<tr><td>WATER</td><td></td><td colspan="2"></td></tr>
<tr><td>GAS</td><td></td><td colspan="2"></td></tr>
<tr><td>COMPRESSED AIR</td><td></td><td colspan="2"></td></tr>
<tr><td>HYDRAULICS</td><td></td><td colspan="2"></td></tr>
<tr><td>OTHER SERVICES</td><td></td><td colspan="2"></td></tr>
<tr><td>OTHER POSSIBLE RISKS</td><td></td><td colspan="2">PRECAUTIONS REQUIRED/TAKEN (INC. PPE)</td></tr>
<tr><td>FLAMMABLE LIQUIDS / GASES</td><td></td><td colspan="2"></td></tr>
<tr><td>LACK OF OXYGEN</td><td></td><td colspan="2"></td></tr>
<tr><td>CONFINED SPACE ENTRY</td><td></td><td colspan="2"></td></tr>
<tr><td>HAZARDOUS SUBSTANCES</td><td></td><td colspan="2"></td></tr>
<tr><td>ACCESS/WORK AT HEIGHTS</td><td></td><td colspan="2"></td></tr>
<tr><td>MATERIAL FEEDS</td><td></td><td colspan="2"></td></tr>
<tr><td>OTHER</td><td></td><td colspan="2"></td></tr>
<tr><td>OTHER RESTRICTIONS ON WORK</td><td></td><td colspan="2"></td></tr>
<tr><td>ACCEPTANCE</td><td>ISSUE</td><td>WORK TERMINATION</td><td>CANCELLATION</td></tr>
<tr><td>I accept this permit to carry out the work described. I understand the requirements and restrictions described above and all persons under my control will abide by them.<br><br>SIGNATURE<br>PERMIT HOLDER<br>Date Time</td><td>I confirm the isolations have been carried out and other precautions described above have been taken.<br>I am satisfied the permit holder understands the restrictions on the work.<br>THE PERMIT IS ISSUED<br><br>SIGNATURE<br>PERMIT ISSUER<br>Date Time</td><td>The work described above has terminated.<br>All persons and equipment under my control are clear of the area which has been left in a safe condition.<br><br>SIGNATURE<br>PERMIT HOLDER<br>Date Time</td><td>THIS PERMIT IS CANCELLED.<br>All isolations may be removed.<br>Other precautions may be withdrawn.<br>Normal activities may then resume.<br><br>SIGNATURE<br>PERMIT HOLDER<br>Date Time</td></tr>
</table>

## CDM health and safety plans

**15.16** The *Construction (Design and Management) Regulations 1994* ('CDM') contain a requirement for a Health and Safety Plan to be prepared for every construction project subject to the Regulations. (The definition of 'construction work' used in the Regulations is so broad that many types of maintenance and installation work also fall within the scope of the *CDM Regulations 1994* – see REF. 1).

The purpose of the plan is to ensure that risks expected to be involved in the project are identified in advance, together with the precautions necessary to control those risks. The framework of the plan must be prepared initially by the 'Planning Supervisor' (a person or organisation appointed by the 'Client').

The 'Principal Contractor' for the project must not be appointed until the 'Client' (on the advice of the 'Planning Supervisor') is satisfied that they are competent to implement the precautions identified in the plan and that they will allocate adequate resources for health and safety. Responsibility for the detailed development and implementation of the plan then passes to the 'Principal Contractor' who also has responsibilities in respect of the competence and health and safety standards of other contractors and self-employed persons working on the project.

Detailed HSE guidance is available on the Regulations themselves, the definitions and responsibilities of the various duty holders and on the content of Health and Safety Plans (see REFS. 1 to 4).

The *CDM Regulations 1994* require the use of risk assessment techniques in the preparation of the Health and Safety Plan and then the application of safety management techniques in its implementation.

The 'Principal Contractor' and other contractors involved in the project should already have *generic risk assessments* relating to their work – the risks normally associated with the work and the precautions available or normally applied. The Health and Safety Plan involves a form of *dynamic risk assessment* in relation to this project including consideration of:

- health and safety standards to be met in the work;
- co-ordination of the contractors involved;
- overall site PPE requirements;
- provision of services, facilities and equipment;
- special requirements of the site or its location;

- special or unusual requirements of the project.

The accompanying Health and Safety Plan checklist was developed primarily to assist those acting as 'Planning Supervisors' or 'Principal Contractors' for engineering and minor building projects in established workplaces such as factories or offices. The content of Health and Safety Plans for other types of work eg major new build or demolition projects will undoubtedly be different. However, the checklist provides at least an illustration of the types of issues which must be addressed in preparation of the plan.

Construction (Design and Management) Regulations 1994

**Health and Safety Plan Checklist**

This checklist is intended to assist those fulfilling roles as Planning Supervisors or Principal Contractors under the *CDM Regulations 1994* but may also help clients in identifying important issues relating to health and safety.

*Planning supervisors* should use it to identify risks and other health and safety issues of relevance to the project and to outline what precautions and other arrangements are likely to be necessary.

*Principal contractors* will need to provide more detail of what precautions actually have been or will be taken. Where appropriate, cross references should be made to other documents (SEE SECTION 2 OF TABLE: RELEVANT DOCUMENTS) and additional detail may be provided on separate sheets.

For small projects the careful completion of this form should provide adequate information but for larger projects, especially those involving significant risk, much more information is likely to be required – including reference to relevant risk assessments, method statements, etc.

| 1 | PROJECT DETAILS | |
|---|---|---|
| 1.1 | Project Title | |
| 1.2 | Expected Commencement Date | |
| 1.3 | Predicted Duration | |
| 1.4 | Project Description | |
| 2 | RELEVANT DOCUMENTS | Give details of relevant documents and standards |
| eg | Project specifications<br>Drawings<br>HSE Guidance<br>BS or CE specifications<br>IEE standards<br>Existing health and safety files | |
| 3 | CONTRACTORS | Contractors must be competent and adequately resourced |
| 3.1 | Principal Contractor | |
| 3.2 | Other Contractors | |
| 4 | COMMUNICATIONS | What arrangements will be made for |
| 4.1 | Monitoring design work | |
| 4.2 | Considering design change implications | |
| 4.3 | Project review meetings | |
| 4.4 | Inducting contractors' employees | |
| 4.5 | Checking contractors' employee training | |
| 4.6 | Monitoring the work location | |

| 5 | PERSONAL PROTECTIVE EQUIPMENT | What will the site requirements be for |
|---|---|---|
| 5.1 | Safety footwear | |
| 5.2 | Safety helmets | |
| 5.3 | Clothing (inc. high visibility) | |
| 5.4 | Eye protection | |
| 5.5 | Hearing protection | |
| 5.6 | Gloves | |
| 5.7 | Other PPE | |
| 5.8 | Signs | |
| 6 | SITE SERVICES AND EQUIPMENT | Arrangements for their provision and maintenance |
| 6.1 | Electrical power | |
| 6.2 | Water supplies | |
| 6.3 | Compressed air | |
| 6.4 | Lighting | |
| 6.5 | Plant or equipment | |
| 6.6 | Other | |
| 7 | TRAFFIC AND TRANSPORT | |
| 7.1 | Traffic routes | |
| 7.2 | Parking | |
| 7.3 | Speed limits | |
| 7.4 | Headroom | |
| 7.5 | Emergency access routes | |
| 7.6 | Separation from moving traffic | |
| 8 | PEDESTRIAN SAFETY | |
| 8.1 | Access to and within site | |
| 8.2 | Access for work at heights | |
| 8.3 | Protection of openings | |
| 8.4 | Protection from falling materials | |
| 9 | SECURITY/SEGREGATION | |
| 9.1 | Segregation from other activities | |
| 9.2 | Perimeter security | |
| 9.3 | Warning signs | |
| 9.4 | Security attendance/patrols | |
| 10 | HAZARDOUS SUBSTANCES | |
| 10.1 | Presence within site | |
| 10.2 | Use in the project | |
| 10.3 | Storage or disposal issues | |

| 11 | OTHER SPECIAL ISSUES | |
|---|---|---|
| 11.1 | Buried or overhead services | |
| 11.2 | Stability of other structures | |
| 11.3 | Need for Permits to Work | |
| 11.4 | Commissioning | |
| 12 | FIRE | |
| 12.1 | High risk materials/activities | |
| 12.2 | Exit routes | |
| 12.3 | Evacuation procedures | |
| 12.4 | Fire fighting equipment | |
| 13 | FACILITIES AND ARRANGEMENTS | |
| 13.1 | Material storage | |
| 13.2 | Waste storage and disposal | |
| 13.3 | Welfare facilities | |
| 13.4 | First Aid | |

Signed Date
Date passed to Principal Contractor (if relevant)

## Method statements

**15.17** A safety method statement is a description of how risks will be controlled or managed in relation to a specific task or activity. It may be incorporated within an overall method statement which describes how the whole task will be performed ie including detailed work methods and specifications of equipment and materials to be used. Method statements are increasingly being required for construction-related projects, with the safety method statement providing an important means of complying with the *CDM Regulations 1994*.

The health and safety plan should normally cover risks in relation to the project as a whole. The safety method statement will normally deal with a task, an activity or a specific health and safety issue identified in the plan and go into much more detail. It will be based on a risk assessment of the relevant task or activity. The content of a method statement might include:

*Identification of key personnel–*

- for overall control and specific operations.

*Training requirements–*

- eg for use of cranes, fork-lifts etc, or the testing or commissioning of equipment.

*Access requirements–*

- for vehicles and pedestrians;
- access equipment needed;
- emergency access issues.

*Equipment requirements–*

- size, weight, type;
- power rating, certification;
- location, stability.

*Site requirements–*

- traffic considerations;
- security/protection of the public or other workers.

*Materials involved–*

- storage, transportation, handling, disposal;
- hazardous substances.

*Work sequencing–*

- need for temporary precautions;
- key scheduling issues.

*Environmental considerations–*

- eg wind speed limits;
- rain, temperature.

*PPE requirements*

*Other precautions–*

- barriers, signs etc;
- fire fighting equipment;
- detection equipment;
- rescue equipment.

## References

### (All HSE publications.)

**15.18**



| | | |
|---|---|---|
| 1 | L 54: | Managing construction for health and safety: *Construction (Design and Management) Regulations 1994.* Approved Code of Practice (1995) |
| 2 | | A guide to managing health and safety in construction (1995) |
| 3 | CIS 42: | *Construction (Design and Management) Regulations 1994.* The pre-tender stage health and safety plan (1995) – free leaflet |
| 4 | CIS 43: | *Construction (Design and Management) Regulations 1994.* The health and safety plan during the construction phase (1995) – free leaflet |

# 16 Looking ahead

**In this chapter:**

**Risk assessment is here to stay**

**Supply-chain pressure**

**Possible changes**

Integration of requirements
Fire safety legislation
Changes to the *CDM Regulations*

**References**

## *Risk assessment is here to stay*

**16.1** Reference was made in CHAPTER 1: INTRODUCTION to some of the recommendations of the robens committee, made in 1972, which eventually resulted in the *health and safety at work etc act in 1974 ('hasawa 1974')*. one of the themes of the robens report was that of 'self regulation' – that employers should address all of the risks involved in their activities rather than just those for which there were specific legal provisions.

To that end *HASAWA 1974* contained a number of general obligations of employers and the self-employed both towards their own employees and to others not in their employment, who might be affected by their work activities. These requirements were qualified by the phrase 'so far as is reasonably practicable'. As was explained in CHAPTER 1: INTRODUCTION, this in effect required employers to carry out a risk assessment in order to identify foreseeable risks and determine what were or were not reasonably practicable precautions. CHAPTER 15: RISK ASSESSMENT RELATED CONCEPTS also explained how the process of risk assessment is fundamental in determining 'a safe system of work' – another basic obligation under *hasawa 1974.*

This progress towards 'self regulation' was further formalised by the requirements contained in the *Management Regulations* and other specific codes of Regulations for risk assessments to be made and (in most cases) to be recorded. In effect the *Management Regulations* oblige employers to carry out a risk assessment to be carried out every time a new statutory requirement applying to their activities is introduced. Risk assessments must also be reviewed whenever any significant change is made to any aspect of those work activities.

*'Revitalising Health and Safety'*, the Strategy Statement published in June 2000 by the Department of the Environment, Transport and the Regions ('DETR'), the parent department of the Health and Safety Executive, also referred to 'self regulation'. One of the ten key points in the Strategy Statement was the need to cultivate 'a more deeply engrained culture of self regulation', particularly in small businesses. Risk assessment by employers must be a fundamental part of that self regulation.

## Supply-chain pressure

**16.2** Since the introduction of *HASWA 1974*, many court decisions, most notably those involving Swan Hunter Shipbuilders and Associated Octel, have emphasised the responsibilities of employers for the activities of employees of other organisations. The structure of *HASAWA 1974* and much subsidiary legislation is such that responsibilities overlap between employers rather than being neatly apportioned between them. Employers must do more than simply not turn a blind eye to the obvious health and safety failings of those with whom they come into contact: they must often take a pro-active interest in the health and safety standards of others.

In recent years a growing number of larger companies, local authorities and other public bodies have had increasingly formalised procedures for checking the health and safety standards of contractors wishing to work for them. This process has been accelerated by the demands of the *Construction (Design and Management) Regulations 1994* ('*CDM 1994*') which require clients to satisfy themselves (via their planning supervisors) that potential principal contractors are capable of dealing with the health and safety issues associated with projects. The Regulations also place responsibilities on principal contractors in respect of sub-contractors. Consequently contractors are frequently required to provide details of their health and safety policies and generic risk assessments together with risk assessments and/or method statements for specific projects or activities. Many clients also take an extremely hands-on approach in policing the work of contractors on their premises.

The importance of supply chain pressure is also stressed in the Strategy Statement '*Revitalising Health and Safety*'. This states:

> 'All public bodies must demonstrate best practice in health and safety management. Public procurement must lead the way on achieving effective action on health and safety considerations and promoting best practice right through the supply chain'.

Whilst this trend is broadly welcomed, it is to be hoped that it results in the full and fair evaluation of risk assessments and method statements, and in monitoring of actual work practices to ensure that precautions identified as being necessary are properly implemented. Sadly much experience of the effects of the *CDM Regulations* has been of a bureaucratic paperchase through which all parties attempt to protect their legal position. As is sometimes demonstrated in the courts, their legal obligations will only be fully met if evaluation of such documents and monitoring of work practices have taken place ie the management cycle has been properly applied.

## Possible changes

### Integration of requirements

**16.3** One change that has already been mooted is the integration of all risk assessment requirements under a single statutory provision rather than the present situation where requirements are contained in several different codes of Regulations. Whilst this might have the benefit of simplifying the law, it would have little tangible impact in practice. As this book should have demonstrated, the techniques involved in carrying out one type of risk assessment are very similar to those necessary for the other types.

### Fire safety legislation

**16.4** Reference was made in CHAPTER 14: FIRE RISK ASSESSMENTS to the possibility of wholesale revision of fire safety legislation in respect of places of work. whilst any simplification of the law is generally to be welcomed, a requirement for a fire risk assessment to be carried out is likely to be contained in any future legislation.

### Changes to the CDM Regulations

**16.5** Concern has been expressed in many quarters at the levels of bureaucracy being introduced as a result of the *CDM Regulations*. The HSE response has been that this was not their intention and careful study of their guidance on the Regulations appears to bear this out. It is to be hoped that any changes, whether to the Regulations or to HSE guidance, will further discourage the bureaucratic tendency.

Nevertheless, all of the parties involved in construction projects will still need to satisfy themselves that other parties involved are capable of taking full account of health and safety issues. All of the means for doing this, including health and safety plans and method statements, involve the application of risk assessment techniques.

## References

### 16.6


| 1 | Revitalising Health and Safety | DETR/HSC (2000) |
|---|---|---|

# Table of Cases

# Table of Statutes

# Table of Statutory Instruments

# European Legislation

**Directives**

# Index